Cleveland
GOLFER'S
BIBLE

4TH EDITION

Cleveland
GOLFER'S
BIBLE

4th EDITION
NOW 198 LISTINGS!

John H. Tidyman
Don Franceski

GRAY & COMPANY, PUBLISHERS
CLEVELAND

For Yoshiro Takaoka, M.D., PH.D.,
a man of grace

Gray & Company, Publishers
1588 E. 40th St.
Cleveland, OH 44103-2302
www.grayco.com

Library of Congress Cataloging-in-Publication Data
Tidyman, John H.–
Cleveland golfer's bible / John H. Tidyman.—4th ed.
Includes index.
1. Golf courses—Ohio—Cleveland Metropolitan Area—
Directories. I. Title.
GV983.C57T53 1997b   796.352'06'877132—dc21
99-6235

ISBN 1-886228-27-2

Printed in the United States of America

10 9 8 7 6 5 4 3 2 1

Contents

Acknowledgements

There we go again. It's a Saturday evening in July, around 7 o'clock. There are only a few players left on the course. Lisa Metro and I, bags on our shoulders, are traipsing down the first fairway at Skyland Golf Course. We are in leisurely pursuit of par. No matter how many times we play like this, the pleasures never wane. We don't keep score. Lisa rarely asks for advice. When she does, I say the same thing or a variation of it: finish your swing. It's getting dark by the time we get to the ninth green. On the way home, we stop for a sandwich and a beer. In weeks filled with myriad delights, none is as delightful as Saturday night golf with Lisa.

Every season I play a round or two with Yoshiro Takaoka, M.D., Ph.D., the brilliant neurosurgeon from Metro Hospital. I rarely play well. My mind doesn't stay on the game. Nearly ten years ago, a problem was discovered on the left side of my brain. The first couple of neurosurgeons who looked at it declared it inoperable and likely fatal. Dr. Tak said, "I can do this operation." He did.

Introduction

This book was researched and written to guide players to the incredible wealth of golf that makes Greater Cleveland a duffer's paradise. There is no instruction between the covers. That's for the professionals. What is presented here is an armchair tour, a smorgasbord of golf.

We live in a region that offers a wealth of opportunity to pursue our favorite pastime. We have golf courses in quantity, and in quality, too. We play in valleys, on plains, and over hills—golfing terrain that was created when the glaciers slid across North America, scooping out water hazards such as the Great Lakes.

Players familiar with these courses will compare notes and perhaps take issue with the author.

Many of us, though, do ourselves a regular disservice by sticking with just a few courses where we are already comfortable. It can take a long time to find out through trial and error which courses we like best, so it's natural to want to spend our playing time on layouts we *know* we're going to enjoy.

This book should help you discover some new places to enjoy.

The data and descriptions are meant to give the inside scoop on courses that can mean the difference between a wasted trip and a pleasant round. No more trips to courses that are pushovers or too difficult; too crowded or too expensive. Anyone who's spent time and money getting to a course where a golf disaster awaited knows how valuable such information can be.

No advertising or sponsorship was solicited for this guide, nobody paid to be in it, and no restraints were placed on the author. Still, it is a bit subjective.

The author thanks all those who called or wrote with suggestions on the first three editions and hopes this fourth edition will inspire additional comment.

Cleveland
GOLFER'S
BIBLE

4TH EDITION

Maps

Areas Covered in this Book:

123 Public Golf Course
123 Private Golf Course

LAKE ERIE

CLEVELAND

Not shown on map:
4 8 34 58 63
65 79 93 125 140
142 143 153 154

Areas

E . . . East	S . . . South
FE . . Far East	FS . . . Far South
FrE . . Farther East	FrS . . . Farther South
W . . . West	SW . . . Southwest
FW . . Far West	SE . . . Southeast
FrW . . Farther West	

MAPS

Far West

N

LAKE ERIE

Lorain

LAKE

3

MILLER

COLORADO

DETROIT

6

ERIE

55

GREENWOOD

ADELBE

BEAVER CREST

JAEGER

45

COOPER FOSTER PK.

N. RIDGE

10

2

LEAVITT

90

133

83

33

GULF

W. RIVER

80

57

20

41

58

20

57

CHESTNUT RIDGE

RUSSIA

44

10

PYLE / S. AMHERST

52

20

102

82

OBERLIN ELYRIA

SLIFE

CAPEL

27

57

DURKEE

511

LAGRANGE

INDIAN HOLLOW

MEDINA ELYRIA

MORGAN

97 Oberlin

HAMILTON

20

303

70

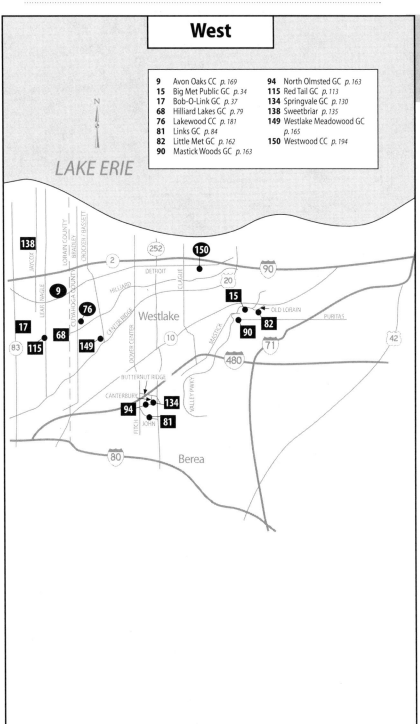

MAPS

West

MAPS

East

1	Acacia CC *p. 167*	**84**	Locust Grove GC *p. 162*
2	Airport Greens GC *p. 23*	**85**	Lost Nation GC *p. 86*
13	Beechmont CC *p. 170*	**88**	Manakiki GC *p. 88*
21	Briardale Greens GC *p. 43*	**91**	Mayfield CC *p. 182*
26	Canterbury GC *p. 171*	**96**	Oakwood Club *p. 183*
36	Country Club, The *p. 175*	**98**	Orchard Hills GC *p. 93*
62	Green Ridge GC *p. 159*	**100**	Pepper Pike CC *p. 184*
67	Highland Park GC *p. 76*	**104**	Pine Ridge CC *p. 101*
72	Johnny Cake Ridge GC *p. 160*	**127**	Shaker Heights CC *p. 190*
74	Kirtland CC *p. 180*	**136**	StoneWater GC *p. 132*

N

LAKE ERIE

Euclid

Mayfield Hts.

Far East

MAPS

4 Ashtabula CC *p. 167*	**86** Madison CC *p. 182*
14 Berkshire Hills CC *p. 31*	**99** Painesville CC *p. 94*
16 Black Brook CC *p. 36*	**101** Pepperidge Tree GC *p. 164*
28 Casement Club *p. 157*	**106** Pleasant Hill GC *p. 103*
30 Chardon Lakes GC *p. 51*	**108** Pleasant View GC *p. 106*
47 Erie Shores GC *p. 62*	**110** Powderhorn *p. 107*
49 Fairway Pines GC *p. 64*	**111** Punderson GC *p. 108*
53 Fowler's Mill GC *p. 66*	**112** Quail Hollow CC *p. 186*
56 Geauga Hidden Valley GC *p. 159*	**116** Reserve at Thunder Hill *p. 114*
78 Legend Lake GC *p. 181*	**124** Sand Ridge GC *p. 188*
83 Little Mountain CC *p. 85*	**135** St. Denis GC *p. 131*

MAPS

Southwest

24	Brunswick Hills GC *p. 47*	**42**	Dorlon GC *p. 58*
25	Bunker Hill GC *p. 48*	**46**	Emerald Woods GC *p. 61*
32	Cherokee Hills GC *p. 55*	**66**	Hickory Nut GC *p. 75*
35	Columbia Hills CC *p. 172*	**87**	Mallard Creek *p. 87*
38	CC Fox Meadow, Meadow Course *p. 176*	**92**	Medina CC *p. 183*
39	CC Fox Meadow, Weymouth Course *p. 176*	**107**	Pleasant Valley CC *p. 104*
		119	Riverside GC *p. 119*
40	Creekwood GC *p. 56*	**122**	Royal Crest GC *p. 120*
		123	Rustic Hills GC *p. 188*

South

MAPS

5	Astorhurst CC *p. 25*	**118**	Ridgewood GC *p. 117*
22	Briarwood GC *p. 44*	**126**	Seneca GC *p. 121*
69	Hinckley Hills GC *p. 80*	**129**	Shawnee Hills GC *p. 123*
71	Ironwood GC *p. 82*	**131**	Skyland GC *p. 125*
77	Leaning Tree GC *p. 160*	**132**	Sleepy Hollow GC *p. 128*
103	Pine Hills GC *p. 97*	**145**	Valleaire GC *p. 136*

MAPS

Southeast

Far South

MAPS

105 Pine Valley GC p.102
109 Portage CC p.185
113 Raccoon Hill GC p.110
114 Raintree CC p.111
117 Ridge Top GC p.116
120 Riverwoods GC p.164
121 Rosemont CC p.187
128 Sharon GC p.191
130 Silver Lake CC p.191
137 Sunny Hill Golf & Rec. p.134
139 Sycamore Valley GC p.164
144 Twin Lakes CC p.193
146 Valley View GC p.137
148 Western Reserve CC p.138
152 Windmill Lakes GC p.139

54 Fox Den Fairways p.69
59 Good Park p.73
61 Green Hills GC p.159
73 Kent State Univ. GC p.83
75 Lake Forest CC p.180
80 Leisure Time Rec. p.160
89 Maplecrest GC p.91
95 Oak Knolls GC p.92

11 Bakers Acres p.30
19 Brandywine CC p.40
23 Brookledge GC p.46
31 Chenoweth GC p.52
43 Ellsworth Meadows p.60
48 Fairlawn CC p.177
50 Firestone CC p.178
51 Firestone GC p.158

Key to Golf Information

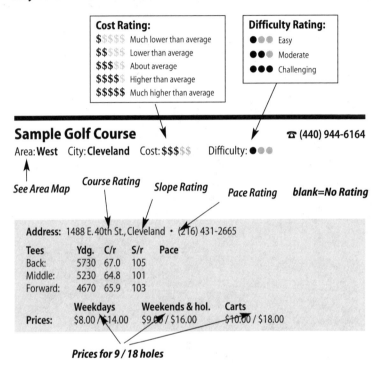

Cost Rating:

$$$$$ Much lower than average
$$$$$ Lower than average
$$$$$ About average
$$$$$ Higher than average
$$$$$ Much higher than average

Difficulty Rating:

●●● Easy
●●● Moderate
●●● Challenging

Sample Golf Course   ☎ (440) 944-6164

Area: **West**   City: **Cleveland**   Cost: **$$$$$**   Difficulty: ●●●

See Area Map   *Course Rating*   *Slope Rating*   *Pace Rating*   *blank=No Rating*

Address: 1488 E. 40th St., Cleveland · (216) 431-2665

Tees	Ydg.	C/r	S/r	Pace
Back:	5730	67.0	105	
Middle:	5230	64.8	101	
Forward:	4670	65.9	103	

	Weekdays	Weekends & hol.	Carts
Prices:	$8.00 / $14.00	$9.00 / $16.00	$10.00 / $18.00

Prices for 9 / 18 holes

Note: Changes Prices, hours and season of operation, and other factual information were carefully verified before this book went to press. However, this kind of information is always subject to change without notice. Golfers should **always call ahead** to confirm important details before heading out to play.

Public Courses
18 Holes or More

Airport Greens Golf Course   ☎ (440) 944-6164
Area: **East**   City: **Willoughby Hills**   Cost: $$$$$ Difficulty: ●●●

Address: 28980 White Rd., Willoughby Hills

Tees	Ydg.	C/r	S/r	Pace
Back:	5730	67.0	105	
Middle:	5230	64.8	101	
Forward:	4670	65.9	103	

	Weekdays	Weekends & hol.	Carts
Prices:	$11.00 / $20.00	$12.00 / $21.00	$11.00 / $21.00

Specials: None

Season: Year-round   **Hours:** 6 a.m.–10 p.m.   **Tee times:** Recommended   **Leagues:** Weekdays 3:30–6:30 p.m.   **Ranger:** Most days   **Practice facil:** Range, Putting Green, Chipping Green, Lighted range   **Clubhouse:** Food, Beer, Liquor, Dining room, Pavilion, 16-acre picnic area with enclosed pavilion   **Outings:** Available (catered or non-catered)   **Lessons:** Available

Directions: I-90 to Exit 187 for Ford Rd./Bishop Rd. in Willoughby Hills; south on Bishop; left (east) on White Rd.; on right.

Description Playing without caution here can cost more than stroke and distance. It can send players to federal prison. While signs on most golf courses are limited to directing cart traffic, at Airport Greens one reads: WARNING. THIS FACILITY IS USED IN FAA AIR TRAFFIC CONTROL. LOSS OF HUMAN LIFE CAN OCCUR FROM SERVICE INTERRUPTION. ANY PERSON WHO INTERFERES WITH AIR TRAFFIC CONTROL, OR DAMAGES OR TRESPASSES ON THIS PROPERTY WILL BE PROSECUTED UNDER FEDERAL LAW. One more distraction while lining up a putt.

This is what happens when a golf course is built on an airport. Dick LaConte, PGA, who designed the course on Cuyahoga County Airport turf, has mixed golf and aviation before. On the clubhouse wall is a copy of a 30-year-old newspaper story about LaConte crashing his light plane into a tree while photographing the 13th hole at the now-defunct Mayfield Heights Golf Club.

"It's a combination of Scottish links in the open areas because we had the restrictions of the airport," said LaConte. "The airport demands that we put nothing through the landing light system area. We can't plant trees there because we have a height restriction and we were restricted in the areas adjacent to the course. It's a unique piece of property."

No one is going to argue with that, though anyone who is reminded of Scottish links after walking this course will likely see the White Cliffs of Dover in the Terminal Tower.

A former pro called the course "sporty," which is golf language for "short." He also suggested that a player needs all the shots to play it well. Could be true, but a long driving game is unnecessary at Airport Greens, and a sand game won't get much of a workout. The real challenge here is concentrating on the stroke while a Cessna takes off.

Highlights The opening hole is a 295-yard par 4 and is pretty typical of the holes here. The fairway is wide and bends softly to the right. Mounds on either side help define the hole. The fairway dips and rolls before arriving at a green elevated about 10 feet.

No. 2, a 215-yard par 3, is an unusual hole for a short course described as "sporty"—a 215-yard par 3 is a pro-length hole. Double bogeys will be posted here far more often than pars. A culvert runs 75 yards in front of the green, which is surrounded by mounds.

No. 6 is a par 3, 170 yards. A hook on this tee will send the ball off the course and across Bishop Road. The green is substantial, and players cross the county line—Cuyahoga/Lake—when walking from one end of the green to the other.

At the No. 7 tee, the sign promising prosecution is attached to the door of a small building used, obviously, for airport business. Landing lights mark the way to the tee. The hole is a 455-yard par 5, the number two handicap on this side.

The last hole before crossing White Road and leaving the airport for a half-dozen holes is No. 10, a short 130 yards from the white tees. Across the road, the course becomes much more attractive. Grass on the fairways will do that. This doesn't alleviate the difficulties of playing with planes in the background (and foreground), however, and players with air combat experience will likely rise to the top.

Nos. 17 and 18 are consecutive par 3s that play around a long and narrow lake. No. 17 is 165 yards with a small lake down its left side. For No. 18, players turn around and play 175 yards back to the clubhouse, water again on the left. Finishing holes like these suggest the designer forgot how much land was available and suddenly realized that two holes had to fit.

Airport Greens has an attractive clubhouse, a good pro shop, and a 60-station practice range.

Astorhurst Country Club   ☎ (440) 439-3636

Area: **South**   City: **Walton Hills**   Cost: $$$$$ Difficulty: ●●●

Address: 7000 Dunham Rd., Walton Hills

Tees	Ydg.	C/r	S/r	Pace
Back:	6342	70.3	120	
Middle:	6075	69.1	118	
Forward:	5945	73.7	124	

	Weekdays	Weekends & hol.	Carts
Prices:	$10.25 / $20.00	$12.50 / $23.00	$12.00 / $21.00

Specials: Seniors Mon–Fri before 3 p.m. $19.00 for 18 holes & ½ cart

Season: Year-round **Hours:** Sunrise–10 p.m. **Tee times:** Taken **Leagues:** Mon–Thu after 3:30 p.m. **Ranger:** Most days **Practice facil:** Putting Green **Clubhouse:** Food, Beer, Liquor, Dining room, Lockers, Showers, Pavilion, Astorhurst Country Place restaurant **Outings:** Available **Lessons:** Available **Pro:** Douglas Smith, PGA

Directions: I-77 to Exit 153 for Pleasant Valley Rd.; east on Pleasant Valley through Cuyahoga Valley National Recreation Area (becomes Alexander Rd. after Canal Rd.); left (north) on Dunham Rd. to the entrance within CVNRA.

PUBLIC 18+

Description One hundred forty-seven acres is not a lot of space for a golf course. But by pushing a few holes against one another, the designers created a reasonable track here. A couple tee shots are off the sides of cliffs, so they've provided some drama, too. Leagues fill the course Monday through Thursday afternoons, and Fridays are popular for outings, so call before coming.

The trees have grown large over the years and now add to the difficulty of keeping the ball in play. Most of the holes are already tight. Fairways and rough are well defined. Yardage markers in the fairways and cart paths are helpful. Twelve of the eighteen have doglegs.

Highlights No. 1, a 359-yard par 4, begins the match with a pine tree–lined, sharp dogleg left; there are trees at the corner turn and the right side of the fairway. Drive through the fairway and more trees will be waiting.

The Astorhurst "Rail Service" takes walking players from this green (and No. 10) to the next tee. It's an open, mechanical lift that clanks up the side of a steep hill.

No. 2 is an awesome 455-yard par 4 that calls for a big drive but offers a wide landing area. The terrain rises and falls as much as 20 feet. Halfway to the green, in the right rough, is an unusual set of sand traps. Not visible from the tee, they are five rectangular traps laid side by side—reminiscent of the famous "church pews" at Oakmont Country Club in Pennsylvania. There is more sand on the left side, but none at the green. On this hole, length is the key.

No. 7 is the only par 5 on the front nine, 590 yards. Its tee looks out over a wide fairway and, off to the right, a practice area. Still, care must be taken in this crowded corner of the course. A pulled tee shot can whistle over the heads of putters on the 5th green or drivers on the 6th tee. The 7th fairway drops from the tee and spreads out for the first few hundred yards. Then it takes a sharp dogleg to the right and rises. The flag is not visible for the second shot, and there is the chance of hitting through the fairway.

Cart riders should be extremely cautious while leaving the tee at No. 8. If you get going too fast and lose control, the thrill rides at Cedar Point would be mild in comparison to what you will experience. (It is an 80-to-100-foot drop.)

No. 13, par 3, plays to two different greens. You hit over a ravine for the longer green—a hole for heroes. Lesser beings play the 105-yard front green.

No. 14, par 4, is short at 305 yards, but it features woods and a deep ravine on the left. A line of trees on the right separates the hole from No.15. A slight dogleg left takes you to a green with a ravine drop-off and trees on both sides.

No. 18, par 5, 498 yards, tees off from the top of a cliff to a landing area 100 feet below. It's a sharp dogleg right with trees right and left of the fairway. Out-of-bounds to the right prevents players from going for the green in two. O.B. in the middle of the course indicates poor design.

This old course is aging well. The two cliffside tee boxes make it fun.

Astorhurst Country Club   (photo: Jonathan Wayne)

Auburn Springs Country Club   ☎ (440) 543-4448

Area: **Southeast**   City: **Chagrin Falls**   Cost: **$$$**$$ Difficulty: ●●●

Address: 10001 Stafford Rd., Chagrin Falls

Tees	Ydg.	C/r	S/r	Pace
Back:	6874	71.9	117	
Middle:	6543	70.3	112	
Forward:	5530	70.7	113	

	Weekdays	Weekends & hol.	Carts
Prices:	$9.00 / $15.00	$13.00 / $22.00	$12.00 / $20.00
	Registration required for discounts		

Specials: Seniors Mon–Fri $8.00 / $14.00; Hot dog & beverage special $25.00 for 1 person, $45.00 for 2 people, $67.00 for 3 people, $88.00 for 4 people

Season: Year-round **Hours:** Sunrise–sunset **Tee times:** Taken weekends **Leagues:** Mon–Fri 4 p.m.–dark **Ranger:** None **Practice facil:** Putting Green, Chipping Green **Clubhouse:** Food, Beer, Liquor, Dining room **Outings:** Available **Lessons:** Not available

Directions: I-271 to Exit 27 for US 422; east on US 422; north on SR 306; right (east) on Bainbridge Rd.; left (north) on Snyder Rd.; right (east) on Stafford Rd.; on right.

Description "Men are usually wild," manager Evelyn Weese says, "they go everywhere." She was explaining high scores on this course. And she knows what she's talking about—Weese turns in scores in the mid-80s on a regular basis. "On the front there's a lot of water and in the back a lot of woods. If you hit a straight ball, you're okay." Well, if you hit a straight ball *long* maybe. The front side measures 6,543 from the whites. From the blue tees, it stretches to 6,874, a length familiar to the Senior PGA Tour.

The course was built in the late sixties on farmland. Ernie Mizda is the builder and owner. This golf course is a tough one, a bit rough around the edges as well. To call it rough-hewn is an act of kindness. (And it would be easy to be kind if the lack of conditioning resulted in low green fees). The men and women who show up at the cashier's desk are here only to play golf. The club has a "basics-only" pro shop. No driving range here, and no rangers on the course. There isn't a pro on the staff, and no lessons are provided. Mizda has two noteworthy rules on the scorecard: no one under 21 may drive a golf cart, and beginners are not allowed on the course during busy periods.

Highlights No. 1 is a 375-yard par 4 that begins from an elevated tee. The fairway drops down to the left. Plenty of players try to cut the dogleg, because hitting straight can send a ball through the fairway. There are trees down the left side and a small pond, too. Behind the well-maintained green is a second pond.

No. 2, a 490-yard par 5, starts rising and doesn't stop rising until it

PUBLIC 18+

approaches the green. It plays much longer than the listed 490 yards. A snap hook off this tee will send a ball into a small lake about 100 yards out. The left side here is thick woods. Down the right side, the hole is marked by a big willow and a line of trees.

Three tough par 4s finish the front side—two of them 440-yarders.

No. 17 is a par 5—570 yards that bend constantly to the right. About halfway to the green there is a small lake on the right side. This is a workingman's par 5; it calls for nothing fancy, only three solid, straight shots to cover the yardage and avoid the hazards. Just like Ms. Weese said.

After putting out on No. 18 and heading for the clubhouse, players run into the original Paul Bunyan driver. It is almost 15 feet tall, carved of two large pieces of wood with a black grip, brown shaft, and black hosel. It is handsome and rough-hewn. Just like the course.

Auburn Springs has the charm of a country picnic; it is not a course that stands on ceremony.

Avondale Golf Club   ☎ (440) 835-5836

Area: **Far West**   City: **Avon**   Cost: **$$**$$$ Difficulty: ●●●

Address: 38490 Detroit Rd., Avon

Tees	Ydg.	C/r	S/r	Pace
Back:	6263	69.9	118	
Middle:	5993	68.5	116	
Forward:	5400	70.7	114	

	Weekdays	Weekends & hol.	Carts
Prices:	$8.00 / $15.00	$9.00 / $16.50	$9.00 / $18.00

Specials: Mon–Fri before 1 p.m. $19.00 for 18 holes & cart; Seniors & Juniors Mon–Fri before 1 p.m. $6.00 / $11.00; Early Bird Special: Mon–Fri before 7:30 a.m., 9 holes $4.50, 18 holes $9.00

Season: Apr–Dec **Hours:** 5:30 a.m.–10:00 p.m. **Tee times:** Taken **Leagues:** Various times **Ranger:** Daily **Practice facil:** Putting Green **Clubhouse:** Food, Beer, Pavilion **Outings:** Available (catered outings: 18 holes & cart, includes lunch or dinner, $43.00 per guest; seating for 200) **Lessons:** Not available

Directions: I-90 eastbound to Exit 153 for SR 83; left (south) on SR 83; right (west) on Detroit Rd. (SR 254); on right, after Long Rd.   OR, I-90 westbound to Exit 148 for SR 254 (Detroit Rd.); east on SR 254; on left, after Moon Rd.

Description George Noll built the front side of Avondale on farmland and opened it for play in 1974. It was his dream to operate the course in his retirement; he had the back nine sketched when he succumbed to a heart attack. His sons built the back nine and today run the operation with their mother, Jane Noll. "It became a family affair," Al Noll said. So if the course looks homemade, it should.

There is some variety in the greens here: a couple are two-tiered, a few are small or unusually shaped (pin placement on the par 3 No. 16 can mean a putt as long as 120 feet), more are big. Many are surrounded by sand and mounds. They are all kept in excellent condition. "That's what we're noted for," Al Noll said. "They're the best greens in the county." A familiar boast of course owners.

Electric lines cut through the course, especially on the front side. Holes were designed to avoid them, though, and landing near poles is no penalty; a two-club length drop is offered.

Highlights No. 1 is a par 5 of 500 yards. Three mounds in the middle of the fairway confront players on the tee, and more mounds come into play for the second shot. The approach must take into account the lake and the sand to the right of the green. For first-time players, this can be a hectic opening hole.

No. 3, a par 3 of 175 yards, is one of many holes studied carefully by Al Noll. When scoring for outings, he sees more high scores on this hole than on any other. Although it is technically the number 15 handicap, he says it plays the hardest. "It's always playing into the wind and most people are short of the green," he explained. Short of the green there is trouble where mounds protect the front. Off to the right is a small pond, and on the right side of the green, sand.

No. 4 is a 360-yard par 4, a dogleg left. In the corner of the turn is The Pit—a mound with a pit in the middle. The corner can still be cut, but only by big and accurate hitters. Missing it and playing the second shot from The Pit will likely add at least one stroke. There is sand beside the green, behind which sits a sizable pond.

No. 12, a par 4 of 365 yards, has three pot bunkers waiting at 210 yards on the right side of the fairway. The hole also has the toughest green on the course, including a two-tiered putting surface and a pair of sand traps.

The only par 5 on the back side is No. 13, a 470-yard hole that tempts players to reach for the green in two. "It doesn't get eagled very often," Al Noll said. The hole bends to the left, and getting on in two calls for clearing a few 50-foot oaks en route. If that shot leaks to the right it will end up in a pond close to the green.

The finishing hole has water in front of the tee. The drive on this 375-yard par 4—the only uphill hole here—has to carry a large pond. Sand lines both sides of the two-tiered green. The putting surface has plenty of action to it and, for reasons not clear, is faster than others here. "It's a knee-knocker," Noll said.

PUBLIC 18+

Bakers Acres   ☎ (330) 928-8728

Area: **Far South**   City: **Tallmadge**   Cost: **$$**$$$ Difficulty: ●●●

Address: 594 Northwest Ave., Tallmadge

Tees	Ydg.	C/r	S/r	Pace
Middle:	5900	65.9	121	
Forward:	4831	68.8	120	

	Weekdays	Weekends & hol.	Carts
Prices:	$9.00 / $16.50	$10.00 / $19.00	$9.00 / $18.00

Specials: Seniors: Mon–Fri 9 holes & cart $11.00 (before 2 p.m.), 18 holes & cart $16.00 (before 12 p.m.)

Season: Year-round **Hours:** Sunrise–sunset **Tee times:** Required weekends
Leagues: Mon–Fri 4 p.m.–6:30 p.m. **Ranger:** Some days **Practice facil:** Putting
Green **Clubhouse:** Food **Outings:** Available **Lessons:** Not available

Directions: I-271 to Exit 18 for SR 8; south on SR 8; east on Howe Ave.; bear right on Northwest Ave.; on left, after Thomas Rd.

Description It is wonderfully common for friendships to begin on golf courses. Less common, though not unusual, for friendships to be rekindled there. At Bakers Acres, two men who had not seen each other since high school—and that was a few decades ago—met when one had a heart attack on No. 12 and the other, a recent graduate of CPR training, was coming in off No. 9. On hearing of the emergency, he ran to the victim and started pounding and pushing and praying. The victim lived. The friendship was rekindled.

Bakers Acres was built in 1978 on farmland originally worked by the Upson family of Connecticut. Mr. Baker knows this because the family burial plot is there. He wonders if Upson Street in Akron is named after them. The graves were moved years ago, but a headstone remains.

Highlights The course is short and tight. There are trees on the front nine, and the back nine was carved out of the woods. There is water, and accuracy is the key to scoring. Greens are medium size and speed, and as easy to read as this book. The hole with the greatest challenge is No. 9, a 380-yard par 4. Getting on in regulation calls for an accurate tee shot and an equally accurate approach. In the elbow of the dogleg stands a tall tree. Missing the green is problematic.

Berkshire Hills Country Club   ☎ (440) 729-9516
Area: **Far East**   City: **Chesterland**   Cost: $$$$$ Difficulty: ●●●

Address: 9760 Mayfield Rd., Chesterland

Tees	Ydg.	C/r	S/r	Pace
Back:	6607	72.1	129	
Middle:	6346	71.0	127	
Forward:	5512	71.8	122	

	Weekdays	Weekends & hol.	Carts
Prices:	$10.50 / $20.00	$14.75 / $26.00	$10.00 / $20.00

Specials: Seniors Mon–Fri 9 holes $9.50 / $17.00 walking (not leagues or outings); Seniors Mon–Fri 18 holes $52.00 for 2 players & cart; $20.00 for full cart Sat–Sun

Season: Year-round **Hours:** Sunrise–sunset **Tee times:** Taken weekends, Until 1pm on weekends, carts required until 1 pm **Leagues:** Mon–Fri **Ranger:** Daily **Practice facil:** Range, Putting Green **Clubhouse:** Food, Beer, Soft drinks, Beer avail. on course **Outings:** Available **Lessons:** Not available

Directions: I-271 to Exit 34 for US 322 East (Mayfield Rd.); east on US 322 through Chesterland; on right, after Heath Rd. (2.5 miles east of SR 306, Chillicothe Rd.)

PUBLIC 18+

Description A player arguing that Berkshire Hills is the most beautiful course in the area would find plenty of supporting evidence between the first tee and the 18th green. The course is only about 30 years old and was designed by Ben Zink, who also designed the layout for Landerhaven (now defunct). Landerhaven was a prairie without features; Berkshire is a roller coaster without tracks.

The winding and hilly drive from US 322 to the parking lot is much like the course itself: lined with trees and given to following the terrain.

The clubhouse is like an old family album: battered a bit, but treasured. Tee times are taken for weekend and holiday mornings. To play at other times, just show up. Not much of a pro shop here, just the basics, and the driving range prohibits the use of woods.

On the other side of the clubhouse is the dining facility for outings: an old dairy barn. It is a splendid setting for prime rib and cloth napkins. Friday is the day for outings.

Highlights Berkshire is a well-manicured and -maintained course, and few starting holes match the grandeur of its No. 1. This par 5, 537-yard dogleg sweeps down from the tee, then veers up and to the right. In the elbow of the dogleg is a large lake. It is a rare player who tries to clear the lake with a tee shot; the fairway is wide, the rough easily playable. When the sky is clear but for a few clouds, the view here belongs on a picture postcard. The big, round green at No. 1 has a couple of slender traps on either side, traps that wrap around the perimeter. This type of trap will be seen the rest of the round.

No. 4 is another par 5, this one a 505-yard uphill hole that will likely confuse the first-time player. A pond rests in front of the tee and the drive must be straight. Few players can reach the top of the hill with their drives, making a second, blind shot necessary. As throughout the course, old hardwoods line the fairway and stand ready to slap down errant shots. More than accuracy is called for here; good scores are often posted by long hitters. The fairway rises towards an aiming flag, where it crests and then rolls straight to the green. The green is half-surrounded in the rear by heavy, heavy brush.

No. 7 is the number one handicap hole, a 448-yard par 4 that demands a straight hit from the elevated tee and an approach shot of great accuracy and length. The fairway rises and dips more than once before nearing the green, where the left side of the fairway precipitously drops off.

Some golfers may choose to go from the 9th green directly to the 10th tee rather than stop for refreshment at the clubhouse; for all the beauty and challenge of the front side, the back side is more beautiful and more challenging. Furthermore, a cart patrols the course with a cooler full of cold beer and soft drinks. A nice touch.

No. 10, a 252-yard par 4, goes up. And up. And up. It's not a difficult hole if players stay on the straight and narrow. If the ball strays left, it finds deep woods. Trees protect the front and right of the green, but even players not known for their length off the tee might be able to drive it.

With No. 12 begin what may be the four best consecutive holes in northern Ohio. No. 12 is a 453-yard par 4 that takes a woodland ride the Headless Horseman wouldn't consider. The tee shot, ideally a soft draw, has to go uphill and slightly left. Deep forest lines the left and plenty of maples and pin oaks line the right. Starting at the 150-yard marker, the fairway descends rapidly, crosses water, and finally comes to the green.

The next tee, No. 13, presents a target only a couple dozen yards wide. The tee shot has to go almost straight uphill; at the crest, trees close in on both sides. This 472-yard par 5 plays down a snug fairway.

No. 14 is a 360-yard par 4, which sounds easy. But this hole calls for careful shotmaking—especially the approach to the green, which is slightly elevated.

No. 15 is a par 5, 509-yard hole that bends right, falls to a creek, then rises sharply up and left to the green. Play outside of the short grass makes this hole especially tough. The walk through the woods to the next tee is a good time to catch one's breath; some interesting golf is played in those last four holes.

The 18th hole looks like it was designed by Andrew Wyeth. It's a par 3, 135 yards from a small, even private, tee box and across a sparkling lake. The green has water on three sides, and to the rear the ground rises dramatically. Players who are walking get to stroll across the wooden footbridge from tee to green. (Carts must use a more substantial bridge.)

Berkshire is a long course: 6,346 for par 72. The blue tees take the course to 6,607, par 73. The women's tees were not provided as an after-

When All Else Fails . . .

There's always new equipment each season for those who have more money than desire to practice.

Recent innovations include:

The Tour Reactive Ball, from Ram. It is allegedly stuffed with some junk called neodymium, said to be a "rare earth metal," which is supposed to transfer energy at a higher rate and give more distance. I think what the ball will do is transfer money at a higher rate from the wallets of golfers to the wallets of Ram Golf executives.

From Cobra come wedges in five lofts with tri-bounce soles. Purchase includes a Phil Rodgers instructional tape. Should be a tape from Will Rogers.

If I offered you a Dual Force FB1, would you report me to federal authorities? Nope; it is yet another putter, this time from Odyssey. The FB stands for Face Balanced. It is an offset putter with a deep cavity and the trademark stronomic insert. Stronomic must be short for astronomic—which is the price certainly is.

Arnold Palmer's company has some updated iron sets. An area in the toe of each iron has had weight removed and filled with a polyurethane insert to reduce vibration. Too bad they can't do that with the executive brains at The King's company.

Sutherland Golf, of Barberton, makes the Sabre golf ball and now the Avant. It is designed for players who swing slowly. The Avant is said to be low-compression and high launch velocity. Players who swing slowly constitute an under-served market because they don't need equipment—they have swings.

Not to be outdone by the other shills, Nicklaus Golf has new stuff worthy of a whole paragraph. The Air Bear M3 is three groups of irons in a single set: the long irons feature titanium and beryllium sole weights; the mid-irons have a titanium insert; the short irons are made of soft nickel chromium and have milled faces for additional backspin. The Player of the Century is clearly vying for Bullshitter of the Century, as well.

You don't have to have a lot of money in order to waste it. For example, Titleist sells a towel with its logo on it for $19.95. Callaway, equally greedy, sells ball mark repair tools, also with its logo, for $14.95. If you feel like carrying a billboard for King Cobras, the umbrella is $49.95. Ralph Lauren offers caps with his name, not yours, on the front and charges only $19.95. (Who told him about golf?) Ping offers a hat with its logo on it for $24.95. For geeks and nerds who still miss the pocket protector, caddy shorts, for $29.95, feature a pocket with outside sleeves for tees, pencil, divot–repair tool, and a snap for a ball marker. Snake Eyes has shirts with its logo on the chest: $59.95.

From the too-little-too-late department, the Ping ISI driver has a 310 cc head. Good for clubbing large rodents, but little else.

Purchase of any of these items will bolster your insanity defense.

—JHT

thought; they are well built and maintained, and they provide reasonable advantage. Water fountains and telephones for emergency use dot the course.

This is a great course for hosting out-of-town guests unfamiliar with the quality of public golf available here.

PUBLIC 18+

Big Met Public Golf Course   ☎ (440) 331-1070

Area: **West** City: **Fairview Park** Cost: **$$**$$$ Difficulty: ●●●

Address: 4811 Valley Pkwy., Fairview Park

Tees	Ydg.	C/r	S/r	Pace
Back:	6356	69.1	110	4:15
Middle:	6125	68.0	108	
Forward:	5870	72.0	113	

	Weekdays	Weekends & hol.	Carts
Prices:	$9.00 / $16.00	$10.00 / $18.00	$10.00 / $18.00

Specials: Golfer's Dozen: 12 rounds for the price of 10; Seniors (62+) & Juniors $7.00 / $12.00

Season: Mid-Mar–Dec **Hours:** Sunrise–sunset **Tee times:** Taken **Leagues:** Women's League on Tuesday **Ranger:** Daily **Practice facil:** Range, Putting Green **Clubhouse:** Food, Beer **Outings:** Available (for small outings Mon, Wed, Fri; call Golf Services at 440-234-8654) **Lessons:** Not available **Pro:** Mike Raby

Directions: I-480 to Exit 9 for Grayton Rd.; north on Grayton; left (west) on Puritas Rd. into Rocky River Reservation; right (north) on Valley Pkwy.; on right.

Description This Cleveland Metroparks course has been a West Side favorite for a couple of generations. It is attractive and playable, and so conveniently located that getting there for many is a matter of 10 or 15 minutes.

Convenience has a downside, however; there are days when the parking lot overflows with cars and the wait to tee off can be excruciating. The course plays very slowly on such days. Management's refusal to send out rangers and speed play is indicative of the regard for players here—if you don't like it, hit the road.

It is not a difficult course, though there are tough holes on it. Sitting in the Rocky River Reservation—"The Valley," to West Siders—this essentially flat layout provides great physical beauty to players. Animals like it, too, including a pair of red fox and dozens of deer. A minor inconvenience is provided by planes leaving and arriving at Hopkins Airport, just south of the course.

Highlights The first hole is a 403-yard par 4 with a generous fairway—often ignored by players who slice their drives into the adjacent No. 2 green. It is a straight hole calling for two long shots. The fairway is lined on the right with small trees, mostly pines. Except for a stand of tall hardwoods, the left side is open. There is sand at the left side of the green. The greens on this course are neither tricky nor fast, but they hold approach shots well and are always in very good shape.

No. 5, the first par 5, measures 452 yards and includes a dogleg left near the green. A small lake was added recently. Again, it's a wide-open fairway. At one time a huge tree stood in the elbow of this dogleg. Lightning eliminated that hazard, but more trees have been planted there, and as time goes on the hole will narrow. Behind the sloped green is the Rocky River.

No. 14 is certainly the most difficult hole on the course, even though No. 9 is designated the number one handicap. At 424 yards, it's a long par 4. A dogleg right turns around the 150-yard mark. To score well on this hole calls for a pro-length drive and great second shot. If the drive leaves the ball on the right side, trees in the elbow of the dogleg will prevent a clear approach. And the green itself is unfair and tricky; it is egg-shaped and has steep sides. It's not unusual to land a ball on the green only to watch it roll off. Whose brilliant design idea was that?

The final two holes are short par 4s more at home on an executive-length course than here. No. 17 is a straight, 289-yard hole with a plateau in the fairway and plenty of room. Big hitters who are also big slicers, however, can land on the 18th tee. No. 18, 293 yards slightly uphill toward the clubhouse, has a mound in front of the green that makes judging the approach shot difficult.

There are occasional surprises on the course. Sometimes the red foxes will raise eyebrows as they take their evening walk. Or a heron swooping down to land in a marsh will hush a foursome. But mostly this course is comfortable, familiar, and convenient. Which explains why Big Met does such big business.

Big Met Public Golf Course   (photo: Casey Batule/courtesy of Cleveland Metroparks)

PUBLIC 18+

Black Brook Country Club

☎ (440) 951-0010

Area: **Far East**   City: **Mentor**   Cost: $$$$$ Difficulty: ●●●

Address: 8900 Lake Shore Blvd., Mentor

Tees	Ydg.	C/r	S/r	Pace
Back:	6216	69.1	118	
Middle:	5870	68.0	116	
Forward:	5398	70.5	117	

	Weekdays	Weekends & hol.	Carts
Prices:	$10.00 / $18.00	$12.00 / $21.00	$11.00 / $22.00

Specials: None

Season: Year-round **Hours:** 6 a.m.–10 p.m. summer; 8 a.m.–5 p.m. winter **Tee times:** Recommended **Leagues:** 4–6 p.m. **Ranger:** Daily **Practice facil:** Range, Putting Green **Clubhouse:** Food, Beer, Pavilion **Outings:** Available (catered for 20–120 guests) **Lessons:** Available **Pro:** Tim Ausperk

Directions: SR 2 to SR 44; north on SR 44 (Heisley Rd.) to exit for Lake Shore Blvd. (SR 283); west on Lake Shore Blvd.; on left.

Description The tee markers here are carved granite. It is an elegant touch and in keeping with Mary Lou Colbow's affectionate regard for the game. The president and owner of Black Brook comes from a golfing family; her father, Robert Shave, was the pro at Manakiki when it was a private club.

Colbow is also a player of some repute and a student of the game. Black Brook, she said, invests heavily in its junior program. Young players who are taught the game and its etiquette will likely always be grateful. Just as important, they will fill courses with golfers who play fast and well, and who take care of the course as they use it.

The course is open all year, and play is permitted according to the weather. Colbow said, "It's a good course for everybody. It's not super long, but it's not short and it has a lot of challenge in it—the back nine, especially, because it's tight." The greens are consistently fast and the course very well maintained. Tees, greens, and fairways are watered.

Highlights No. 4 is the only par 5 on the front side and, at 444 yards, it is quite short. There is plenty of room to fit a slice before reaching the white o.b. stakes on the right side. This hole has one of the tougher greens. Plenty of sand around and in front of it, so rolling the ball on it is not possible. The green itself has tough hills. It is easy enough to three-putt here (maybe more).

The back side is slightly longer and more difficult than the front. The terrain changes are marked by shallow and not-so-shallow valleys and much more water. The toughest hole is saved for last.

No. 11, a 185-yard par 3, is a gorgeous hole, calling for a big iron shot over valley and creek to a large green. Sand traps prevent big hits from bouncing into the woods behind the green.

No. 18, the most challenging hole on the course, is equally beautiful. The tee shot on this 425-yard par 4 is blind; players have to go out a hundred yards to see the green. There are only a few trees on both sides, but the target area for the drive is not large. A straight hole, it starts dropping about 200 yards from the green. On the right of the valley floor is a lake. The terrain rises quickly to a green with three traps and deep woods behind it. Separating the woods from the green is a split-rail fence.

Black Brook is an old, and old-fashioned, layout with holes that can delight the average player and holes that can confound. It is a little gem, off the side of the road, where management's commitment to the game is clearly evident.

Bob-O-Link Golf Course   ☎ (440) 835-0676

Area: **West**   City: **Avon**   Cost: **$$$**$$ Difficulty: ●●●

Address: 4141 Center Rd. (SR 83), Avon

| Tees | Red & White | | | | Red & Blue | | | | Blue & White | | | |
	Ydg.	C/r	S/r	Pace	Ydg.	C/r	S/r	Pace	Ydg.	C/r	S/r	Pace
Back:	6263	68.1	108	3:42	6052	68.0	115	3:44	6383	69.6	115	
Middle:	5911	66.7	105		5656	66.3	111		6023	67.9	112	
Forward:	5050	66.6	107		4808	66.7	112		5102	68.4	115	

	Weekdays	Weekends & hol.	Carts
Prices:	$9.00 / $16.00	$10.00 / $19.00	$10.00 / $20.00

Specials: Seniors & Juniors Mon–Fri $6.00 / $11.00

Season: Mar–Dec **Hours:** 6 a.m.–10 p.m. **Tee times:** Taken weekends **Leagues:** Various times **Ranger:** Most days **Practice facil:** Range, Putting Green, Chipping Green, Sand **Clubhouse:** Food, Beer, Liquor, Pavilion, (3 pavilions, 2 enclosed) **Outings:** Available (also regular course events) **Lessons:** Available **Pro:** Joe Kris

Directions: I-90 to Exit 153 for SR 83 in Avon; south on SR 83 (Center Rd.); on left, after Riegelsberger Rd.

Description Bob-O-Link features 27 holes (all watered), three pavilions (one totally enclosed), 85 riding carts, a driving range, and a rule that should appear on all scorecards: Rule No. 9, under Local Rules, reads, "This is a fun game; play with courtesy."

More than 40 leagues play here, and a great outing business is done on Wednesdays and Saturdays. The new clubhouse, built in 1986, is roomy and comfortable and includes the pro shop, which carries the essentials only. Weather permitting, play continues all year.

Manager Bill Fitch remembers his first foursome. The original owners of the course gave this foursome the keys to the clubhouse. They were always out playing before the owners showed up. They even made coffee for the owners. The foursome played together steadily from 1969. Two members are dead now, both killed by heart attacks. "One was on the 14th hole and one was on the 16th," Fitch said. "The coincidence of that happening. . . ." The survivors continue to play.

The nines are designated by colors: Red, White, and Blue Links. The 150-yard markers are 4 x 4s with yellow numerals. The greens are not lightning fast but not slow either. Except for the occasional gully or mound, the course is built on flat terrain.

Highlights No. 3 is a pro-length 440-yard par 4, and it's the number one handicap hole on this nine. (Each of the three nines has handicaps 1 through 9.) Nothing fancy, just straightaway and long. All down the left side, however, are dense underbrush and tall trees, which hide an 8-foot-deep gully. Water courses through the gully, and balls hit into this jungle often stay there, waiting for the sharp-eyed hawker.

Then it's a short walk over a covered bridge to the next tee, shared by a hole from the Red nine. Look before you hit to make sure you don't switch nines by accident. When standing on the tee, it's difficult to see where No. 4 goes. The par 4 is 395 yards, and halfway out begins a serious dogleg right. A large sand trap marks the elbow of the dogleg, and more sand is on the right of the green. To the left, for players who skipped breakfast for an early tee time, stands a pear tree. At the right time of year the branches are filled with fruit.

No. 9, a 515-yard par 5, opens straight then turns sharply left near the approach. There, the Bob-O-Link version of the Eisenhower tree sits, a huge cottonwood on the right side of the fairway. In addition, mounds line the right side. On both sides, pines guide to the hole. There is a spot of sand directly in front of the green and a small pond there, as well. The pond cannot be seen until players get close.

The first two nines are fun to play but have no real signature holes. The third nine, the newer Blue Links, is not the longest of the three but is the most interesting. Only 3,086 yards, none of the par 4s on this nine is longer than 375 yards. The two par 5s make up the yardage, measuring 520 and 573. This nine calls for greater golf skills.

No. 1, for instance, is only 320 yards long and could be reached with two mid-iron shots. But no one is likely to pull a mid-iron from their bag on the tee. The hole narrows as it nears the green. Tall hardwoods line the left side of the fairway. Forty yards in front of the green a creek crosses the fairway. With more hardwoods leaning in on the right side, the tee shot and approach shot have to fly true. The greens here are much different from those on the Red and White Links; they are faster and have a great deal of shape to them. Double-break putts are common. If bets are made on this nine, it would pay to bet on the player with the best short game.

Bob-O-Link is a good layout for the average golfer, but one that takes a little getting used to. That isn't a fault of the course so much as it is a fact of the terrain. And one of the best things about Bob-O-Link is the number of teenagers playing the course. A course with a future.

Boston Hills Country Club   ☎ (330) 656-2438

Area: **Southeast**   City: **Boston Heights**   Cost: **$$$$**$ Difficulty: ●●●

Address: 105 East Hines Hill, Boston Heights

Tees	Ydg.	C/r	S/r	Pace
Back:	6167	68.3	110	4:12
Middle:	5865	65.9	106	
Forward:	4987	67.4	105	

	Weekdays	Weekends & hol.	Carts
Prices:	$11.00 / $20.00	$13.50 / $25.00	$11.50 / $22.00

Specials: Seniors Mon–Fri before 3 p.m. $7.00 / $9.50

Season: Year-round **Hours:** 6 a.m.–7 p.m. **Tee times:** Taken **Leagues:** Mon–Thu afternoons **Ranger:** Most days **Practice facil:** Range, Putting Green, Chipping Green, Sand, Covered heated practice tees (across street from club at The Range at Boston Hills, see separate entry). **Clubhouse:** Food, Beer, Liquor, Dining room, Pavilion, 1,400 sq. foot outing facility **Outings:** Available (for up to 250 people) **Lessons:** Available **Pro:** Ron Burke, PGA

Directions: I-271 to Exit 18 (SR 8); south on SR 8; right (west) on E. Hines Hill Rd.; on right. OR, Ohio Turnpike (I-80) to exit 12, to exit 12 (SR 8), ¼ mile north on SR 8; left (east) on E. Hines Hill; on right.

Description There is lots of activity at this old course, built in 1924 by Wink Chadwick (perhaps the quintessential yuppie name). Much of it has to do with marketing golf and golf services. A driving range with heated units for year-round practice and partnership with a discount golf store are good examples.

The entire course tilts down to Route 8, and holes play uphill, downhill, and sidehill. The elevation is gentle, never steep, and this is a good course to walk and carry. Most of the holes have generous landing areas, and the greens are medium speed. A dress code is strictly enforced.

Highlights It is a wide and comfortable layout. No. 3, a 449-yard par 5, is a good example. An aiming flag guides players to the optimum landing area from the tee. Though it is a decided dogleg right with a huge old maple tree in the elbow of the bend, it's not a particularly challenging par 5 but a beautiful one. On both sides of the broad fairway are hardwoods. The shallow green is egg-shaped and set at an angle. The approach shot here may be the most challenging.

The first par 3, No. 5, is under 100 yards. Many players would score better if they just threw the ball. Between the tee and the green is a tiny lake. The green has old hardwoods on the right and left sides. Bunkers are on both sides, too, and the rear of the green falls steeply away. Only 98 yards, it is an unfair hole, jammed in only because the number of holes called for is 18 and not 17.

No. 11, a 411-yard par 4, is the number one handicap hole. It used to be a par 5. A blind tee shot leads to a very wide fairway that bends sharply to the left. Trees define the hole and prevent cutting the dogleg. The approach is generally a long one to a small green in a forest of hardwoods.

Brandywine Country Club   ☎ (330) 657-2525

Area: **Far South**   City: **Peninsula**   Cost: $$$$$ Difficulty: ●●●

Address: 5555 Akron-Peninsula Rd., Peninsula

Tees	Ydg.	C/r	S/r	Pace	Par 3 Course Ydg.	C/r	S/r	Pace
Back:	6470	70.2	113					
Middle:	6088	68.4	110		1003	27.0		
Forward:	5625	70.5	113					

	Weekdays	Weekends & hol.	Carts	
Prices:	$11.00 / $20.00	$12.50 / $25.00	$11.00 / $22.00	*1998 prices

Specials: Mon–Fri before 9 a.m. $40.00 for 2 players & cart (18 holes); Mon–Fri until 2 p.m. $32.00 / $54.00 for 2 players & cart; Sat–Sun after 4 p.m. $32.00 for 2 players & cart; Seniors: Mon–Fri before 2 p.m. $9.00 / $13.00, carts $9.00 / $18.00, or 2 seniors Mon–Fri 18 holes & cart $21.00

Season: Year-round, weather permitting **Hours:** Sunrise–sunset **Tee times:** Taken, up to 2 weeks in advance **Leagues:** Mon–Thu 3:45–6 p.m. May–Aug **Ranger:** Weekends **Practice facil:** Putting Green **Clubhouse:** Food, Beer, Liquor, Pavilion **Outings:** Available **Lessons:** Available **Pro:** Jim Bricker

Directions: I-271 to Exit 12 for SR 303 (Streetsboro Rd.); east on SR 303; right (south) on Akron-Peninsula Rd. (also called S. Locust St.); on left.

Description In the parking lot on a summer day, license plates give an indication of this course's drawing power: Cuyahoga, Ashtabula, Stark, Summit, Trumbull, Portage, Huron, and Wayne counties are all there.

The front side offers a rolling, tree-lined, and well-maintained nine holes; the back side is legendary for its unusual holes that claw up and down hillsides, drop over cliffs, and steal balls from all but the most accurate players. In the pro shop is a shirt emblazoned with "I Survived the Back Nine at Brandywine."

If the Z-hole here—the 545-yard par 5 that is impossible to eagle—is legendary, it's also, like other holes on the back side, a novelty. The tee shot is a short iron, and the green is hidden and unreachable for the second shot. Approaches from sidehill/uphill lies are not uncommon on the back nine.

Peninsula is a pretty little town off the beaten path. And Brandywine's drama is attractive.

Highlights For players taken with the sensual beauty of courses, get the first tee time on a weekday. The gorgeous, deep-green front nine, sparkling with dew and framed on one side by tall, tree-covered hills, is awe inspiring. The game begins with a straightaway 376-yard par 4. The fairway rises past a century oak on the right side. Even though it should not come into play, it may stay in players' memories: it is a magnificent old tree. The fairway is generously wide on this hole, and the green slopes slightly forward. Sand marks the right edge.

The front nine is lovely, but the heroic shots and bragging rights come from the back nine. It opens with a 347-yard par 4. From a slightly elevated tee the fairway is straight, though narrow as it nears the green. Woods on either side and an equipment barn on the right emphasize the importance of staying in the fairway. Water comes into play in the last 100 yards, where a creek runs parallel to the fairway. There is sand at the right side of the green.

No. 12 is short, a 277-yard par 4. Cottonwood and poplars provide shade on the tee; hickories and oaks fill the woods on either side. To the left rear of the green, and not visible from the tee, is a lake. The ground behind the green falls away to the water. It's at this hole players realize the game is moving deeper into the hills that previously only lined the fairways.

At No. 13, the fairway dips in front of the tee, then shoots up and veers right. It's a 350-yard dogleg to the right and not one that tempts drivers to clear the elbow. The first couple hundred yards are all up—at about a 45-degree angle. On both sides of the fairway, tee to green, mature hardwoods begin where rough ends. Leaving the narrow fairway at any point can add a substantial number of strokes.

No. 15 is only 148 yards, but it can be reached with a well-hit short iron; the tee box is virtually the edge of a cliff and the green is 150 feet below. Maintenance and conditioning are problematic on the back nine and this tee is a good example, with its rubber mats. This is one of the signature holes here and is pictured on the scorecard.

Between the 13th tee and the 16th green is the Ohio version of the Khyber Pass. The famous Z-hole—No. 16, a 545-yard par 5 (and number two handicap)—is played on a valley floor. Its fairway goes out straight about 200 yards, takes a sharp right to the 150-yard marker, then an equally sharp left toward a green with sand on the left side. The fairway on this hole is narrow and seems more so because the valley walls rise on both sides. Walking off this green with a 5 is wholly satisfactory.

On the other side of the road is a par 3 course recently created by the Yesberger family on what had previously been a practice area.

Brandywine has a juniors program that should be copied and instituted at every course. Lee Yesberger and her corps of teachers and rangers give kids the opportunity to learn well and play fairly the greatest game in history. She runs tournaments, holds parties, and keeps records for her junior players at the log-cabin clubhouse built in front of

PUBLIC 18+

the practice green. Lots of golfers, years from now, are going to think warm thoughts about the grandmotherly Mrs. Yesberger, the woman who introduced them to golf.

PUBLIC 18+

Brentwood Golf Club
☎ (440) 322-9254

Area: **Far West**   City: **Grafton**   Cost: **$$**$$$ Difficulty: ●●●

Address: 12415 SR 57, Grafton

Tees	Ydg.	C/r	S/r	Pace
Back:	5148			
Middle:	4695			
Forward:	4223			

	Weekdays	Weekends & hol.	Carts
Prices:	$7.75 / $14.50	$8.50 / $16.00	$8.50 / $16.75

Specials: Seniors Mon–Fri before 3 p.m. $4.75 for 9 holes; Juniors Mon-Fri before 3 p.m. $5.00 for 9 holes

Season: Mar–Oct **Hours:** Sunrise–sunset **Tee times:** Taken weekends **Leagues:** Various times **Ranger:** Weekends **Practice facil:** Range, Putting Green, Chipping Green **Clubhouse:** Food, Beer, Pavilion **Outings:** Available **Lessons:** Available **Pro:** Andrew Bobrock

Directions: I-480 to SR 10 (I-480 ends here); west on SR 10 to SR 57; south on SR 57 (Medina–Elyria Rd.); on left.

Description   The Brothers Jalowiec—Bernard, Henry, and Walter—caddied as kids at Spring Valley Country Club, just north of Elyria. While rearing their own families in the late sixties, they built Brentwood during vacations, on weekends, and at night. The property was originally farmland.

Brentwood has a comfortable clubhouse and a super driving range. The course is mostly flat and easy to play.

It is a course popular with older golfers. "We have a lot of senior citizens, being that the course is a little shorter," Jalowiec said. "We give them a special rate, they don't abuse the course. They enjoy themselves." Some mornings the clubhouse looks like God's Waiting Room.

The course has no sand, but water comes into play.

Highlights   Greenskeeper Joe Yourkiewicz likes No. 4 on the front side, normally a 180-yard par 3 with a sizable green. It can play as short as 130 or as long as 245, he said. On the back nine, he selected No. 15 as the signature hole. It's a 370-yard par 4 with a narrow landing area. This dogleg left has a tricky green, he added.

The layout gets a bit crowded on the back nine, but it's a nice walk in the woods. The owners are notably gracious. The back of the scorecard says it well: "A Family-Owned Golf Club for Friendly Golfers."

Briardale Greens Golf Course   ☎ (216) 289-8574

Area: **East**   City: **Euclid**   Cost: **$$$**$$ Difficulty: ●●●

PUBLIC 18+

Address: 24131 Briardale Ave., Euclid

Tees	Ydg.	C/r	S/r	Pace
Back:	6127	70.5	122	
Middle:	5754	68.4	119	
Forward:	4977	68.4	108	

	Weekdays	Weekends & hol.	Carts
Prices:	$9.75 / $17.50	$11.00 / $19.50	$11.00 / $19.00

Specials: Seniors Mon–Fri $7.25 / $12.50; weekend rates apply to all holidays

Season: Mar–Nov **Hours:** Sunrise–sunset **Tee times:** Required **Leagues:** Mon–Fri 8–10 a.m., 3:30–6 p.m. **Ranger:** Daily **Practice facil:** Range, Putting Green, Chipping Green **Clubhouse:** Food, Beer **Outings:** Available (Weekends only) **Lessons:** Available **Pro:** Tom Sloat

Directions: I-90 to exit for Babbitt Rd.; north on Babbitt; right on Briardale Ave.

Description The first sign golfers read as they drive into Briardale Greens says, "You play at your own risk here." In the parking lot, the sign reads, "You park at your own risk here." Is there something we should know? On the property is one of the Euclid senior citizen activity buildings, and lots of older players tee it up here. The flat course, opened in 1977, is not distinguished but is inexpensive and accessible. Situated in the middle of this densely populated East Side suburb, it is a very busy course. Tee times are taken for weekday as well as weekend play. A half dozen or more leagues line up for play on weeknights. The small clubhouse seats only a handful before strangers rub elbows; the pro shop is similarly small. For outings, however, the pavilion seats more than a hundred and still has room for grills.

Highlights No. 1 is a no-frills par 4, 337 yards long. It is representative of what is going to follow. The fairway is defined by a few small stands of trees on both sides and a few bushes. Behind the green is a little lake.

No. 3 is a 350-yard dogleg right around a lake, which is inexplicably marked o.b. Cattails fill the bank on the green side of the water, and there is sand on the left side of the green. The sand slows some balls from bouncing to the chain-link fence that marks the edge of the course and the beginning of a residential area.

The number one handicap hole is No. 7, a par 5 of 495 yards, two lakes, tall trees, and a well-bunkered green. There are backyards all along the left side and a few trees on the right. About 170 yards from the green, a small lake appears on the right and a second lake behind it. If the lakes don't grab balls sliced from the fairway, tall sycamores on the right side will knock them down. The green has a large trap in front and a smaller trap in the rear.

No. 8 is a 170-yard par 3. Behind the tee is Babbitt Road, from which drivers of cars sometimes critique drivers of golf balls. The second body of water on the previous hole shows up on the right side here. Mallards raise families at water's edge. A brace of sand traps rests on the right side of the green.

Briardale is successful for a short list of reasons. It is not pretentious. It's a muny course for muny players, men and women from the neighborhood who enjoy the game. It is fun and inexpensive.

Briarwood Golf Course
☎ (440) 237-5271

Area: **South**   City: **Broadview Hts.**   Cost: **$$$$$**   Difficulty: ●●●

Address: 2737 Edgerton Rd., Broadview Hts.

Tees	Ben & Glen				Lochs & Glen				Lochs & Ben			
	Ydg.	C/r	S/r	Pace	Ydg.	C/r	S/r	Pace	Ydg.	C/r	S/r	Pace
Back:	6405	70.2	117	3:35	6985	72.8	125	3:45	6500	70.8	117	3:35
Middle:	5930	68.0	112		6330	69.5	119		5930	68.0	111	
Forward:	5355	69.9	110		5860	71.6	115		5930	68.9	108	

	Weekdays	Weekends & hol.	Carts
Prices:	$11.00 / $20.00	$13.00 / $25.00	$11.00 / $22.00

Specials: None

Season: Opens in Apr   **Hours:** Sunrise–sunset   **Tee times:** Taken weekends   **Leagues:** Mon–Fri various times   **Ranger:** Most days   **Practice facil:** Range, Putting Green **Clubhouse:** Food, Beer, Liquor, Lockers, Showers, Banquet rooooms   **Outings:** Available **Lessons:** Available

Directions: I-71 to Exit 231 for Royalton Rd. (SR 82); east on SR 82; right (south) on Broadview (SR 176) past Valley Pkwy.; right (east) on Edgerton Rd.; on right, after State Rd. (SR 94).

Description   Briarwood is not a historic course, but some golfing greats have played there. The first nine opened in 1966 and the greens fee was $1.50. That was Lochs. A year later, the Glens nine opened. And in 1972, Ben was opened. In 1971 an exhibition match was played between Miller Barber, Bobby Cole, and Jack Nicklaus. Jack lost. New ownership will mean some changes, but not likely anything drastic. Dozens of leagues call Briarwood home, and the course does a very good trade in outings. The clubhouse, completed in 1989, seats 160. There is also a pavilion.

The nines combine to offer three distinct rounds: Ben-Glens, Lochs-Glens, and Ben-Lochs. Very little sand on this course. The nine holes known as Ben are treated like a kid brother at a neighborhood baseball game, which is to say tolerated but not admired. That's too bad. Ben is a delightful little nine and, if played from the back of the tee boxes, no pushover for most golfers.

Highlights The first par 5 on Ben is the opening hole and is 460 yards from tee to green. It has a wide fairway that bends to the left. Down the right side, woods come into play; down the left, hidden from view, is a sizable lake. Before launching the approach shot, players have to watch for other players crossing the fairway—it's the only way to get from the 8th green to the 9th tee.

The rough is playable here and the fairways are lush. The greens are manicured and challenging. The population of Canada geese is substantial; so are its goose droppings.

No. 4 is a simple 330-yard par 4, but interesting. It is straight for about 200 yards, then abruptly turns left. Down the left side of the fairway are deep and thick woods, high enough to prevent anyone from cutting the corner. Down the right side, trees guide the player and the terrain drifts off and down. The green has a great deal of action on it. There's a grass bunker in front and deep woods behind.

No. 6 is a 490-yard par 5 where the drive must carry a narrow lake and climb. The fairway bends slightly and rises slowly but steadily. About a hundred yards from the green, a grass bunker sits in ambush in the right rough. There is no sand here—and very little sand anywhere on the three nines. Then it's off—across the No. 1 fairway—to the 9th tee.

The other two nines, Glens and Lochs, constitute the usual 18-hole round here.

The No. 2 tee box offers seasonal flowers and a difficult tee shot. The hole, a par 4 that plays 380, starts flat, then drops off to a valley in front of the elevated green. There is water on the right side of the valley. But that's not the difficult part. At about 165 yards from the green in the right side of the fairway is the local Eisenhower tree—actually two shagbark hickories. They effectively cut the width of a fairway that wasn't all that wide to begin with. The rough on the left side is filled with an assortment of trees.

No. 7, a par 5 of 490 yards, has been described by Jim Chorba as one of the best par 5s in the area. Chorba is president of the Inter-Club Public Golf Association and has played a lot of par 5s. One hundred yards from the tee the turf drops to a valley. Woods line both sides and are especially heavy on the left. The left side of the fairway rises and falls while the right is reasonably flat. A fast-moving creek crisscrosses the fairway on a diagonal, then lines the right side. At the green, which is elevated, the wide creek runs in front and left. This is the number two handicap hole on this nine.

After the turn, No. 4 on Lochs is a beautiful par 5. A lake sits in front of the tee box, willows leaning over the far shore on the right side. The lake is only 120 yards across, and where the fairway begins it bends slightly to the left and begins a long, slow rise. A few trees define the hole, and there is pitch and roll to the fairway. From the 150-yard marker, it falls slightly to a green with no sand.

A split-rail fence and well-tended flower garden make the 7th tee

PUBLIC 18+

especially attractive. It is a rising 365-yard par 4. The green is off to the right and only the top of the flag is visible until the last 100 yards, when the fairway levels.

Briarwood is a lush course thanks to a multitude of creeks and lakes. The layout successfully exploits the terrain, and the three nines and several tees adapt well to many types of golf game.

Brookledge Golf Club

☎ (330) 971-8416

Area: **Far South**   City: **Cuyahoga Falls**   Cost: **$$**$$$ Difficulty: ●●●

Address: 1621 Bailey Rd., Cuyahoga Falls

Tees	Ydg.	C/r	S/r	Pace
Back:	6254	68.9	107	
Middle:	5701	66.4	102	
Forward:	5326	66.2	103	

	Weekdays	Weekends & hol.	Carts
Prices:	$9.25 / $17.00	$11.00 / $20.00	$9.00 / $18.00

Specials: Seniors Mon–Fri $6.75 / $12.50, carts $7.00 / $14.00; Seniors Mon–Fri before noon $16.00 per person and ½ cart

Season: Mar 1–Nov 30 **Hours:** 6:30 a.m.–sunset **Tee times:** Recommended, Taken up to 2 weeks in advance **Leagues:** Mon–Fri evenings **Ranger:** Daily **Practice facil:** Range, Putting Green, Chipping Green, Sand, 2 ranges (mat & grass tees) **Clubhouse:** Food, Beer, Pavilion **Outings:** Available **Lessons:** Available **Pro:** Steve Black

Directions: I-271 to Exit 18 for SR 8; south on SR 8; left (east) on Howe Ave.; "soft" left (north) on Bailey Rd. at six-point intersection; right (east) on Kennedy Blvd. to entrance.

Description Up until the late 1980s, this course had only nine holes. Management asked Arthur Hills to stretch it out to 18, and when he did he made a very playable course. There is only one par 5 on the back side, but it is the par 3s that are the holes of note, especially No. 12, which measures 165 yards from the whites, 188 from the blues. The ball has to carry a ravine while slipping through a tree-lined passageway. Hills does not overdo anything. He wants courses to be playable for all levels. When a sand bunker is put in on one side of the green, the other side will have a grass bunker or mound.

Three teaching pros here stay busy at the range, a first-rate facility open year round. During the wintertime, heated stalls are open. During the warm weather, grass tees are moved every day. On either end are chipping and putting greens, and there is a new teaching tee. There are also five target greens

Brunswick Hills Golf Course   ☎ (330) 225-7370

Area: **Southwest**   City: **Brunswick**   Cost: $$$$$ Difficulty: ●●●

Address: 4900 Center Rd. (SR 303), Brunswick

Tees	Ydg.	C/r	S/r	Pace
Back:	6538	70.8	119	
Middle:	6198	69.1	113	
Forward:	5096	69.1	110	

	Weekdays	Weekends & hol.	Carts
Prices:	$10.50 / $18.00	$11.50 / $20.00	$9.50 / $18.00

Specials: Seniors (60+) & Juniors (under 17) Mon–Fri before 3 p.m. $6.00 / $11.00; Season memberships: individual senior, $550; individual junior, $450

Season: Year-round **Hours:** 5:30 a.m.–10 p.m. (peak season, weather permitting) **Tee times:** Taken **Leagues:** Mon–Fri, various times **Ranger:** Most days **Practice facil:** Putting Green **Clubhouse:** Food, Beer, Liquor **Outings:** Available (seating for 120 people) **Lessons:** Not available

Directions: I-71 to Exit 226 for SR 303; west on SR 303 (Center Rd.) to entrance on left.

PUBLIC 18+

Description In the late sixties, a group of golfers pooled their loot, bought this farmland, and had the first nine holes of Brunswick Hills built. They got an easy nine, with generous fairways and level ground. The stockholders built most of the second nine themselves. What a difference. It's a hilly, beautiful romp through woods of hawthorn, ash, maple, cottonwood, and pines. Many of the holes on the back side, though, while beautiful and often fun to play, lack good design and are penal, a style of design replaced by strategic design long ago, and with good reason. Brunswick Hills is one of the longer courses in the area. It stays open year round. League play is scheduled every day of the week but is not heavy. The front nine here is especially nice for mixed twosomes playing twilight golf.

Highlights Play begins on a 355-yard par 4 across a valley to a wide and trouble-free fairway. The valley, which cuts across the fairway, has a stream coursing through it and will affect play on holes 5, 7, and 9, too. On the back side, the stream will influence play on more than half the holes. The first green is slightly elevated but has no sand.

The front nine is fun, wide open, and not difficult. The back nine is fun, tight, and tough. Players lulled by the front side are brought up short with No. 10, a big dogleg to the left of 355 yards. Attempts to cut the corner are thwarted by a stand of tall trees. Along the right side, the course property ends and o.b. begins. And the sloped green is not easy to hold.

No. 12, a 399-yard par 4, is a beautiful hole. What appears to be a tree farm bounds the right side, and a couple of stands of trees on the left make this fairway narrow. It is not only narrow, but fast headed downhill, where it crosses a creek then rises to a lovely green balanced on the side of a hill.

No. 14, a 325-yard par 4, continues the roller-coaster ride. Missing the fairway can prove costly, but even being on the fairway, with its uneven lies, calls for concentration. This is clearly a side that favors experience.

No. 15, a long, 568-yard par 5, has all the virtues and beauty of the previous three holes—in spades. Not only does the creek have to be cleared, it has be watched, too. After crossing the fairway, it sneaks up the right side. The fairway narrows in the last 200 yards. It ends at a small green; three very good shots are needed to reach it in regulation.

The designers of this back nine just followed Mother Nature and let her have her way. There is nothing forced or artificial about the holes; each takes advantage of the terrain. So there are holes that are both aesthetically pleasing and very challenging.

Bunker Hill Golf Course ☎ (888) 749-5827

Area: **Southwest**   City: **Medina**   Cost: **$$$$$**   Difficulty: ●●●

Address: 3060 Pearl Rd., Medina

Tees	Ydg.	C/r	S/r	Pace
Back:	6643	70.9	117	
Middle:	6134	68.6	113	
Forward:	5074	68.2	110	

	Weekdays	Weekends & hol.	Carts
Prices:	$12.00 / $21.00	$13.50 / $27.00	$11.00 / $22.00

Specials: Mon–Fri Seniors & Juniors specials

Season: Mar–Nov **Hours:** Sunrise–sunset Sat, Sun; 7 a.m.–10 p.m. Mon–Fri **Tee times:** Taken **Leagues:** Mon–Fri evenings; some mornings **Ranger:** Daily **Practice facil:** Putting Green **Clubhouse:** Food, Beer, Liquor, Pavilion **Outings:** Available (large pavilion for special events) **Lessons:** Not available **Pro:** Todd Ingraham

Directions: I-71 to Exit 222 for SR 3; right off the highway; right (west) on Hamilton Rd.; left (south) on US42 (Pearl Rd.); on right.

Description The ad says it all: if you haven't played Bunker Hill lately, you haven't played it. The newest old course in the area, which was farmland until its transformation to a 9-hole golf course in the 1920s, and an 18-hole course in the 1940s, has undergone another transformation.

The original clubhouse was a small part of a restaurant, well known at the time as the Bunker Hill Inn. A fire destroyed the building in 1959; it was rebuilt as a clubhouse only in 1960. The Ingraham family, which purchased the property in the 1940s and was responsible for adding the second nine holes, still runs the operation. Arnold Ingraham is at the helm.

Bunker Hill might once have been regarded as a second- or third-tier track, but the improvements have not only stretched the course out—they've given it some personality, too.

The major changes start with the switching of the nines. The former No. 17, now No. 8, remains a par 3 but now features tees built back into the hillside and a rebuilt, larger green. New tees have been added to No. 9. No. 12 and No. 13, are completely new, built around a seven-acre lake. The former Nos. 3 and 4 were combined to make No. 14. No. 15 has been shortened from a par 5 to a par 4, but it still has a severe dogleg left to contend with. For No. 18, holes 8 and 9 were combined to create a par 5. The old No. 8 green was taken out, and the hill behind it leveled.

The clubhouse and snack bar have also been remodeled. The sausage sandwich here is worthy fare and, for the sophisticates among us, cappuccino is served. You can't get this much change out of a parking meter.

The pavilion area is private, with its own parking, and will accommodate 140–150 people. A historical note of interest: the current maintenance building is a 150-year-old barn that serves as a backdrop for tees No. 1 and No. 10.

Changes in the future will not be as dramatic, but will be important. Superintendent Scott Brickley's work is cut out for him: rebuild and enlarge the greens and add some new tees.

One thing that hasn't changed is Bunker Hill's laudable support of Junior Golf, which provides instruction and playing opportunities for more than 100 kids.

Highlights Soft spikes are mandatory. You will first see a new practice putting green. Remember the old No. 1 tee? That's it. Ten holes feature doglegs of various degrees. If you like carts, the paths here make riding in wet or otherwise inclement weather possible. Paths are marked at 200, 150, and 100 yards. (On par 5s, 250 yards is marked, too.) There are now four sets of tees and monument-type tee markers that add a touch of class.

No. 1 is a big and hilly par 5 of 525 yards. You need a good drive to get over the first hill to reach a flat area in the ravine. Another big hill awaits your next shot. After the second shot, don't forget to ring the bell letting the golfers behind know you cleared the area.

No. 3, par 3, 188 yards. A good-sized tree in front of the green will be the target of a lightning strike if the Great God of Golf hears our prayers.

No. 8, par 3, 130 yards. The changes have made this hole an interesting one; the tees are moved back in to the hill, and three sand traps on the hill lead up to an elevated green that is two-tiered and double-width.

No. 9, par 4, 396 yards, is the signature hole (though No. 18 is also a legitimate candidate). Woods and water on the right; trees on the left. Then the first of two creeks crossing the fairway. And as if you needed any more challenge, the green is steeply elevated. And there's a bell to ring here, too.

No. 12 is a short yet demanding par 5 of only 484 yards. The seven-acre lake on the right runs the length of the hole. A smaller lake on the left shouldn't be overlooked either. Hitting into a narrow green adds to the challenge.

No. 15, a par 4 of 367 yards, was a longer hole—and a par 5—in a previous life. Shortening it and lowering par didn't do away with the sharp dogleg left, though. Thick woods on the left go all the way to the corner turn. A small green is surrounded by trees.

Bunker Hill is a beautiful and scenic course, with natural terrain that has been enhanced. Right now, it could be the best-kept secret on the west side of town. It won't be for long.

PUBLIC 18+

Carlisle Golf Course

☎ (440) 458-8011

Area: **Far West**   City: **Grafton**   Cost: $$$$$ Difficulty: ●●●

Address: 39709 Slife Rd., Grafton

Tees	Ydg.	C/r	S/r	Pace
Middle:	5860	71.2		
Forward:	5540	72.3		

	Weekdays	Weekends & hol.	Carts
Prices:	$7.50 / $14.00	$8.50 / $15.50	$9.00 / $17.00

Specials: Senior and Junior discounts available Mon-Fri before 3 p.m. (except holidays)

Season: Year-round **Hours:** 7 a.m.–sunset **Tee times:** Not taken **Leagues:** Various times **Ranger:** Daily **Practice facil:** Putting Green **Clubhouse:** Food, Beer, Liquor, Dining room, Pavilion **Outings:** Available **Lessons:** Available

Directions: I-480 to SR 10 (I-480 ends here); west on SR 10; merges with US 20 and SR 301 (LaGrange Rd.); continue on SR 301 south 1 mile; left (east) on Slife Rd.; on right.

Description Few things smell as good as Carlisle Golf Course in late autumn. At this rough-hewn course, leaves are raked and burned, wafting an olfactory reminder that summer has passed. After the round, there is a fire to be found in the clubhouse, too. Additions to the wooden clubhouse, a two-story affair, have become annual projects.

Getting to Carlisle is a pleasant trip, because State Route 301 glides past scenic farms; one does not have to go far from the city to enjoy rural delights. A local celebration at the course is Boog Smith Day. Mr. Smith loved golf and he loved a pitcher of beer. One day after having both, he keeled over and introduced himself to his Maker. Owner Jim Mullins said ol' Boog wanted to go that way. In Boog's honor, players gather to drink beer and play golf.

Highlights Nothing fancy here. It is a homemade, neighborhood course for locals. The front side opens with a straight and unassuming par 4 of 365 yards. The first green is nearly two-tiered, and tricky. Fairways tend to brush up against one another here, and it takes a couple rounds to get comfortable with club selection.

There are riding carts available, but only the aged and infirm should be using them. This is a course made for walking.

The back side is more interesting than the front. The four holes before Norton's Knoll take advantage of the century oaks and a couple manmade lakes. The physical beauty of the course peaks from Nos. 12 through 15.

It is not a long course, at 2,785 out, 3,075 in, par 71. And it is not an especially challenging course. But it can be a fun place to chase the ball. And golfing dreams can come true here—just ask about Boog Smith.

PUBLIC 18+

Chardon Lakes Golf Course ☎ (440) 285-4653

Area: **Far East**   City: **Chardon**   Cost: **$$$$$**   Difficulty: ●●●

Address: 470 South St., Chardon

Tees	Ydg.	C/r	S/r	Pace
Back:	6789	73.1	135	
Middle:	6190	70.2	129	
Forward:	5685	73.0	130	

	Weekdays	Weekends & hol.	Carts
Prices:	$11.00 / $22.00	$16.00 / $32.00	NA / $20.00

Specials: Season pass available; Seniors Mon–Fri $25.00 for 18 holes & ½ cart

Season: Apr 1–Nov 15 **Hours:** 7 a.m.–9 p.m. weekdays; 6 a.m.–9 p.m. weekends **Tee times:** Taken, Up to 7 days in advance **Leagues:** Mon–Thu 4–6:15 p.m.; Thu a.m. (Ladies League) **Ranger:** Daily **Practice facil:** Range, Putting Green, Sand **Clubhouse:** Food, Beer, Liquor, Lockers, Showers, Pavilion **Outings:** Available **Lessons:** Available **Pro:** Tom Bond

Directions: I-90 to Exit 200 for SR 44; south on SR 44 (becomes South St. in Chardon); on right.

Description This tough and pretty course opened in 1931. It has a wonderful history graced by great names: Tom Weiskopf, Jack Nicklaus, and Arnold Palmer have gone around here more than once. Weiskopf's parents were members throughout the sixties. And Nicklaus holds the course record, a 67 shot during an American Cancer Society benefit in 1974.

Par is 72 over 6,174 yards. Out-of-bounds appears on the first five holes and again on the back side. Aprons in front of the greens add a country-club touch to the course. Another such touch is yardage marked on sprinkler heads. The 150-yard markers are Norway spruces.

Highlights No. 1 is a 348-yard par 4 that begins at a tee with a sign reading: "No Mulligans." No hitting 'til you're happy here.

No. 2 is the only par 5 on the front side and is a short 473 yards. A lake on the right side of the tee should not come into play. Pines are on both sides of the fairway and on the right is a housing development. A big slice can put the ball into a sunroom. The straight fairway rises gradually to a green with sand on the right front.

No. 4 is a long 205-yard par 3 uphill all the way. On the right, o.b. leads into a field with a sign promising "You'll Be Prosecuted to the Fullest Extent of the Law" for trespassing. Sounds like looking for a ball is a felony. A rude touch to a game marked by civility.

At No. 6, a beautiful hole, stone steps lead up to the blue tees. The hole leaves straight from the tee, then turns sharply left toward the green. This 384-yard par 4 has plenty of creek defining the right side. For the last stretch into the green, pines mark the left side and water marks the right. It's a very narrow fairway coming in, only 18 yards across. Little wonder this is the number one handicap hole.

No pushover, this little course, and it is in good hands. Shooting for a record held by Nicklaus adds glamour.

Chenoweth Golf Course

☎ (330) 644-0058

Area: **Far South**   City: **Akron**   Cost: $$$$$ Difficulty: ●●●

Address: 3087 Chenoweth Rd., Akron

Tees	Ydg.	C/r	S/r	Pace
Back:	6109	69.0	113	
Middle:	5613	66.6	109	
Forward:	4750	67.0	108	

	Weekdays	Weekends & hol.	Carts
Prices:	$10.00 / $20.00	$12.00 / $24.00	$10.00 / $20.00

Specials: Seniors Mon–Fri before 11 a.m. $7.00 / $13.00

Season: Year-round **Hours:** Sunrise–sunset **Tee times:** Taken **Leagues:** Mon–Fri evenings **Ranger:** Daily **Practice facil:** Range, Putting Green **Clubhouse:** Food, Beer, Liquor, Pavilion **Outings:** Available **Lessons:** Not available

Directions: I-77 to Exit 120; north on Arlington Rd.; right (east) on Chenoweth Rd.

Description This young course was started in 1991; the second nine was added two years later. Although a short course, it's certainly not executive length; the two best holes are longer than 500 yards. Fairways are tight here, and the rolling terrain has plenty of trees. There's only a bit of water and bunkering is light. No. 5 is worthy of note. This dogleg par 5 is 532 yards long, and the water that runs down the right side from the tee crosses the fairway at the elbow. The home hole is another challenge. It's 502 yards, and a dogleg shows up for the second shot. Water in front of the green. Eagles are rare, indeed.

You Need Lessons

Among the many mysteries of golf is this, the greatest mystery of all: Why do so many of us think we can improve without lessons? Most players who have enjoyed the benefits of a good teacher would agree that money is far better invested in lessons than in a new driver.

Bob Bourne, PGA, is the director of instruction at StoneWater Golf Club in Highland Heights. A player for the University of Houston and a PGA Tour player for a few years in the early seventies, he brings almost three decades of private club teaching experience to the range.

"The first thing I want students to understand is that we're forming a relationship that will go from teacher/student to coach/player. We both want the same thing: for the player to develop a game that provides pleasure."

Teachers can do more today than ever before. Improvements such as cavity–back and perimeter–weighted irons make it easier to hit. Ranges are often designed with a teaching program in mind. Videotaping allows the student to see what the teacher has been describing.

Even with these improvements, however, "Learning a repeating swing calls for a commitment to the game," Bourne says. And with him, it calls for a commitment of $300 for his basic teaching package.

For $300, Bourne videotapes the student, teaches the basics, and provides drills over a total of three hours. Many teachers give 30-minute lessons. Bourne believes the 45-minute lesson is often better.

As the relationship begins, it is truly teacher/student. Bourne studies the student.

"My first job is to figure out how a particular student learns. Some are right-brain, some are left-brain. Some learn best with demonstration, others with verbal teaching."

Like all teachers, Bourne wants to know what talent or experience you've arrived with. He wants to make sure the basics are in place, to make sure the grip is sound, the address is proper, and alignment is accurate.

Then the fun begins: Swinging the club.

It's at this point that the value of a teacher appears. The golf swing, after all, is far closer to cabinet making than pile driving.

"If you have a teacher right in front of you, setting up ball after ball, and talking you through the lesson, success comes quickly," Bourne said. "But I remind students that they're on the teaching range, not on a course where every shot counts."

It's the teacher who explains how easy it is to come over the ball, to hit slice after slice, to push or pull the ball.

"With most students, they're learning not only how to swing the club; they're also learning what goes into a swing. It's one of the hidden benefits. If you understand the swing and the subtle differences in it, you take your understanding of the game to another level."

Mr. Bourne's basic lesson package includes driving, short irons, and putting. "That's because almost three-quarters of a beginner's game will be with those three shots.

If a beginner shoots 100, he or she uses the driver 14 times. That score probably has 40 putts. And the pitching wedge was used 16 times. That's 70 strokes right there, so I want the student to build the foundation of the game with those three shots."

Bourne doesn't ignore the importance of golf etiquette. But instead of lecturing, he takes students on the course, shows them where to stand on the tee, in the fairway, and on the green. When to maintain silence. When and how to handle the flag. "It seems to make more sense to students if we go out and do it instead of just talking about it."

Etiquette and playing the game at a brisk pace are important. For players who take too long to address the ball and swing, Bourne has a drill. He counts, "One-one-thousand, two-one-thousand, three-one-thousand . . . . Before I count to ten, I want them to hit it and they do. Sometimes they're surprised at how easy it is to play 'ready' golf."

Once the basic program is completed, Bourne recommends playing with accomplished players. "I suggest a practice regimen for them and my advice about playing is designed to make playing fun, even at a basic skill level. I suggest they play with accomplished players. And if their tee shot is a bad one, I tell them to pick it up and drop it by the ball closest to the green. That way they're not going to slow anyone down. I also tell them for all their shots to put it on a tee. Remember, they're learning, not playing for the rent money."

Once the basics are in place and a practice and playing schedule is established, teachers are there for remedial lessons, for tune-ups, and for golf talk. It's the teacher who can recommend the best equipment for the player, and who shares the pride in a good swing.

"That's when you know you're a coach, no longer a teacher," Bourne said.

—JHT

TIDYMAN'S TIDBITS #1

Courses with front sides so different from the back it's hard to believe they're related:

• Painesville CC
• Brandywine GC
• Brunswick Hills GC

Cherokee Hills Golf Club

☎ (330) 225-6122

Area: **Southwest**   City: **Valley City**   Cost: **$$$**$$ Difficulty: ●●●

Address: 5740 Center Rd. (SR 303), Valley City

Tees	Ydg.	C/r	S/r	Pace
Back:	6210	68.3	109.2	3:45
Middle:	5880	67.0	109.2	
Forward:	5420	70.3	116.2	

	Weekdays	Weekends & hol.	Carts
Prices:	$10.00 / $17.00	$11.00 / $21.00	$10.00 / $20.00

Specials: Cart special Mon–Fri before 2 p.m., Sat–Sun after 2 p.m. (tee times required) $24.00 for 18 holes & ½ cart (seniors $20.00); Seniors & Juniors Mon–Fri before 2 p.m. $9.00 / $18.00

Season: Year-round **Hours:** Sunrise–sunset **Tee times:** Taken **Leagues:** Various times **Ranger:** Most days **Practice facil:** Putting Green, Chipping Green **Clubhouse:** Food, Beer, Liquor, Dining room, Private rooms **Outings:** Available (a specialty) **Lessons:** Available

Directions: I-71 to Exit 226 for SR 303 (Center Rd.); west on Center Rd.; 5 miles on left.

Description A handsome red barn has served as clubhouse at Cherokee Hills for many years. Ed Haddad owns this 30-year-old course and keeps it open as much as Ol' Man Winter allows. They play the game at a quick pace here; at the third tee, for example, a sign reads: "If it has taken you more than 25 minutes to get here, you are playing too slowly." Though this is not a particularly long course—6,010 yards, par 69 (only one par 5 on each side)—it offers some tough holes.

Highlights The opener, a 340-yard par 4, starts at an elevated tee. It's a lovely view, one of the higher spots on the course. It is lined on both sides with trees. Closer to the green, a creek shows up on the left side in the rough, and a huge old willow stands at the left side of the green.

No. 6, or The Hole from Another Planet, is a 510-yard par 5 played on ground high and low, wide and very narrow. A huge sycamore stands in the middle of the fairway. From the tee, the hole begins innocently enough by stretching straight out for 250 yards. A lake appears on the right side but should not come into play. The surprise is on the left, where the fairway falls over and down a steep hill and then shoots off to the right. In the middle of this low ground is the sycamore. Behind it a hundred yards or so is the green, stuck in the base of a hill. Making matters more interesting is a creek down the left side of the last part of the fairway that then cuts across in front of the green. This hole can likely be played a dozen different ways, and scoring well on it has to be a matter of experience with the hole as well as excellent shotmaking.

No. 10 is a 410-yard par 4, a hole with generous fairway and water at the green. It finishes at the low point on the course, and getting back out

PUBLIC 18+

and up to the next tee can wind players not used to hauling their own clubs over hill and dale.

A stepladder on the tee is a good indication that the shot will be blind. So it is at No. 13, where a 390-yard par 4 rolls and rises to the 150-yard marker before heading downhill. Sand is on both sides of the green and, more dangerous, a good-sized lake rests on the left.

Creekwood Golf Club   ☎ (440) 748-3188
Area: **Southwest**   City: **Columbia Station**   Cost: $$$$$ Difficulty: ●●●

Address: 9691 N. Reed Rd., Columbia Station

Tees	Ydg.	C/r	S/r	Pace
Middle:	6117	68.8	116	
Forward:	4775	69.1	112	

	Weekdays	Weekends & hol.	Carts
Prices:	$9.25 / $16.50	$10.75 / $20.00	$9.50 / $19.00

Specials: Mon–Fri (times vary) $46.50 for 2 players and cart; Seniors Mon–Fri $7.00 / $12.00, carts $8.50 / $17.00; Seniors Mon–Fri (times vary) $38.50 for 2 players and cart

Season: Year-round **Hours:** Sunrise–sunset **Tee times:** Required weekends
Leagues: Various times **Ranger:** Daily **Practice facil:** Range, Putting Green
Clubhouse: Food, Beer, Pavilion, Patio **Outings:** Available **Lessons:** Not available

Directions: I-480 to Exit 1B for Lorain Rd.; west on Lorain Rd. to Root Rd.; left (south) on Root; bear right onto N. Reed Rd.; on left.

Description David Sandvick, who built this course, was a bricklayer who loved the game. Sandvick needed three years to build the front nine, which opened in 1960. Six years later, the back side was completed. Sandvick died in 1967, and succeeding management of the course was not what it should have been.

But the Sandvick family has been rebuilding this course for over a dozen years, and it looks like it. The course is in good shape: the drainage problem of years ago grows smaller every year. Fairways, tees, and greens are watered.

Highlights The first hole is wide open and long, a 430-yard par 4. Like a number of holes here, it is not well defined. Water is on the right near the green but should not be a problem. Sand is used judiciously here and seems to be of a finer grain than that of other clubs. This is a good warm-up hole with a green that is easily chipped to.

Several of the greens here have steep sides to them; missing the green and hitting the side can send a ball 30 or 40 yards, a design feature that is penal—and on this course, with these league players, penal design doesn't help.

While No. 10 appears wide open, the 365-yard dogleg to the left calls for some accuracy off the tee. The elbow of the dogleg, which veers to the left, is filled with tall hardwoods and sits on the edge of a creek running across the fairway. It is here that the women's tee is placed, one of the few women's tees on this course that looks like it was not designed as an afterthought. Going down the right side of the fairway is o.b. A rail fence marks the end of the course property, and the farm there—fields, silo, barn—is beautiful.

Holes 13, 14, and 15 constitute Amen Corner as designed by Bizarro. No. 13 is a 330-yard par 4. Only 150 out and then 150 to the left, it is a suspiciously short 330 yards. The trouble is the corner of the dogleg; it holds the next tee, and players trying to cut the corner run the risk of killing someone teeing off on No. 14. White stakes make the area out of bounds.

No. 15 is a 455-yard par 5 that is straight until the final 50 yards, at which point the fairway lurches to the right. In the elbow of the tight dogleg is a stand of tall hardwoods. To get on in two calls for a shot not found in most bags: a high, long fade that drops suddenly. And while chipping the last shot to the green, one runs the risk of getting clobbered by players on the 13th tee. A very crowded corner. The final holes play on more open territory, though.

PUBLIC 18+

Deer Track Golf Club ☎ (440) 986-5881

Area: **Far West**   City: **Elyria**   Cost: **$$$**$$ Difficulty: ●●●

Address: 9488 Leavitt Rd., Elyria

Tees	Ydg.	C/r	S/r	Pace
Back:	6410	70.3	124	4:10
Middle:	6159	69.1	122	
Forward:	5350	68.7	115	

	Weekdays	Weekends & hol.	Carts
Prices:	$10.00 / $19.00	$11.00 / $21.00	$10.00 / $20.00

Specials: Mon–Fri before 1 p.m. $19.00 for 18 holes & ½ cart; Seniors Mon–Fri before 1 p.m. $16.50 for 18 holes & ½ cart; Seniors Mon–Fri before 3 p.m. $6.00 / $11.00

Season: Year-round **Hours:** 6 a.m.–10 p.m. Apr–Oct; 8 a.m.–4 p.m. Nov–Mar **Tee times:** Taken **Leagues:** Various times **Ranger:** Some days **Practice facil:** Range, Putting Green, Chipping Green, Sand, 5 target greens **Clubhouse:** Food, Beer, Liquor, Pavilion **Outings:** Available (also regular course events) **Lessons:** Available **Pro:** Tony Dulio, PGA

Directions: SR 2 to SR 58 (Amherst/Oberlin); south on SR 58 (Leavitt Rd.); on right.

Description Deer Track is a course that grew up. It started as a par 3 and driving range in 1958. In 1970, it was turned into an executive-length, nine-hole layout. In 1972, Tony Dulio and his late father, Jim, bought the place and remodeled it, making it a regulation par 36. The second nine opened in July of 1989. The course name was originally Midway; it was renamed when the back nine was built. The name comes from the con-

PUBLIC 18+

struction period, when the owners would walk the course early in the day and find deer tracks. On the back side lives a fox family; its breadwinner often steals balls from the greens and takes them home. Why? The fox mistakes them for eggs, it is theorized. Someplace on the edge of the course is a fox den filled with Titleists, Slazengers, and Pinnacles.

Highlights No. 2 is a 371-yard dogleg left, a par 4 that calls for an accurate drive and a more accurate second shot. The greens here are well cared for and challenging. At this green, sand lies on both sides. The use of manmade lakes and mounds adds a great deal to an otherwise flat layout.

No. 8 is the number one handicap hole, a very difficult dogleg left. It calls for a minor tee shot but an approach of heroic proportions. It is 398 yards and, depending on location of the tee, the drive can be anywhere from 180 to 230 yards. There is a long and narrow lake along the left side of the fairway from the tee. After less than 200 yards, the fairway abruptly turns left. From the tee, players look down a fairway with tall trees on both sides. These narrow the fairway considerably. So it's a tough—some might call it confusing—tee shot. The second shot has to be a long iron or fairway wood down a narrow fairway. Behind the green is plenty of water.

Hole Nos. 1, 9, 10, and 18 are parallel and close together. Sharing fairways on these straight and hazard-free holes is common.

Dorlon Golf Club
☎ (440) 236-8234

Area: **Southwest**   City: **Columbia Station**   Cost: $$$$$ Difficulty: ●●●

Address: 18000 Station Rd., Columbia Station

Tees	Ydg.	C/r	S/r	Pace	Women's tees Ydg.	C/r	S/r	Pace
Back:	7154	73.1	125	4:15				
Middle:	6475	70.3	118		5431	70.1	115	
Forward:	5691	66.3	107					

	Weekdays	Weekends & hol.	Carts
Prices:	$8.50 / $17.00	$9.00 / $18.00	$9.50 / $19.00

Specials: Breakfast Special Mon–Fri 7 a.m.–1 p.m.: $22.00 18 holes & ½ cart (breakfast included); Seniors (65+) 7 a.m.–3 p.m.: 2 players $18.00 18 holes & ½ cart; "Dorlon Dozen"—play 12 for the price of 9.

Season: Year-round **Hours:** Sunrise–sunset **Tee times:** Taken, holidays **Leagues:** Mon–Thu 4–6 p.m. **Ranger:** Daily **Practice facil:** Range, Putting Green, Chipping Green, Sand **Clubhouse:** Food, Beer, Dining room, Pavilion **Outings:** Available **Lessons:** Available

Directions: I-71 to Exit 231 for SR 82 (Royalton Rd.); west on Royalton for 6.8 miles; left (south) on Station Rd. for 1.5 miles; on right.

Description A new sign and new landscaping greet golfers at the entrance of Dorlon Golf Club, formerly known as Dorlon Park Golf Course. There's a new owner, too: Deborah Lontor-Bonham has taken over for her late father. Other things are changing here, including the clubhouse, which is being fixed up as part of an ambitious $300,000 renovation. The course is also receiving attention—notably the reconstruction of sand traps and major improvements on the driving range. Future plans include continuous cart paths, improved irrigation, and tee reconstruction.

Like your golf courses long? Pack a lunch and tee it up on the blues here. They measure 7,154 yards, par 72.

PUBLIC 18+

Highlights The course opens with a par 5, though an easy one. It is 472 yards and has a small lake on the right side about 50 yards from the tee. Water shows up again a couple hundred yards out, also on the right side and reachable. Getting on this green in regulation is often dramatic. There is a big trap on the left front and the green itself is slightly elevated. It falls off steeply in the rear. The greens here are not slow by any means.

No. 7 is a 518-yard par 5 that begins with a long and narrow lake right in front of the tee box. The water is almost a hundred yards long, 20 yards across, and in the shape of a C. Beyond the water, a generous fairway bends a bit to the left. The back and sides of this green fall away sharply. All the greens here call for a steady hand, a sharp eye, and patience.

No. 14 is a 364-yard par 4 from an especially beautiful tee box. Surrounded by oaks more than 100 feet tall and far from the clubhouse, this part of the course seems to encourage players to be quiet. This is a sharp dogleg to the right, and no chance of shooting over the corner here unless one of the 14 clubs is a mortar. Both sides of the fairway lead to deep woods. Grass bunkers show up close to the green.

The greens here tend to be hilly and fast, and many are protected by sand traps. They can teach caution to rash players. It is a long and challenging 18 holes, a course for men and women who have no need for pro shops or lessons.

TIDYMAN'S TIDBITS #2

Courses where taking a riding cart is not always wimpy:

- Ironwood
- Hinckley
- Brandywine
- Thunder Hill

PUBLIC 18+

Ellsworth Meadows Golf Club ☎ (330) 656-2103

Area: **Far South**   City: **Hudson**   Cost: **$$**$$$ Difficulty: ●●●

Address: 1101 Barlow Rd., Hudson

Tees	Ydg.	C/r	S/r	Pace
Back:	6456	70.5		
Middle:	6161	69.0		
Forward:	5167	65.9		

	Weekdays	Weekends & hol.	Carts
Prices:	$13.00 / $20.00	$16.00 / $25.00	$7.00 / $10.00

Specials: Seniors (limited hours) $10.00 / $17.00; Hudson residents receive $3.00 discount (NA for carts)

Season: Apr–Nov **Hours:** Mon–Fri 7:30–sunset; Sat, Sun 6:30–sunset **Tee times:** Required **Leagues:** Available **Ranger:** Daily **Practice facil:** Putting Green, Chipping Green **Clubhouse:** Food, Beer, Liquor **Outings:** Available (for weekend groups only) **Lessons:** Available **Pro:** Denny Smith, PGA

Directions: I-271 to Exit 18 for SR 8; south on SR 8; left (east) on SR 303; right (south) on Terex Rd.; left on Barlow Rd.; on left, past Nicholson Dr.

Description Ellsworth Meadows Golf Club is now city owned, and that's a good thing here. Before the purchase in 1997, the course was known as Big Springs, and playing conditions were less than optimal. That was then. This is now. Denny Smith, PGA, is the pro and manager, so the course and club are in excellent hands.

The Ellsworth name is a prominent one in Hudson. James W. Ellsworth was born here and left much of his fortune here—in Hudson Academy, the clock tower, the underground utility system ... you get the idea.

Players who avoided Big Spring in recent years would be well advised to play again. Almost three quarters of a million dollars is being invested in the course, including clubhouse renovation, the beginning of cart paths, drainage on the west side of the course where rainwater was problematic, a new pump house, and a watering system. Smith brags about the greens being handled as they are, "Each one has been aerated, seeded, top-dressed with loving care. And the results are showing already."

Highlights This has always been a shotmaker's course, with demanding landing areas and narrow fairways. The trees here define many of the holes and the par 5s are all risk/reward holes. You can leave your driver in the bag for lots of tee shots here; accuracy rules.

No. 7, a par 3, is all water and a 160-yard carry.

Among other changes, the nines have been reversed. Good. With the old layout, the home hole was a 330-yard par 4. With the new layout, players charge down a 500-yard par 5 to the clubhouse.

Always a joy to see a course saved; a toast is in order. To Hudson!

Emerald Woods Golf Courses   ☎ (440) 236-8940

Area: **Southwest**   City: **Columbia Station**   Cost: **$$$**$$ Difficulty: ●●●

Address: 12501 N. Boone Rd., Columbia Station

Tees	Audrey's-Heatherstone				Pine Valley-St. Andrew's			
	Ydg.	C/r	S/r	Pace	Ydg.	C/r	S/r	Pace
Back:	6673	71.7			6629	72.1		
Middle:	6165	69.1			6058	69.1		
Forward:	5295	69.2			5080	69.4		

	Weekdays	Weekends & hol.	Carts
Prices:	$10.00 / $18.50	$12.00 / $22.00	$10.00 / $20.00

Audrey's-Heatherstone

Specials: Mon–Fri before 10 a.m. free cart w/ 18 holes (2 players); Mon–Fri 10 a.m.–1 p.m. $10.00 for a cart when playing 18 holes (2 players)

Season: Year-round   **Hours:** 7 a.m.–sunset weekdays; 6 a.m.–sunset weekends
Tee times: Taken weekends   **Leagues:** Mon–Fri 4:30–6 p.m. (one 9-hole layout always available for public)   **Ranger:** Most days   **Practice facil:** Putting Green   **Clubhouse:** Food, Beer, Pavilion   **Outings:** Available (Large groups welcome; incentives for weekday outings; 3 pavilions.)   **Lessons:** Not available

Directions: I-71 to Exit 231 for SR 82 (Royalton Rd.); west on Royalton; right (north) on N. Boone Rd.; on right.

Description In this neck of the woods—farmland for most of its settled history—there are lots of golf holes. Within five minutes of each other are Dorlon Park, Royal Crest, Hickory Nut, Mallard Creek, and this 5-nine course. The first nine opened in 1965, and that was Audrey's. Heatherstone opened in 1967, Pine Valley opened in 1969, and St. Andrew's in 1977. A fifth nine, called A Walk in the Park, is the latest (and is actually a separate executive-length layout). That's a lot for event coordinator George Flynn, whose background is not golf. He was a manufacturing engineer for the better part of two decades. When his layoff was announced, he told his wife it was time for a career change.

There is irrigation here, but it is often used only once a week, so the dry weather can have a terrible effect on the course. "We're not as lush as some other places that water every day, but we're not burned out."

Many leagues play here, and there are plenty of outings as well. "Some people at other courses tell me they're dropping outings. But I enjoy doing them, working and planning with the people who call and say 'this is my first outing.' Before I got here, I did six outings of my own."

Highlights Audrey's is listed as the No. 1 course. Its No. 2 is a 382-yard par 4, a dogleg left that begins with a pine-lined fairway then gives way to hardwoods. In the last 130 yards to the green, the fairway is made more narrow by Lake Deborah on the right side. There is sand at this green, as well. That is a representative hole here, with woods, water, and sand getting between players and birdies.

No. 4, a soft dogleg left, is a 400-yard par 4. It is the longest par 4 on

PUBLIC 18+

this nine and for that reason alone the number two handicap. No. 6, a 355-yard par 4 is open, but Lake Deborah guards the left side of the green and sand sits on the right. No. 8, a 385-yard par 4, has Lake Celestine on its left.

The scorecard matches Heatherstone with Audrey's to make a round. No. 13 is a long par 3; at 194 yards, more golfers will miss than hit the green. A hook can send the ball into an adjacent backyard, despite a wooden fence erected to prevent such shots. A sign on the fence reads: PLEASE, DO NOT ENTER YARD FOR YOUR BALL. PICK UP GOOD BALL AT PRO SHOP COUNTER. THANKS. On the left side of the green stands a handsome locust tree, one of many that dot the course.

The number one handicap on the Audrey-Heatherstone layout is No. 15, a par 4 of 445 yards. It calls for a huge drive to get in position for the approach shot. It is a soft dogleg left, and trees on both sides can slow progress to the egg-shaped green.

The next nine is Pine Valley, known to some players as The Nine Holes From Hell. Jungle combat experience provides the best training for this nine, which begins with the number one handicap hole, a par 4 of 353 yards. The terrain here is hilly and best covered by jeep. The woods get thick enough at times for inexperienced players to need directions to the next tee. Many pack sandwiches and leave a trail of crumbs. It has some unusual holes. In short, it's a lot of fun to play.

Emerald Woods, though it doesn't have any long nines, does have some very tough holes. It also has great variety and a friendly, professional staff.

Erie Shores Golf Course   ☎ (440) 428-3164; (800) 225-3742

Area: **Far East**   City: **Madison**   Cost: $$$$$$ Difficulty: ●●●

Address: 7298 Lake Rd. East, Madison

Tees	Ydg.	C/r	S/r	Pace
Back:	6000	68.2	116	
Middle:	5823	67.2	114	
Forward:	5053	67.0	108	

	Weekdays	Weekends & hol.	Carts
Prices:	$9.50 / $16.00	$10.25 / $17.75	$11.00 / $22.00

Specials: Mon–Fri $34.00 w/cart, Sat–Sun $36.00 w/cart; Season pass available; Winter rates Nov–Apr; Seniors Mon–Fri $19.95 for 18 holes, cart, hot dog, soft drink

Season: Year-round **Hours:** Sunrise–sunset **Tee times:** Required weekends, Taken daily **Leagues:** Daily, various times **Ranger:** Daily **Practice facil:** Range, Putting Green, Chipping Green, Sand **Clubhouse:** Food, Beer, Lockers, Pavilion, Indoor patio **Outings:** Available (up to a year in advance) **Lessons:** Available **Pro:** Terry Clark, PGA

Directions: I-90 to Exit 212 for SR 528; north on SR 528; right (east) on US 20; left (north) on Bennett Rd. for 3 miles; right (east) on Lake Rd. East; on right.

Description Erie Shores' management completed a $1-million renovation in 1993 that changed and improved this course owned and operated by Lake County Metroparks. Players will be pleased. So will other animals.

"We're certified by the state as a backyard wildlife habitat," Tom Weiss, PGA, said. "To qualify, we planted flowers and ferns. Thirty-three species of flowers are laid out strategically to accommodate the life cycles of hummingbirds and butterflies. We have purple martin houses and bat houses and squirrel houses, as well."

They also have golf. This short course was developed in 1957 from two farms; the chicken barn from one was turned into the first clubhouse.

After the park board assumed title 15 years ago, it hit the ground running and has not stopped. At present, Erie Shores (you can reach Lake Erie with a driver and a 6-iron) is a pretty course, well maintained, and staffed with friendly, helpful employees. The courtyard in front of the clubhouse is brick and decorated with flowers. Every tee also has a flower bed, most of them in wooden barrel halves. When not playing, Sherri Dugan serves as gardener for the course.

New practice areas have been built, including a 28-station driving range, and the cart paths have been redone.

Calling for tee times is an especially good idea here, as the course schedule is filled with league play, including women, juniors, seniors, mixed couples, and, every Sunday morning, a weekend league of stalwarts. The Sunday morning league, 50 strong, is out before 7:30 a.m. And that is more than "rain or shine." It is year round. When the greens are covered with snow, the players take shovels along with clubs. At least once a month, Weiss puts on some sort of tournament. Night-light tourneys, the nine-hole matches played after dark, are well attended.

Few courses treat "family golf" as warmly as this one.

Highlights The terrain at Erie Shores is flat, but the course offers some very pretty holes. The greens here are not very fast, but they are healthy. Around most of them, groundskeepers maintain an apron of short grass about seven feet wide.

The course plays easy, and it's a pleasure to walk. It's a pleasure to look at, as well, thanks to the care taken with the flora. At No. 3, a soft dogleg left, the tee looks out over two small lakes in front, and there is a home for purple martins. The 355-yard par 4 has a wide fairway. On some days, a ball hawker sits in the left rough and offers used balls to players.

The No. 8 tee is often completely in shadow. This par 4 of 379 yards bends softly to the left. Bird houses for chickadees and bluebirds show up here.

Erie Shores steadily improves. It's a wonderful course for family golf, where skill levels can differ greatly but the pleasures of the course can be enjoyed equally.

PUBLIC 18+

PUBLIC 18+

Fairway Pines Golf Course

☎ (440) 357-7800

Area: **Far East**   City: **Painesville**   Cost: **$$$**$$ Difficulty: ●●●

Address: 1777 Blase-Nemeth Rd., Painesville

Tees	Ydg.	C/r	S/r	Pace
Back:	6619	70.9	112	
Middle:	5910	67.3	107	
Forward:	5081	68.1	106	

	Weekdays	Weekends & hol.	Carts
Prices:	$10.25 / $17.00	$11.75 / $20.50	$10.00 / $20.00

Specials: Seniors Mon–Fri $20.25 for 18 holes & cart; Seniors (walking) $7.50 / $12.50

Season: Mar 15–Nov 15 **Hours:** 8 a.m.–sunset Mon–Fri; 7 a.m.–sunset Sat, Sun **Tee times:** Taken weekends, holidays **Leagues:** Mon–Thu evenings (one nine only) **Ranger:** Daily **Practice facil:** Range, Putting Green **Clubhouse:** Food, Beer, Lockers, Showers, Banquet room **Outings:** Available (air-conditioned clubhouse accommodates 20–200) **Lessons:** Available **Pro:** Milt Johnson, PGA

Directions: SR 2 to exit for SR 535 (Fairport/Nursery Rd.); left off exit across freeway; right on Blase-Nemeth Rd.; on left past Greenside Rd.

Description While still a young course, Fairway Pines looks and plays as if it has been around much longer than a decade. Fast greens with aprons in front, much water, judicious use of sand traps, and a very challenging layout are among its virtues; yet this course will not intimidate average players. The front side has only one par 5, and that is shorter, at 435 yards, than many par 4s in the area. The course can be dramatically lengthened, though, by playing the blue tees.

"Slow play will not be tolerated," the scorecard reads, and one of the local rules calls for playing o.b. shots stroke only, the ball to be dropped at the point of entry. While disrespectful of the USGA, it will speed play.

Highlights A grove of sycamores and willows leads to the first tee. There, next to an old-fashioned and comfortable park bench, are twin garbage cans; players are asked to separate their trash for recycling.

No. 8, a 372-yard par 4, looks open from the tee but tightens with trees in the last 100 yards. This is one of many tee boxes here that are especially handsome by public course standards. It is 42 yards long and only 8 yards wide. The course can play much longer and with much more challenge using the back of the box. A creek cuts across the fairway before the green, which is surrounded on three sides by tall trees.

The back side begins with a straight par 4 of 353 yards. As on many holes here, stands of trees on both sides add to the physical beauty of the course and insist on play in the fairway. Trees surround a big green, including a stand of white birch on the left side.

No. 15 is only 338 yards from the white tees but no easy par. It's a dogleg left, and blocking players who want to try cutting the corner is a stand of tall trees. An accurate tee shot is vital because the approach must clear a sizable lake waiting in front of the green. The water continues on the right side of the green.

Fairway Pines was designed and built with the modern public player in mind. Neither a pushover nor a U.S. Open layout, these 18 holes offer players plenty of opportunities for par.

PUBLIC 18+

Forest Hills Golf Course   ☎ (440) 323-2632

Area: **Far West**   City: **Elyria**   Cost: **$$**$$$ Difficulty: ●●●

Address: 41971 Oberlin Rd. (US 20), Elyria

Tees	Ydg.	C/r	S/r	Pace
Back:	6280	69.7	117	
Middle:	6035	68.6	115	
Forward:	4825	67.6	104	

	Weekdays	Weekends & hol.	Carts
Prices:	$7.50 / $11.50	$9.00 / $13.00	$10.00 / $20.00

Specials: Seniors Mon–Fri $4.75 / $7.50; Sat–Sun after 5 p.m. $6.50 for 9 holes; Mon–Fri before 1 p.m. $33.00 for 2 players 18 holes & cart

Season: Mar 14–Dec 30, weather permitting **Hours:** 7 a.m.–sunset **Tee times:** Taken weekends **Leagues:** Various times **Ranger:** Weekends **Practice facil:** Range, Putting Green **Clubhouse:** Food, Beer, Liquor, Pavilion **Outings:** Available **Lessons:** Available **Pro:** Thomas Porter, PGA

Directions: I-480 to SR 10 (I-480 ends here); west on SR 10; merges with US 20 and SR 301 to exit for Lagrange Rd.; right (north) on Lagrange; left (west) on Butternut Ridge Rd.; right (north) on Oberlin Rd.; on right.

Description Forest Hills is owned by Lorain County and leased to Tom Porter, PGA, who started playing here as a youngster and worked on the maintenance crews during high-school summers.

The course has the Black River running through it and a wealth of trees, including cottonwood, walnut, buckeye, and ash.

Players should take care on arrival to pull into the Forest Hills driveway and not the drive next door, which belongs to the Elyria Country Club. At Forest Hills, play can be had for around $20; next door, the initiation is more than 20 grand.

Highlights The first hole is a par 5 of 565 yards. It is a wide-open hole and straight. There is an apron in front of the green, and an apron, when cared for, always provides a country-club look to a hole. There is sand on the left side of the green, which slopes to the rear. The greens here are very well maintained and often fast.

No. 2 shares a tee with No. 16. This 330-yard par 4 sweeps into a valley from an elevated tee. The green is off to the right and is eerily beautiful: in front is a moat-like water hazard and behind, a stand of trees. Nos. 4 and No. 6 also share a tee, and both holes (like many others on the course) play alongside the Black River.

No. 7 can confound and delight. The tee shot here is crucial. It must go far enough to leave a clear approach to the small elevated green, but not so far that it tumbles into the boomerang-shaped lake that is straight out from the tee. At that point, the fairway turns left and rises. Pines guide the hole to the green.

No. 11, a gorgeous par 3, is only 135 yards. The tee is elevated, the green at the bottom of a valley. Both sides of the hole are wooded, and there is a small pond to the right of the green.

Fowler's Mill Golf Course

☎ (440) 729-7569

Area: **Far East**   City: **Chesterland**   Cost: **$$$$$**   Difficulty: ●●●

Address: 13095 Rock Haven Rd., Chesterland

	Lake/River				Maple/Lake				River/Maple			
Tees	**Ydg.**	**C/r**	**S/r**	**Pace**	**Ydg.**	**C/r**	**S/r**	**Pace**	**Ydg.**	**C/r**	**S/r**	**Pace**
Back:	7002	74.7	136	4:01	6595	72.1	128		6385	70.7	125	
Middle:	6623	72.8	133		6375	70.6	126		6226	69.5	122	
Forward:	5950	73.9	122		5913	73.6	123		5797	73.0	123	

	Weekdays	**Weekends & hol.**	**Carts**
Prices:	$30.00 / $51.00	$35.00 / $61.00	Prices include cart

Specials: Mon–Fri before 8 a.m. $38.00 for 18 holes & cart, after 3 p.m. $38.00 for 18 holes & cart; Seniors Mon–Tue before 10 a.m. $35.00 for 18 holes & cart. Carts are $3.00 per person (fee included in total price).

Season: Mar–Nov **Hours:** Sunrise–sunset **Tee times:** Taken, credit card guarantee for Fri, Sat, Sun, hol. **Leagues:** Mon–Fri 4–6 p.m. on Red nine only **Ranger:** Daily **Practice facil:** Range, Putting Green **Clubhouse:** Food, Beer, Liquor, Dining room, Lockers, Pavilion **Outings:** Available (Indoor banquet space for 200+ guests) **Lessons:** Available

Directions: I-271 to Exit 34 for US 322 (Mayfield Rd.); east on US 322 for 10 miles, through Chesterland; right (south) on Rock Haven Rd.

Description   What do you think about a public course that has a rough-renovation program? Fowler's Mill, the course designed for TRW in 1970, often acts like a private club, and that renovation project is a good example of the management's commitment to a great course. TRW operated the course exclusively for employees. When American Golf Corporation bought it in 1986, Fowler's Mill was opened to the public. The course was designed by Pete Dye, and the signature par 4 is the 438-yard No. 4, a hole for heroes. There are just a couple of ways to succeed on that hole but a hundred ways to get in trouble. It is only one of a number of rewarding holes here. Fowler's Mill is not a course for beginners or for those with short tempers. Lessons are available on the grass driving range and sizable practice green. Even with such help, the average score here hovers around 101. The greens here are maintained as well as any in this area. Conditioning is exemplary. A new clubhouse opened in 1998; the guest of honor was Mr. Dye himself.

Fowler's Mill Golf Course

(photo © D² Productions, Murphy/Scully)

Highlights The infamous No. 4 fairway is narrow and dangerous. It runs along the side of a large lake on the right. An inadvertent slice, however slight, can be the beginning of disaster. But bailing out to the left means no chance for par. From the tee, players must stay straight. Even a great drive is just a beginning. The approach shot, a long iron, has to be equally great. About 200 yards out, the fairway takes a 90-degree right turn and continues to hug the lake. The green is protected by plenty of sand and fortified with Dye's trademark railroad ties. It would be interesting if management measured the average score on this one.

No. 5, the only par 5 here under 500 yards, is a 483-yarder with a fairway that bends first to the left and then back to the right. It's hilly, and there's plenty of sand at the green. This hole is representative of the course in that it can't be played well by first-timers. The pleasures of playing here grow with subsequent visits, but the first round can be confounding.

No. 9 is the first hole since No. 4 to have water, and unusual water it is. A wide creek cuts diagonally across the fairway, creating two landing areas. This 366-yard par 4 calls for an accurate tee shot. The approach shot also calls for judgment. The water and sand are hazards on the left.

A number of area courses are distinguished by having one side far more difficult than the other. Not so here. Both sides are hard. The front nine is called the Blue Nine, the back nine is called the White Nine. There is a third nine, the Red Nine, which is treated by most players as an oddity. It will be covered below.

The White Nine has holes numbered and handicapped one through nine. The fact that it is almost always played as the back nine is not considered on the scorecard.

A real premium is placed on the tee shot on No. 6, a 405-yard par 4 and the number one handicap on this nine. Trees guide the hole down the left side and a few tall hardwoods stand on the right. Also down the right are sand traps. The fairway is narrow and it slopes left to right. Unusual lies are not unusual here.

No. 9 is a hard one to win matches on. It's a long and tough par 5 that sees few birdies. It is 544 yards long and almost impossible to reach in two. From the tee, it looks wide open, and it is, but this dogleg left has sand on the right and left sides of the fairway as well as around the green. The sand continues down the left side and the green is elevated. A par here is a great way to finish a round.

Many of the players here are ardent fans of Pete Dye's layout but know little or nothing about the third (Red) nine. That's a shame—it's gorgeous.

Across Rock Haven Road, the Red No. 1 is wide and comfortable (though occasional car traffic behind the tee can be noisy). This par 4, 351 yards, is a dogleg left with deep woods down the right side and a few trees on the left. In the last 100 yards the fairway narrows, turns sharply left, and rises 15 or 20 feet to the green.

After leaving the road behind, this nine is much quieter, most of the noise supplied by crickets.

No. 3, a magnificent par 5, is 516 yards. The fairway rises slowly and crests about 220 yards from the green. It slips gradually down to the green and narrows. Trees stand up in the left rough and create a place for Canada geese to mill about. Sand is on the left side of the green and an old hardwood grows next to it. The hole is magnificent not for the degree of difficulty but for the physical beauty of its surroundings.

What a delightful difference between the Red Nine and the other two on the other side of the road. But it shouldn't be hard to believe the same designer dreamed up all three. The aim of golf design, after all, is to create both challenging and playable courses. That was certainly done here at Fowler's Mill.

Fox Den Fairways

☎ (330) 673-3443

Area: **Far South**   City: **Stow**   Cost: **$$$$**$ Difficulty: ●●●

Address: 2770 Call Rd., Stow

Tees	Ydg.	C/r	S/r	Pace
Back:	6447	70.4	115	3:40
Middle:	6136	68.0	112	
Forward:	5473	69.0	114	

	Weekdays	Weekends & hol.	Carts
Prices:	$10.75 / $21.00	$13.75 / $26.00	$10.00 / $20.00

Specials: Mon–Thurs before 3 p.m., all day Friday $24.00 for 18 holes & ½ cart; Seniors Mon–Thu before 3 p.m. $22.00 for 18 holes & ½ cart

Season: Mar 25–Dec 1 **Hours:** Sunrise–sunset **Tee times:** Required weekends, suggested weekdays **Leagues:** Tue–Thu 8–9:45 a.m; Mon–Thu 4:30–6:30 p.m.
Ranger: Most days **Practice facil:** Range, Putting Green, Chipping Green, Sand
Clubhouse: Food, Beer, Pavilion, Picnic area **Outings:** Available (limited to 32 or fewer) **Lessons:** Available **Pro:** Tom McKinney

Directions: I-271 to Exit 18 for SR 8; south on SR 8 to exit for Hudson/SR 303; east on SR 303 (E. Streetsboro Rd.) into Hudson; then right (south) on SR 91 (Main St.) into Stow; left on Fishcreek Rd.; left on Call Rd.; on right.

PUBLIC 18+

Description Fox Den has a comfortable clubhouse, a very good juniors program, and a solid layout. It was built in 1966 and is today an important part of the Stow/Akron community. It is home to the Memorial Four-Person Scramble to benefit Edwin Shaw Hospital, the Junior Championship, a couple of pro-ams, and the Akron Amputee Open.

The sand here seems to be of particularly high quality, clean and light and fluffy. A number of holes are too close to each other. Three tees have been relocated: 2, 12 and 13. This will stretch the blue tee course to nearly 6,500 yards and the regular tees to 6,136.

Highlights The first tee box is notable for its gorgeous flower garden. Throughout the course, well-tended and colorful flower boxes show up at tees. There are no white tees here. Instead, yellow marks the middle tees. Blue is the championship length, red for forward markers.

The course gets prettier with each hole. The tee box at No. 3 backs into tall hardwoods. On No. 4, the number two handicap hole, the Arbor Committee tends to locusts, willows, oaks, and firs.

No. 5 is an unfair par 5 that goes out only 165 yards before turning right and chugging uphill. It is unfair because there is no chance for players to get on in two, and the drive—only 165 yards—is not important.

For players using the blue tees, the difference really comes into play on No. 8. It's a 320-yard downhill par 4 from the yellow tees. But from the blues, it suddenly stretches to 414 and calls for a Trevino fade.

On the back side, players again march uphill. But the pleasant surprises there are worth the walk. At No. 12 is a flower box 4-$\frac{1}{2}$ feet deep, 30 feet long, and 10 feet wide. With that kind of investment, you know it will be well tended, and it is.

PUBLIC 18+

FoxCreek Golf and Racquet Club
☎ (440) 282-9106

Area: **Far West**   City: **Lorain**   Cost: **$**$$$$ Difficulty: ●●●

Address: 5445 Beavercrest Dr., Lorain

Tees	Ydg.	C/r	S/r	Pace
Back:	6407	71.5	131	
Middle:	6004	69.8	127	

	Weekdays	Weekends & hol.	Carts
Prices:	$9.00 / $17.00	$11.00 / $20.00	$7.00 / $13.00
	Annual membership: $1,300		

Specials: Limited membership $100 plus tax (does not include greens fees); Senior specials available (limited times)

Season: Apr–Nov **Hours:** Sunrise–sunset **Tee times:** Required **Leagues:** Mon–Fri, one side 5 p.m.–close **Ranger:** Daily **Practice facil:** Putting Green **Clubhouse:** Food, Beer, Liquor, Dining room, Lockers, Showers, Tennis, Racquetball, Health club
Outings: Available **Lessons:** Available **Pro:** Mike Masterson

Directions: SR 2 to exit for SR 58 (Leavitt Rd.); north on SR 58; left (west) on Jaeger Rd.; right (north) on Kolbe Rd.; left (west) on Beavercrest Dr.; on left.

Description FoxCreek (formerly known as Lorain Country Club) is a value rarely matched among the best public golf courses in northern Ohio. Lorain CC was started in 1958 when Curley DeBracey designed the front nine. The next year the back nine was designed by local builder Frank Nardini. Both men took advantage of Beaver Creek, which does more twisting and squirming than a member of Congress. It provides water hazards on 13 holes.

The course records were set by a couple of professional players, Sam Snead and Charley Coody. Snead hung on for a while with a 66, fired during a pro-am. Local auto dealer Ed Mullinax figured that number was safe and offered a car to anyone who could break that record. Along came Charley Coody, who fired a 63 and drove away happy.

Highlights No. 1 quickly introduces players to the course's virtues. The view from the elevated tee is magnificent and inspiring. Inspiration helps, because the drive on this 492-yard par 5 really has to get out there. It's a dogleg left, and the approach is made more challenging by huge willows on the left side and Beaver Creek ambling across the fairway in front of the green. All that is necessary to par this opening hole is a big and accurate drive, a very accurate second shot (move the ball to the right side of the fairway, but keep it out of Beaver Creek), and a wedge to the green. Oh, and good putting, too.

No. 3, the number one handicap hole, is a 420-yard par 4 that bends around to the left. About 90 yards from the green, the fairway suddenly rises. Snead and Coody knew how to hit a long iron and make it stop, but for the rest of us course management will be important here.

The back nine, said to be tougher than the front, starts with a 355-yard par 4 from an elevated tee. It's another tough tee shot, and the pro here says the rough on the right is better than the fairway on the left.

There is more water on this nine, and accuracy is more valuable. There are no holes for coasting here.

The two finishing holes are short, but each calls for control. No. 17 is only 306 yards, but with water to the right and a very narrow landing area before hitting to an elevated green, it is demanding just when player fatigue becomes a factor. No. 18 is a par 3 of only 128 yards, and with the clubhouse in the background, novices tend to hit short.

Don't expect liveried doormen here or formal dining. But to play a challenging course with players of like mind, it's well worth the trip and the expense.

PUBLIC 18+

Gleneagles Golf Club   ☎ (330) 425-3334

Area: **Southeast**   City: **Twinsburg**   Cost: **$$$$$**   Difficulty: ●●●

Address: 2615 Glenwood Dr., Twinsburg

Tees	Ydg.	C/r	S/r	Pace
Back:	6545	72.2	121	
Middle:	5918	69.6	118	
Forward:	5147	69.4	115	

	Weekdays	Weekends & hol.	Carts
Prices:	$12.00 / $24.00	$14.00 / $28.00	$10.00 / $20.00

Specials: Seniors Mon–Fri before noon $20.00 for 18 holes

Season: Open mid-Apr **Hours:** Sunrise–sunset **Tee times:** Required **Leagues:** Mon–Fri 4–6:00 p.m. **Ranger:** Daily **Practice facil:** Range, Putting Green **Clubhouse:** Food, Beer, Pavilion, Covered porch **Outings:** Available (for corporate or group outings–provide own caterer, cookouts, buffets; party tent for up to 200 people) **Lessons:** Available **Pro:** Michael Brown, PGA

Directions: I-480 to Exit 37 for SR 91 (Darrow Rd.); north on SR 91; right (east) on Glenwood Dr.; on left.

Description The patron saint here is Lazarus, who knows a thing or two about coming back from the dead. Gleneagles, the Twinsburg track named after the course at the Gleneagles Hotel in Perthshire, England, struggled its first few years. Maintenance and conditioning were not high on the to-do list, and enjoying the wonderful design of Ted

McAnlis was difficult. The driving range was more suited to goat farming than golf practice.

When the city fathers decided to buy the young course a few years ago, Gleneagles was on its way to becoming a very good municipal course. But, for some reason, the nines have been reversed. In McAnlis's original design, the opening hole was a wide-open, lazy par 5 of only 460 yards—a great hole to warm up with. And the home hole was a dandy: a par 4 that hung on the edge of a lake and virtually insisted on a dramatic finish. Such disregard for the designer's wishes is shameful—some would call it a capital crime. Now instead of the course being played as it was meant to be played, which in this case means building to a climax, it is just two very nice nines.

Highlights The front side starts off like a roller coaster and hints the course will be exciting. The first tee looks out on a fairway racing steadily downhill and sloping right. Such downhill/sidehill lies can challenge the most experienced player in any foursome. Only 371 yards, this hole has trouble spots enough to upset a good round. A creek crosses 40 yards in front of the green.

The elevated tee at No. 3, a par 4 of 393 yards, encourages thought and concentration. It faces a steep drop to a valley bottom and water, after which the fairway veers sharply left and up. The large green is surrounded by tall trees. This hole calls for consecutive good shots and offers little margin for error.

No. 9 is dramatic. It begins easily enough, a straight shot from the tee, but suddenly the fairway drops steeply off to the left and the remainder narrows like a corset-cinched waist. The big lake on the left reaches up the left side of the green, and suddenly the approach shot takes on another dimension.

The back side starts with a big, lazy par 5 and ends with a big, lazy par 4. With the original design, the course was exciting, even memorable, but with the nines switched, the magic isn't there.

TIDYMAN'S TIDBITS #3

Cliffside tee boxes:
- Nos. 8 & 18 at Astorhurst
- No. 15 at Brandywine
- No. 17 at Tanglewood CC

Good Park Municipal Golf Course   ☎ (330) 864-0020
Area: **Far South**   City: **Akron**   Cost: **$$$**$$ Difficulty: ●●●

Address: 530 Nome Ave., Akron

Tees	Ydg.	C/r	S/r	Pace
Back:	6663	72.0	123	3:50
Middle:	6270	70.3	119	
Forward:	5094	69.1	115	

	Weekdays	Weekends & hol.	Carts
Prices:	$10.50 / $20.00	$11.50 / $22.00	$10.00 / $20.00

Specials: Seniors & Juniors Mon–Fri before 11 a.m. $7.50 / $13.00

Season: Apr–Nov **Hours:** Sunrise–sunset **Tee times:** Taken weekends **Leagues:** Mon–Fri 4–6 p.m. **Ranger:** Most days **Practice facil:** Putting Green, Chipping Green **Clubhouse:** Food, Beer, Lockers, Showers **Outings:** Available **Lessons:** Not available

Directions: I-77 to Exit 132; north on White Pond Dr.; right (east) on Mull Ave.; right (south) on Hawkins Ave.; right (west) on Sunsetview Dr.; left on Nome Ave.; on right.

Description J. E. Good Park is sneaky tough. It is tight and green and softly rolling. It's beautiful for the strong hardwoods that frame the holes and the care provided for the flora. It is a snug course and hemmed in on all sides by avenues and drives . . . and one major interstate. But thanks to the efficacious use of trees it never feels crowded or tight.

Soft doglegs and straightaways make up this course, which is a great track for golfers who walk and carry their bags. The rough is hardly a bother. If you can't control your tee shots, you won't lose many balls here. But you won't get honors, either.

TIDYMAN'S TIDBITS #4
Government-owned courses:
- Gleneagles (Twinsburg)
- Springvale (North Olmsted)
- Briardale Greens (Euclid)
- Seneca & Highland (Cleveland)
- Big Met, Little Met, Manakiki, Mastick Woods, Shawnee Hills, Sleepy Hollow (Cleveland Metroparks)
- Erie Shores and Pine Ridge (Lake County MetroParks)
- Ridgewood (Parma)
- Grantwood (Solon)
- Good Park (Akron)

PUBLIC 18+

Grantwood Recreation Park   ☎ (440) 248-4646
Area: **Southeast**   City: **Solon**   Cost: $$$$$ Difficulty: ●●●

Address: 38855 Aurora Rd., Solon

Tees	Ydg.	C/r	S/r	Pace
Back:	6374	70.7	124	
Middle:	6063	69.7	122	
Forward:	5607	69.1	119	

	Weekdays	Weekends & hol.	Carts
Prices:	$12.00 / $22.00	$13.75 / $26.50	$12.00 / $20.00

Specials: Seniors: Mon–Fri (before 3 p.m.) 18 holes & cart $24.00 per player.

Season: Apr–Nov **Hours:** Sunrise–sunset **Tee times:** Required **Leagues:** Mon–Fri 3:30–6:30 p.m. **Ranger:** Daily **Practice facil:** Putting Green, Chipping Green **Clubhouse:** Food, Beer, Pavilion, Banquet room **Outings:** Available **Lessons:** Available

Directions: I-271 to Exit 27 for US 422; east on US 422 to Solon; south on SR 91; left (south) on SR 43 (becomes Aurora Rd.); near intersection of Aurora and Pettibone Rds.

Description In the mid-1980s, the city of Solon purchased 18 holes on Aurora Road from private owners and created Grantwood Recreation Park. The course, originally built as a nine-hole layout in the twenties, used an old barn for its clubhouse.

In 1981, a new clubhouse and banquet facility went up; a party was held to celebrate the opening. Among the honored guests were members of the Solon Fire Department. And a highlight of the party was the burning down of the old clubhouse.

Though it is owned by the city, Grantwood is not subsidized by taxpayers. Operating funds come only from greens fees, services of the banquet facilities, and pro shop receipts.

Since the town bought it, the course has undergone substantial change. The change continues. New red tees were installed because the original tees were not fair. Other work included planting 200 trees, expanding some greens, and installing more sand traps. It is a busy course and most of the work was done not to make play more difficult, but to make it safer.

Tee times are strongly recommended here. More than 35,000 rounds are played every year, and leagues account for a good part of that; industrial, seniors', women's, and traveling leagues all enjoy Grantwood.

The clubhouse does a good banquet business, and golf outings and fund-raisers are often held here. The facilities, the location, and the excellent parking make it useful year round.

The rough is allowed to grow to about three inches and water comes into play on eleven holes. The course is bisected by a railroad line, which players cross under via an old tunnel. One golfer tells of landing a drive in a slow-moving coal car headed east—his longest drive ever. It must be pointed out, though, that eventually that drive went out of bounds. And out of state. The railroad line is no longer in use, but the tunnel under it still adds a bit of charm to the layout.

Highlights No. 1 is wide open with a trap about 140 yards out. It plays 390 yards, a good warm-up hole. It's difficult to lose a ball on this hole, though the second shot is blind because of the rolling fairway. Better here to ignore the checkered aiming flag and instead shoot for the birdhouse, designed for those great mosquito-eaters: purple martins. Traps protect both sides of the green.

After the first five holes, it's through the tunnel, where traffic to many holes converges. The holes run parallel on this side, but there is enough space between fairways to minimize shooting into (and from) adjacent fairways. This side of the course is carved out of rich farmland and the thick growth and old hardwoods around its edges give it a stadium-like feel. Much more impressive than the other, open side of the tracks.

The two par 5s on the front nine are consecutive. No. 6 is almost 100 yards longer than No. 7, which plays 465 yards. It is No. 7 that is the more interesting, however, because it tempts big hitters to send the second shot to the green, and that shot is blind. The fairway rises gently, dips and bends softly left, and narrows all the way to the green.

Grantwood is an amiable course and shows what muny government can do when it puts its mind to running a golf course.

PUBLIC 18+

Hickory Nut Golf Club ☎ (440) 236-8008

Area: **Southwest** City: **Columbia Station** Cost: **$$$**$$ Difficulty: ●●●

Address: 23601 Royalton Rd., Columbia Station

Tees	Ydg.	C/r	S/r	Pace
Middle:	6424		126	

	Weekdays	Weekends & hol.	Carts
Prices:	$10.00 / $16.00	$11.00 / $19.00	$10.00 / $20.00

Specials: Seniors $1.00 off per 9 holes

Season: Apr 1–Oct 31 **Hours:** Sunrise–sunset **Tee times:** Not taken **Leagues:** Mon–Fri 4–6 p.m. **Ranger:** Weekends **Practice facil:** Putting Green **Clubhouse:** Food, Beer, Pavilion **Outings:** Available **Lessons:** Not available

Directions: I-71 to Exit 231 for SR 82 (Royalton Rd.); west on Royalton Rd.; on left, past Marks Rd.

Description The course is flat and easy to walk. The arbor committee did well (trees planted when the course was built in 1961 have grown to thick woods), and the greens are especially well conditioned. Tall grass in the rough gives Hickory Nut a bit of a Links course feel.

Highlights The first two holes are a good indication that the course is long: the opener is a 440-yard par 4 with an elevated green; No. 2 is a 545-yard par 5.

No. 8 is another long par 5, this one 530 yards. Watch out for a large tree on the right side of the fairway, only a few yards from thick woods. If you aim left, there are more trees to combat. As you work your way down the fairway you will notice the approach to the green narrowed by a tree on the left with overhanging limbs and sand traps on the right. Both the tree and traps are about 20–30 yards from the green. The approach is almost like trying to split the uprights on a 40-yard field goal attempt.

Highland Park Golf Course   ☎ (216) 348-7273

Area: **East**   City: **Highland Hills**   Cost: **$$**$$ Difficulty: ●●●

Address: 3550 Green Rd., Highland Hills

	Red Course				Blue Course			
Tees	Ydg.	C/r	S/r	Pace	Ydg.	C/r	S/r	Pace
Middle:	6341	69.7	113	3:40	6709	71.7	119	3:42
Forward:	5945	73.1	119		6289	75.7	125	

	Weekdays	Weekends & hol.	Carts
Prices:	$8.00 / $15.00	$8.50 / $16.00	$9.00 / $18.00

Specials: Seniors & Juniors Mon–Fri before 3 p.m. $5.00 for 9 holes; Seniors & Juniors Sat–Sun after 3 p.m. $9.00 for 18 holes

Season: Mar 1–Dec 31 **Hours:** Sunrise–sunset **Tee times:** Taken weekends
Leagues: Various times **Ranger:** Daily **Practice facil:** Putting Green, Chipping Green
Clubhouse: Food, Beer, Lockers, Showers **Outings:** Available **Lessons:** Not available

Directions: I-271 to Exit 29 for US 422 (Chagrin Blvd.); west on Chagrin Blvd.; left (south) on Green Rd.; on right.

Description Highland, where it once appeared no capital improvements had been made since the sand wedge was invented, is now undergoing important changes. Fairway irrigation has been completed and a new clubhouse is open. And the biggest change of all is rumored: privatization of this course owned (and abused) by the City of Cleveland. More than one mayor used the course as a cash cow and failed to have it properly maintained.

Highlights The Blue course does not turn at the clubhouse and so does not lend itself to nine-hole play. It opens with a 393-yard par 4 from an elevated tee that looks down on a fairway lined with trees. The terrain continues down until, at about the 150-yard mark, a creek cuts across. On the other side, the ground rises suddenly to a green with sand around the right side and rear.

10 Reasons Kids Should be Banned from Golf

1. They can't afford it. Any 12–year–old with loot enough for greens fees probably runs an extortion business at school.

2. Their fathers think it's cute.

3. Most of them have five-minute attention spans. 'Nuff said.

4. Kids need only three pairs of shoes: black, brown, and tennies. Don't get them started on waterproof saddle shoes with soft spikes.

5. The game has to be taught by adults. Kids have enough adults in their lives; don't saddle them with any more.

6. They need transportation to and from the course. What do we look like, chauffeurs?

7. Kids have their own variations on language; no sense in letting them share our golf jargon.

8. They don't have time to play golf. If they have five hours on a Saturday, let them blacktop the driveway.

9. They're not worth anything at the 19th hole.

10. I have enough trouble playing guys in their 60s. The last thing, and I do mean the last thing, I need right now is to have a 7th–grader with a great short game beat me in a $2 Nassau.

—JHT

The number one handicap, No. 3, is a par 4 of 454 yards. The fairway rolls a bit on this and many holes at Highland, but the only drama here is provided by length. The fairway is generous and straight to the green, which has a grass bunker in front and seven white oaks like sentinels behind.

The 18th hole on the Blue course is only the number four handicap hole, but it is a true match-decider hole. A long and dangerous par 4 of 449 yards, it begins with a tee shot into a valley that has a creek running diagonally across the fairway. On the other side of the creek, the fairway leans to the left and rises to an elevated green. A finishing hole of U.S. Open proportions. The strength of the Blue course is definitely the length of many of its holes.

The Red course is decidedly different. The hilly terrain comes into play more than it does on the Blue. Both nines finish at the clubhouse. And the Red course winds up with a pair of par 4s totaling only 729 yards.

No. 1 is a blind tee shot. A par 4, it is 388 yards over an up-and-down fairway. It rises from the tee and crests at about 200 yards, then falls steadily until 50 yards from the green, where it rises again. This hole could use a bell to ring to let players on the tee know when it is safe to hit. A ranger could fill the same need, but neither is provided.

The 4th tee is reached after a short walk through the woods. This par 5 is 480 yards and straight as the crow flies. For golfers, however, the wide fairway drops suddenly at the 150-yard marker. All the way down the right side are deep woods; a line of trees marks the left side. Forty yards from the green, a long and narrow trap runs down the right rough and continues past the green.

No. 8 begins with a tee box obviously used for tank maneuvers. It is yet another blind tee shot with thick woods down the left side and open area on the right. A 402-yard par 4, it's the number one handicap hole on the Red course. It is number one because it has a blind tee shot, a hilly fairway, and a green that cannot be safely reached except by air. About 40 yards in front of the green, the left side of the fairway suddenly drops, cliff-like, about a dozen feet. Bouncing the ball onto the green is out of the question. And the green, sitting in a shallow valley, is the toughest at Highland. The right side is two or three feet higher than the left. At the left rear, the ground suddenly rises, and on the right is a stand of trees. A tough pin placement can easily add three or four strokes to a score. A par on No. 8 is something to talk about.

All in all, Highland could again become one of the area's best public courses. Lots of well-designed holes and a convenient East Side location are two of its many virtues. But it needs a commitment to golf on the part of the owners. The players are ready and waiting.

Hilliard Lakes Golf Course

☎ (440) 871-9578

Area: **West**   City: **Westlake**   Cost: $$$$$ Difficulty: ●●●

Address: 31665 Hilliard Blvd., Westlake

Tees	Ydg.	C/r	S/r	Pace
Middle:	6600	69.5	122	
Forward:	6200	71.5	120	

	Weekdays	Weekends & hol.	Carts
Prices:	$10.50 / $18.50	$13.00 / $24.00	$10.00 / $20.00

Specials: Seniors Mon–Fri 10 a.m.–3 p.m. $8.50 / $16.00

Season: Mar–Dec **Hours:** Sunrise–sunset **Tee times:** Taken **Leagues:** Mon–Thur 4:30–6 p.m. **Ranger:** Daily **Practice facil:** Putting Green, Practice fairway **Clubhouse:** Food, Beer, Liquor, Dining room **Outings:** Not available **Lessons:** Not available

Directions: I-90 to Exit 156 for Crocker-Bassett Rds.; south on Crocker Rd.; right (west) on Hilliard Blvd. to dead end at Lincoln Rd.

Description On a flat piece of land with a little water going through it, Matthew Zaleski built this course in 1967. His son Ron manages it. Part of the land was once officially listed as Avon Airport. The 18th hole was the runway, and in World War II military pilots trained here.

No outings here. "Just room for golfing only," Zaleski says.

The blue tees are 6,665 yards and the whites are 6,183 yards. The forward tees are 5,611 yards, long by most standards for forward tees.

Highlights "The whole back nine is different," Zaleski says. No. 11 used to be a par 5, now it's a long par 4 at 426 yards. No. 12 is a par 5, 548 yards—the combination of a former par 4 and par 3; number 15 is a new par 3. Tees are being moved back on some of the holes on the front side. It will make them longer, of course.

TIDYMAN'S TIDBITS #5
Best courses for beginning players:

- Pine Brook GC
- Riverside GC
- Brentwood GC
- Little Met GC
- Mastick Woods

PUBLIC 18+

PUBLIC 18+

Hinckley Hills Golf Course

☎ (330) 278-4861

Area: **South**   City: **Hinckley**   Cost: **$$$$$**   Difficulty: ●●◐

Address: 300 State Rd., Hinckley

Tees	Ydg.	C/r	S/r	Pace
Back:	6846	71.6	125	3:55
Middle:	6253	69.2	120	
Forward:	5478	70.9	118	

	Weekdays	Weekends & hol.	Carts
Prices:	$12.50 / $25.00	$12.50 / $25.00	$12.00 / $24.00

Specials: 2 players & cart Mon–Fri & Sat, Sun, hol. after 2 p.m. $31.00 / $62.00

Season: Apr 1–Nov 15 **Hours:** Sunrise–sunset **Tee times:** Taken **Leagues:** Daily **Ranger:** Daily **Practice facil:** Putting Green, Chipping Green, Driving net **Clubhouse:** Food, Beer, Liquor, Pavilion, Party room **Outings:** Available **Lessons:** Not available

Directions: I-71 to Exit 226 for SR 303; east on SR 303 (Center Rd.); left (north) on State Rd.; 2 miles, on left.

Description This challenging and hilly course is a tough one to walk. Designed by the late Harold Paddock, Sr., and opened in 1963, it plays 6,248 yards, most of them uphill, downhill, or sidehill. Those numbers are from the white tees. From the blue tees, it plays 6,846 yards, par 73 (there is a second par 5 on the back). It's a powerful course from the white and blue tees, and women golfers have no pushover in front of them: the ladies' tees play 5,478 yards, par 72. Unless groups have lots of good players, outings will have a hard time on this course. The pro shop/clubhouse has been expanded and improved in recent years and combines with a nearby pavilion to provide services, including outings, that are first rate. The course is filled with hills, water, big greens, sand, and, on two holes, natural gas wells. Free drops from the wells.

Highlights The course wastes no time in showing off its virtues. No. 1 is a 510-yard par 5 from an elevated tee. The wide fairway sweeps up and down, then up and down again as it makes its way to an elevated green. Trees fill both sides of the last 100 yards. While neither short nor easy, Hinckley does play wide open. Length here is slightly more valuable than accuracy. Twenty-four yards of turf, the difference between the white tees and the blue tees, is substantial yardage if the hole is a par 3 or par 4, but on the legendary par-5 No. 9, it's not much. Hitting from the white tees begins a journey of 592 yards. Hitting from the blues, it's 630 yards. Regardless of starting point, the hole is tough. Not just because of the length, but because the fairway provides players with difficult uphill and downhill lies. It is a straight hole, o.b. all the way down the left side. To make it more scenic, a three-acre lake bed was excavated and allowed to fill with springwater and runoff. Hinckley Hills is one of five public courses in tiny Hinckley, Ohio.

Hinckley Hills Golf Course

(photo: Jonathan Wayne)

Indian Hollow Lake Golf Club

☎ (440) 355-5344

Area: **Far West** City: **Grafton** Cost: **$$**$$ Difficulty:

Address: 16525 Indian Hollow Rd., Grafton

Tees	Ydg.	C/r	S/r	Pace
Middle:	5910			
Forward:	4865			

	Weekdays	Weekends & hol.	Carts
Prices:	$8.00 / $14.00	$10.00 / $17.00	$9.50 / $19.00

Specials: Mon–Thu until 2 p.m.& all day Fri: 2 golfers & cart $17.00 each, Seniors $15.50 each

Season: Year-round **Hours:** Sunrise–sunset **Tee times:** Taken weekends **Leagues:** Various times **Ranger:** Most days **Practice facil:** Putting Green, Chipping Green **Clubhouse:** Food, Beer, Liquor, Snack bar **Outings:** Available **Lessons:** Available

Directions: I-71 to Exit 226 for SR 303; west on SR 303 past SR 83 and across the Black River; right (north) on Indian Hollow Rd.; on right.

Description The Black River graces the back nine of this very playable layout put together by Don Gardner, golf fanatic and mechanic by trade, in 1968. It remains a family-run operation.

No. 13, a par 4 of 340 yards, is a dogleg left with the Black River on the right. The tee shot doesn't have much landing room, and the approach has to take into account a grove of black walnut trees. The course has specials every weekday until 2 p.m. On Fridays, the special goes on all day. A third nine is being constructed.

Ironwood Golf Course

☎ (330) 278-7171

Area: **South**   City: **Hinckley**   Cost: **$$$$$**   Difficulty: ●●●

Address: 445 State Rd., Hinckley

Tees	Ydg.	C/r	S/r	Pace
Back:	6360	69.7	118	
Middle:	6042	68.3	115	
Forward:	5785	72.8	124	

	Weekdays	Weekends & hol.	Carts
Prices:	$11.00 / $22.00	$12.50 / $25.00	$11.00 / $22.00

Specials: Seniors Mon–Fri before 3 p.m. $26.00 for 18 holes & cart

Season: Apr–Oct **Hours:** Sunrise–sunset **Tee times:** Taken weekends, until 2 p.m. **Leagues:** Mon–Fri 3–6 p.m. **Ranger:** Daily **Practice facil:** Putting Green, Chipping Green **Clubhouse:** Food, Beer **Outings:** Available (for golf only) **Lessons:** Not available **Pro:** Mark Bell

Directions: I-71 to Exit 226 for SR 303 (Center Rd.); east on Center Rd. to SR 94 (State Rd.); left (north) on State Rd.; on right, after Eastwood Rd.

Description Ironwood was laid out by the late Harold Paddock, a designer who also helped create Hinckley Hills and other courses. He was in a wheelchair by the time he worked on Ironwood. The first nine holes opened in 1967; the back nine opened a year later. Even unable to play, he laid out a track with a lot of personality. In addition to the usual golf skills, stamina and endurance help here.

The only worrisome element at Ironwood is the lightning. Owner Bob Brown explained, "We've been hit a number of times. We're sitting on top of the hill, so high that it's blown the transformer off. It's blown out the telephones. I mean it literally blew the wires apart. It's blown out the wall pump in our water well, and the heating element in the hot dog cooker. We're just high on the ridge here. In fact, over there across the valley is the highest point in the county and we're definitely not much under it."

That causes few to shy away from this first-rate track, though. More than 20,000 rounds are played here each year. There is plenty of league play, including traveling leagues on the weekends. Tee times are taken for weekend play but are unnecessary weekdays. The pro shop is in one end of a clubhouse that seats more than 80.

From the white tees, it plays 6,042, par 71. If that sounds short, players should know that three of the par 4s on the front side stretch more than 420 yards. And Ironwood takes advantage of its many hills.

Highlights No. 1 is one of the long par 4s—431 yards, all downhill, to a green that falls away on the sides. The entire right side of the hole is o.b. and trees mark the left side. The view of the valley from the first tee is magnificent. The first green is sizable.

Behind the first green is the tee for No. 2, a par 3 of more than 200 yards, again downhill. On both sides of the steep fairway are woods. So the tee calls for more than a big hit—it also has to be accurate. This green is also substantial. But it is sloped steeply and getting a tee shot to stick here is no guarantee of par. The sides of the green, especially in the back, fall away.

To play the second nine, it's back into the valley: Nos. 10 and 11 are all downhill.

Players may not usually brag about getting on a 359-yard par 4 in regulation, but No. 14 might be an exception. The tee shot on this 359-yard par 4 must avoid water in front of the tee and more water on the right side of the narrow landing area. The approach shot has to reach a much-elevated green. To make the shot more interesting, at the bottom of the green on the left is a sizable pond. The fairway narrows to 30 yards. At the green, woods line the rear and right side. No sand here, but that adds small comfort.

Ironwood opens April 1 and closes November 15. Outings are no longer held here ("They're a hassle"), though Bob Brown welcomes small golf parties. He has enough to worry about. Maintaining the course, with its hills and valleys and ponds, is job enough. The ponds supply water for the course, so it suffers much less during drought periods than courses with only municipal water.

Kent State University Golf Course   ☎ (330) 673-4000

Area: **Far South**   City: **Franklin Township**   Cost: $$$\$\$ Difficulty: ●●●

Address: 2346 SR 59, Franklin Township

Tees	Ydg.	C/r	S/r	Pace
Middle:	5327	64.9	107	
Forward:	4524	64.2	109	

	Weekdays	Weekends & hol.	Carts
Prices:	$9.50 / $17.00	$12.00 / $21.00	$10.00 / $20.00

Specials: KSU faculty & staff: Mon–Fri before 1 p.m. $7.50 / $12.75; KSU students: Mon–Fri $6.00 (9 holes)

Season: Mar 1–Dec 24 (weather permitting) **Hours:** Sunrise–sunset **Tee times:** Recommended **Leagues:** Various times **Ranger:** Weekends **Practice facil:** Putting Green **Clubhouse:** Food, Beer, Pavilion **Outings:** Available **Lessons:** Available **Pro:** Mike Morrow, PGA

Directions: I-480 to SR 14 east (I-480 ends here); right (south) on SR 43; (Cleveland-Canton Rd.) left (east) on SR 59; past KSU campus.

Description With its small greens and thousands of trees, this course makes winners out of golfers good with their irons. It's a great place for outings, because skilled shooters win and hackers are not overwhelmed. The trees here shape a number of holes and provide back settings at lots of greens. The place is old, built in 1929 by a local designer. Mike Morrow, PGA, brags about these small greens, claiming that they sometimes approach the quality found only in private clubs. It is No. 6 that will always challenge him, a 225-yard par 3 with a very small green. Missing the green leaves no good approach angle. "It's very hard to make a 3," the pro said.

Kent State University Golf Course

Links Golf Club   ☎ (440) 235-0501

Area: **West**   City: **Olmsted Twp.**   Cost: **$$**$$ Difficulty: ●●●

Address: 26111 John Rd., Olmsted Twp.

Tees	Ydg.	C/r	S/r	Pace
Back:	5000	63.6	107	3:19
Middle:	4500	60.6	96	
Forward:	3570	60.1	96	

	Weekdays	Weekends & hol.	Carts
Prices:	$9.00 / $14.50	$9.50 / $16.50	$9.00 / $18.00

Specials: Seniors $5.50 / $10.00; Mon–Fri until 2 p.m. $24.00 / $36.00 for 2 players & cart, Seniors $16.00 / $25.00

Season: Year-round   **Hours:** Mon–Fri 7:30 a.m.–9:30 p.m.; Sat, Sun 6 a.m.–9:30 p.m.; shorter hours in winter   **Tee times:** Required weekends, Recommended weekdays **Leagues:** Mon–Fri 4–6 p.m.   **Ranger:** Daily   **Practice facil:** Range, Putting Green, Chipping Green, Sand   **Clubhouse:** Food, Beer, Liquor, Dining room, Pavilion, (men's showers only)   **Outings:** Available   **Lessons:** Available   **Pro:** Vince Mastro

Directions: I-480 to Exit 6 for SR 252 (Great Northern Blvd.); south on SR 252 (becomes Columbia Rd.); right (west) on John Rd.; on right.

Description Going out, it plays into a trailer park; coming in, it wanders through the backyard of an old folks' home. This course was long a poorly maintained executive-length course (where they sometimes sprayed the greens . . . well, green). It now rates—barely—as a full-length 18. Management is trying to repair a reputation for nonexistent customer service.

PUBLIC 18+

Little Mountain Country Club   ☎ (440) 358-PUTT
Area: **Far East**   City: **Concord**   Cost: Difficulty: ●●●

Address: 7667 Hermitage Rd., Concord

Tees	Ydg.	C/r	S/r	Pace
Back:	6809			
Middle:				
Forward:	5332			

	Weekdays	Weekends & hol.	Carts
Prices:	New course: call for prices		

Specials: Call for specials

Season: Opening August 1999 **Hours:** Call for hours **Tee times:** **Leagues:** None **Ranger:** **Practice facil:** None **Clubhouse:** None **Outings:** **Lessons:** **Pro:** Jimmy Hanlin, PGA

Directions: I-90 to exit 200 for SR 44); left (south) on SR 44; right (west) on Auburn Rd.; right (northwest) on Girdled Rd. (becomes Hermitage Rd.); 1 mile on right.

Description The first rounds are tentatively scheduled for late 1999 at Little Mountain, a new club and course in Concord Township.

It will be the second course created by the Fry/Hurdzan Design Group. (StoneWater was the first).

Carved out of 244 acres of rolling woodland, the course will have four sets of tees; bent grass in the fairways, greens, and tees; Kentucky bluegrass in the rough; a three-acre lake; and a stream that meanders across five holes. The property falls 200 feet from south to north, and the finishing hole will be the longest in the area at 620 yards. From the tee, players will gaze at Lake Erie, seven miles away.

TIDYMAN'S TIDBITS #6
Friendliest staffs:
• Painesville CC
• Skyland GC
• Powderhorn GC
• Erie Shores
• Legends at Massillon

PUBLIC 18+

Lost Nation Municipal Golf Course   ☎ (440) 953-4280

Area: **East**   City: **Willoughby**   Cost: $$$$$ Difficulty: ●●●

Address: 38890 Hodgson Rd., Willoughby

Tees	Ydg.	C/r	S/r	Pace
Back:	6440	69.4	113	
Middle:	6095	67.8	110	
Forward:	5700	70.9	112	

	Weekdays	Weekends & hol.	Carts
Prices:	$9.25 / $17.00	$10.25 / $18.00	$12.00 / $22.00
	Winter rates: $6.00 / $10.00 (Nov 1–Mar 31)		

Specials: Mon–Fri $21.00 per peson for two players, 18 holes with cart

Season: Year-round **Hours:** Spring–fall: Mon–Fri 6:30 a.m.–sunset, Sat–Sun 6:15 a.m.–sunset; Winter hours: 8 a.m.–5 p.m. **Tee times:** Taken **Leagues:** Mon–Fri 4–6 p.m. **Ranger:** Daily **Practice facil:** Range, Putting Green **Clubhouse:** Food, Beer **Outings:** Available **Lessons:** Available **Pro:** Dave Moskalski

Directions: SR 2 to Lost Nation Rd.; north on Lost Nation; right on Hodgson Rd.; on right.

Description Lost Nation, built in 1928, has weathered wars, the Depression, good times and bad, and . . . weather. Every once in a while, someone bounces a ball on the ice in front of No. 7 and aces the par 3. In fact, a great deal of winter golf is played here. That sounds unlikely, given the easterly location and nearness to the snowbelt, but the winds coming in off the lake push the snow farther south.

Highlights It's a relatively flat course, and, except for Nos. 1 and 9, the front nine is played on the other side of Hodgson Road. No. 1 is a 385-yard par 4. It begins just outside the clubhouse and heads for the Lost Nation Airport in the distance. It bends to the right toward a small green with a couple of traps on the right side. The hole is fairly open, with a driving range on the left and the entrance drive on the right.

At No. 4, the golf gets more challenging. It's a 400-yard par 4, a slight dogleg left. The left side is filled with thick woods and, before the 150-yard markers, big grass bunkers sit on both sides of the fairway. A few more bunkers appear at the green—one grass and one sand.

No. 5, a 475-yard par 5, has a sneaky little water hazard that begins as a creek cutting across the fairway in front of the women's tees. When it finds the left rough, it turns up toward the green. On the right side of the fairway, big grass bunkers slow balls headed for the adjacent sixth fairway. Players with well-developed slices will share fairways on these two holes.

The back nine opens and closes with par 5s. It is the more difficult nine, because woods and water play a more important role and the terrain rises and falls more on this side of the road.

Some people say the name of the course comes from an Indian tribe that found itself lost in these parts. That's hard to believe, given the nearness of both State Route 2 and Interstate 90.

Mallard Creek

☎ (440) 236-8231

Area: **Southwest**   City: **Columbia Station**   Cost: $$$$$ Difficulty: ●●●

Address: 34500 Royalton Rd. (SR 82), Columbia Station

Tees	Ydg.	C/r	S/r	Pace
Back:	6622	69.9	106	4:30
Middle:	6199	70.1	114	
Forward:	5754	71.1	113	

	Weekdays	Weekends & hol.	Carts
Prices:	$12.00 / $19.00	$14.00 / $24.00	$10.00 / $20.00

Specials: Seniors Mon–Fri before 3 p.m. $16.00 (walking), $21.00 (riding); Mon–Fri before 7:30 a.m. carts free (other rates don't apply) $12.00 / $19.00

Season: Year-round **Hours:** Sunrise–sunset **Tee times:** Required **Leagues:** Mon–Fri 3:30 p.m.–6:30 p.m. **Ranger:** Daily **Practice facil:** Range, Putting Green, Chipping Green **Clubhouse:** Food, Beer, Pavilion **Outings:** Available **Lessons:** Available **Pro:** Jeri Reid

Directions: I-480 to Exit 1B for Lorain Rd.; west on Lorain Rd. (becomes Butternut Ridge Rd. after crossing Root Rd.); left (south) on Island Rd.; left (east) on SR 82 (Royalton Rd.); on left.
I-71 to Exit 231 for SR 82/Royalton Rd.; west on SR 82; on right.

Description Mallard Creek opened its first two nines on Memorial Day weekend, 1992. The third nine joined the family on Memorial Day weekend in 1995. Formerly farmland, the property consists of 350 acres. It is now one of the busiest courses in Northeast Ohio.

Ron Palmer, former owner of Sweetbriar Golf Course in Avon Lake, is the owner. His father built the Sweetbriar, Thunderbird, Willow Creek, and Cherry Ridge golf courses. Ron's brother is the current owner of Thunderbird. Son Chris Palmer, along with John Knezevich, manages Mallard Creek.

The course has gone through many changes over the past few years—not in the layout but in overall conditioning and improvements. For example, there are now cart paths throughout the entire 27 holes. This feature has taken some of the wear and tear off the fairways and allowed a more defined fairway/rough cut. Also, the maturing and treatment of the turf has resulted in a solid and healthy growth of grass. Plate or disc yardage markers have been added in the fairways at 200, 150, and 100 yards. Course drainage problems have been addressed.

A fourth nine is scheduled to open in 2001. This nine will be similar to the third nine, with a lot of water from a newly built 14-acre lake as the cornerstone of its design. Ron Palmer is the primary designer.

In the past, adequate water supply for course irrigation was a problem. That situation has been corrected with the addition of the new lake.

A beverage cart (with snacks) roams the course—a nice touch and good revenue producer. Three separate pavilions accommodate 150 people each and can be combined for larger groups.

Highlights More than half the 27 holes here are doglegs. No. 2 is a long par 4, at 424 yards, with a dogleg left. Trees on the right and left corner turn require length and accuracy off the tee. Trees continue on both sides to the green. No. 8, a par 4 of 318 yards, is not long but starts with a dogleg right. The key decision here is whether to lay up before the water or drive the corner towards the green.

No. 10 is a long dogleg right, a 438-yard par 4 with trees right and left, continuing from the turn all the way to the green. No. 12, a slight dogleg right, is a par 5 of 518 yards, and has trees on the right and left. A major obstacle is the large tree left of center in the fairway 300 yards from the tee. This signature-hole candidate has some water left off the tee but this shouldn't be a problem.

No. 20, a dogleg left, is a par 5 stretching 526 yards. It plays tough, with a lake on the right and trees located at the corner turn. These trees are about 250 yards from the tee. Failure to place the tee shot on the right side will bring the trees into play.

Mallard Creek is open every day except Christmas.

Manakiki Public Golf Course   ☎ (440) 942-2500
Area: **East**   City: **Willoughby Hills**   Cost: $$$$$ Difficulty: ●●●

Address: 35501 Eddy Rd., Willoughby Hills

Tees	Ydg.	C/r	S/r	Pace
Back:	6625	71.4	128	4:30
Middle:	6189	69.9	125	
Forward:	5390	72.8	121	

	Weekdays	Weekends & hol.	Carts
Prices:	$13.00 / $15.00	$22.00 / $24.00	NA / NA

Specials: Golfer's Dozen: 12 rounds for the price of 10; Seniors (62+) & Juniors $8.00 / $15.00; carts are $11.00 per person.

Season: Mid-Mar–mid-Dec **Hours:** Sunrise–sunset **Tee times:** Taken, 5 days in advance, beginning at noon **Leagues:** Mon–Fri, various times **Ranger:** Daily **Practice facil:** Putting Green, Chipping Green, Sand **Clubhouse:** Food, Beer, Liquor, Dining room, Showers, Party rooms, Catering **Outings:** Available (Mon, Wed, Fri, Sat after 1 p.m.; call 440-942-2500) **Lessons:** Available **Pro:** Tom Kochensparger

Directions: I-90 east to Exit 189 for SR 91 (SOM Center Rd.); south on SR 91; left (east) on Eddy Rd.

Description Donald J. Ross, the Scotsman from Dornoch, designed the course in 1928. (Ross apprenticed at St. Andrews under Old Tom Morris—the father to Young Tom Morris, but no relation to Big Tom Morris, current Metroparks manager of golf operations.)

Originally a private club, Manakiki has been turned into one of the premier public courses in the area. A great deal of work has been completed in recent years and much more continues. A watering system is in place, as are cart paths, and several tees have been completely rebuilt. The challenging blue tee at No. 8, the number one handicap hole, was retrieved from the woods. Few players hit from that tee, however, because it calls for a drive few can produce on demand: a big, long, soft draw. No hook, please, or the ball is lost in the woods or water. No fade or slice, either, or the ball goes through the fairway and rattles around an equipment shed. No, this blue tee on No. 8 demands a great tee shot and there's no negotiating.

In addition to a first-rate course, the club has a ballroom and recently gave the food concession to the restaurant company that operates Sammy's and the Metropolitan Club, among others. Prices for food at the turn doubled, but so did the quality and selection. Many foursomes finishing the last hole on Saturday afternoons climb the last few yards from the green and see newlyweds posing for wedding pictures while a reception awaits in the ballroom.

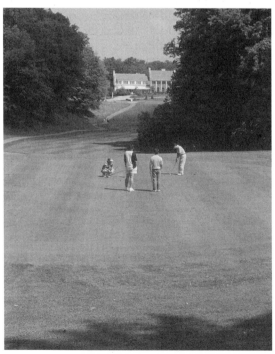

Manakiki Public Golf Course   *(photo: Casey Batule/courtesy of Cleveland Metroparks)*

PUBLIC 18+

Highlights No. 1 is the only homely hole on the course. A 375-yard par 4, it begins with a blind tee shot up a wide fairway. To the left front of the tee is the practice green; the practice range (available for a dollar) is to the right. A line of pines separates fairway from range, which is not o.b. About 170 yards from the tee is a large trap in the left rough, an easy hazard to find. The rising fairway crests near the 150-yard marker (4 x 4s with easy-to-read numerals—another improvement of recent vintage). There is sand on the right front of the green, which is flat.

No. 3 is one of four terrific par 5s on this layout. The driving area is very generous on the left side, but missing to the right can send the ball over the edge of a valley and into another fairway. Getting back can be difficult. From the tee of this 451-yard hole, the fairway dips and then rises until, about 225 yards from the tee, it drops away into a valley. Water cuts across the bottom of the valley 130 yards from the green. On the other side of the water, the ground rises just as suddenly as it fell, then levels toward the green. This green has a great deal of action in it; a huge dip in the front can make two-putting a monumental task.

To speed play, the course sometimes provides a ranger on this hole. The ranger staff is volunteer, mostly retirees who get to play in exchange for their service. By and large, they are a considerate and understanding lot. They spot balls and offer encouragement.

No. 16 calls for extra thought before swinging. It is a 310-yard par 4 that starts left to the 150-yard mark, then drops into a valley. The hole bends back to the right and rises to the green. Missing the fairway to the left sends the ball into deep brush. Missing the fairway to the right puts tall trees between the ball and the green.

No. 18 resembles No. 10 because it plays in the same type of narrow, deep valley. At 392 yards its length is similar, too. But this valley is sun drenched, and players getting drives in the fairway have shots to the smallest green on the course. Instead of being intimidating, it is an exciting hole. There is water crossing the fairway at 50 yards from the green. From there, the ground rises severely.

The approach shot at 18 is fitting. Manakiki is a dramatic course marked by great golf history and provides a wonderful ride over 18 very different holes.

TIDYMAN'S TIDBITS #7
Most handsome clubhouses:

• Painesville CC
• Pine Ridge GC
• Manakiki GC
• Pine Brook GC
• Western Reserve G&CC

Maplecrest Golf Club

☎ (330) 673-2722

Area: **Far South**   City: **Kent**   Cost: $$$$$ Difficulty: ●●●

Address: 219 Tallmadge Rd., Kent

Tees	Ydg.	C/r	S/r	Pace
Back:	6312	69.2	111	
Middle:	6016	67.9	108	
Forward:	5285	69.8	113	

	Weekdays	Weekends & hol.	Carts
Prices:	$10.00 / $20.00	$13.00 / $25.00	$10.00 / $20.00

Specials: None

Season: Mar 15–Dec 1 **Hours:** Sunrise–sunset **Tee times:** Recommended **Leagues:** Mon–Fri 3:30 p.m. **Ranger:** Daily **Practice facil:** Range, Putting Green **Clubhouse:** Food, Beer, Liquor, Lockers **Outings:** Available (outside banquet area only) **Lessons:** Available **Pro:** Karen Rainieri

Directions: I-271 to Exit 18 for SR 8; south on SR 8 to I-76 east (in Akron); I-76 to Exit 31 for Tallmadge Rd.; left (west) on Tallmadge; on right.

Description Manager Jim Irving knows more about this course than anyone else, having caddied here as a kid and worked here since adolescence. Sensitive about the slope rating of 108, which would indicate a less-than-average golf challenge, he says, "Don't believe it. It's a helluva lot harder than that." He's right. It is. With five par 3s, par is 71. And what par 3s! On the front side, No. 3 is 210 yards, No. 6 is 184 yards, and No. 8 is 228 yards. On the back side, No. 13 is 182 yards and No. 17 is 159. If you play the par 3s in par, you have a magnificent round going.

Highlights The course is lined with all sorts of trees, including flowering varieties, pines, maples (of course), the odd sycamore, and plenty of oaks. A stream meanders through and comes into play on five holes. In addition to the par 3s, two other holes are worthy of note: Nos. 7 and 10. The gorillas get out their clubs for the tee shot at No. 7. The creek is out there 213 yards, and driving it is a challenge difficult to ignore. No. 10 is a par 5 of 502 yards, and the creek is out about 260 yards from the tee; the dogleg left has o.b. down the right side. Three traps guard the green, which is noticeably narrow.

A hole in one on a par 4 is always noteworthy, and it occurred here a couple decades ago when a player on No. 1 let fly and his sliced ball finally bounced in the cup on No. 2.

PUBLIC 18+

Oak Knolls Golf Club

☎ (330) 673-6713

Area: **Far South**   City: **Kent**   Cost: **$$$$**$ Difficulty: ●●●

Address: 6700 SR 43, Kent

Tees	East Ydg.	C/r	S/r	Pace	West Ydg.	C/r	S/r	Pace
Back:	6882	71.8	118	4:15	6373	69.0	112	4:00
Middle:	6486	70.2	114		6172	68.0	110	
Forward:	5508	70.1	111		5681	71.3	112	

	Weekdays	Weekends & hol.	Carts
Prices:	$10.50 / $19.00	$13.00 / $25.50	$10.00 / $20.00

Specials: Mon–Thu before noon, all day Friday $24.00 per person, 18 holes with cart; Sat–Sun & holidays after 1 p.m. $10.50 / $20.00; (9-hole cart special all day Fri and Sat–Sun, holidays after 1 p.m. $27.00 per couple); Seniors & students Mon–Fri before 4 p.m. $8.00 / $14.00

Season: Year-round **Hours:** Sunrise–sunset **Tee times:** Required **Leagues:** Various times **Ranger:** Daily **Practice facil:** Range, Putting Green, Chipping Green **Clubhouse:** Food, Beer, Lockers, Showers, Pavilion **Outings:** Available **Lessons:** Available **Pro:** Jon Wegenek

Directions: I-480 to SR 14 east (I-480 ends here); south on SR43 for 5 miles

Description Oak Knolls Golf Club, Inc., a privately held company, built the East Course in 1961. When land became available across the street in 1968, they built the West Course. State Route 43 bisects the tracks. The terrain is similar on both, though water shows up only on the West Course. More than 70,000 rounds are played here per season—a lot of golf. Older players in particular are courted here.

Highlights Howard Morrette designed the East Course, and he put in a couple exceptional par 5s: Nos. 1 and 9. The only way to play them is from the blues, from which the opening hole stretches 638 yards and No. 9 measures an even 600. The first hole sees more eagles because it plays slightly downhill and often has a bit of a tailwind. No. 9 plays uphill and into the wind. Trees planted in 1961 are big enough to add shape to the holes.

A couple of holes were improved in 1998: No. 6 was changed from a par 3 to a par 4 by cutting a fairway through the trees, and No. 7 was lengthened by 50 yards (to 400) by pushing the tee back—way, way back. There are two pavilions here for outings, and there's lots of league play on weeknights.

Jon Wegenek, PGA, designed the West Course; it is a finely balanced layout with generous landing areas and flat, medium to medium-fast greens. This is the side preferred by older players, a market segment important to management here.

Orchard Hills Golf Course   ☎ (440) 729-1963

Area: **East**   City: **Chesterland**   Cost: **$$$$$**   Difficulty: ●●●

Address: 11414 Caves Rd., Chesterland

Tees	Ydg.	C/r	S/r	Pace
Back:	6409	71.1	126	3:42
Middle:	6200	70.2	124	
Forward:	5651	72.6	122	

	Weekdays	Weekends & hol.	Carts
Prices:	$10.50 / $21.00	$12.00 / $24.00	$12.50 / $24.00

Member prices ($28.00 membership fee); daily guest pass available for non-members: additional $3.00 for 9 holes, $6.00 for 18 holes

Specials: Senior specials with Buckeye card

Season: Mar–Nov **Hours:** Sunrise–sunset **Tee times:** Required **Leagues:** Evenings **Ranger:** Most days **Practice facil:** Putting Green, Chipping Green, Sand **Clubhouse:** Food, Beer, Lockers, Showers **Outings:** Available **Lessons:** Available **Pro:** Gary Lyman

Directions: I-271 to Exit 34 for US 322 (Mayfield Rd.); east on Mayfield; left (north) on Caves Rd.; on left, one mile north of Wilson Mills Rd.

PUBLIC 18+

Description With a slope rating of 124 and the lovely, heavy scent of apples in the air, Orchard Hills in autumn must bear a strong resemblance to the fantasy some players have of heaven. It is as close to a private golf club as most golfers are likely to get without a sponsor and a substantial initiation fee. This semi-private layout, part of Patterson's Fruit Farm, has much to recommend it.

Orchard Hills attracts serious players, men and women who want to play the game well. It has a good little pro shop and a separate snack bar. When apples are in season, golfers play 18 holes, then grab a peck or two of apples and a gallon of cider before leaving the parking lot.

It is a very challenging layout, one that calls for course management, accuracy, and a deft touch on the greens. Ah, yes, the greens. Striking the ball well with woods and irons doesn't count for much here if the putting game is not decent. The greens roll fast and true.

It is a course notable for its physical beauty. The staff obviously works hard to keep it in excellent condition.

Highlights Players who walk this course regularly will be in good condition, too. The cardiopulmonary system gets a workout here, especially on No. 8, a 446-yard par 4, and its evil twin, No. 18—434 yards uphill.

Not all holes are as long or as demanding as these two, though. There are a few short, tempting par 4s: No. 1 (313 yards); No. 10 (290 yards); and No. 16 (306 yards). Nos. 1 and 10 are easy holes. No. 16 calls for two iron shots, the second over a small pond to a canted green. It was on the No. 16 tee many years ago that a player was shot to death. His assailant had lain waiting in the brush next to the tee box for hours. Police called it a gangland slaying and no one argued.

Orchard Hills shares an important quality with a select number of courses: exciting design. Playing here is like a roller-coaster ride for grownups. And after playing the two last holes, players nod in agreement on hearing "It ain't over 'til it's over."

Even if the length and strength of the course discourage some players from walking, golfers are in for a treat each time they tee it up here.

Painesville Country Club   ☎ (440) 354-3469

Area: **Far East**   City: **Painesville**   Cost: **$$$**$$ Difficulty: ●●●

Address: 84 Golf Dr., Painesville

Tees	Ydg.	C/r	S/r	Pace
Middle:	5956	69.0	120	3:48
Forward:	5435	71.3	120	

	Weekdays	Weekends & hol.	Carts
Prices:	$10.25 / $18.25	$12.75 / $22.50	$10.00 / $19.00

Specials: Seniors Mon–Fri before 2 p.m. $7.25; Juniors Mon–Fri before 2 p.m. $8.00

Season: Year-round **Hours:** Mon–Fri open 7 a.m.; Sat–Sun open 6 a.m. **Tee times:** Taken **Leagues:** Mon–Fri afternoons; some traveling leagues on weekends **Ranger:** Weekends; weekday evenings **Practice facil:** Range, Putting Green, Sand **Clubhouse:** Food, Beer, Liquor, Dining room, Lockers, Pavilion, Club rental **Outings:** Available (steak roasts a specialty) **Lessons:** Available

Directions: I-90 to Exit 205 for Vrooman Rd.; north on Vrooman across Grand River; left (west) on Riverside Dr.; left on Golf Dr.

Description Family-owned businesses are supposed to self-destruct by the third generation. Not so here, where C. J. Alden's grandson, Rich, continues to improve on the original. Rich Alden's touch with a mower is remarkable, and he turns ordinary fairways and rough into well-defined holes with eye appeal.

Much has changed since 1928, when the opening of the Painesville Country Club was featured in *The Telegraph*. A clothing store ad on the same page offered men's suits for $22.50—an extra pair of trousers cost six bucks.

Much remains the same. It was a great little course then, and it's a great little course now. It looks and plays just as it did when it opened. It was designed by a Mr. Lamoran, according to old and yellowing news clips. He was the pro at Kirtland Country Club and supervised construction. This layout is a good example of the adage about designers discovering courses rather than building them—it is fitted to the land. The back is tighter than the front and both enjoy dramatic changes in elevation.

The course and stone clubhouse were developed by C. J. Alden, then president of the Painesville Metallic Binding Co. His son, Dick, and grandson, Rich, run them today. The clubhouse has a snack bar and pro shop, as well as a large dining room with hand-carved woodwork saved from one of Cleveland's Millionaire's Row mansions. The mantel is easily 12 feet high. On one wall rests a huge moose head. Dick Alden likes to nod toward the beast and say in a confidential tone, "Shot him on the 14th fairway."

Notes for the 19th hole: the barroom here is the most comfortable in the area. It is not big. The bar itself could hold a dozen only if they were related. But the old wooden bar is handsome, and the windows on two sides make the room bright. Service is fast and friendly.

Highlights The opening hole is a 521-yard par 5. The tee is elevated, and the hole plays first across a shallow valley. The fairway rolls up and down until the 150-yard marker, where it swoops down to the green. Well behind the green is a ravine. There is plenty of sand on this hole—and on this course. Its small greens are of average speed.

It is a walk over the ravine to get to the tee at No. 2, a 394-yard par 4. This was designed as a straight hole, but over the last 50 years a couple of trees near the fairway have grown up and out; they make it look like it bends to the left. As at many of the greens here, mounds surround the putting surface. On this hole, losing the ball to the right or over the green sends it crashing down a ravine. Behind the green is the Grand River. It is at the bottom of a 100-foot cliff and encircles much of the course.

One of many virtues of this course is the dearth of development. There is but a single building visible to players on the round. And when the trees are in foliage, even that structure can't be seen. Play here is quiet, secluded, and beautiful.

There are two tees on No. 8, the famous "bell hole," to allow faster play. When the course is crowded (or when the original tee box just needs some time to recover from play), the second tee is used and it takes 50 yards off the 181-yard hole. There are two ponds, also, so there is water to clear regardless of the tee used. The green was originally cut in the shape of a bell with the bottom facing the tee. To serve as a clapper, a small evergreen was planted in front of the green. According to old news clips, some members disliked the hazard; others were charmed by it. The shape of the green has changed over the decades, but the doughty evergreen remains. It is substantial but not towering, and clearing it is not difficult.

No. 9 is a 340-yard par 4 that seems to wind to the green because of elevated terrain on the left side. But though mowed as a dogleg, it really isn't one. Playing a drive off the side of the hill is common. There is sand in the fairway, in the rough, and at the green. On this hole (and on several others) what is called an "extended approach" is cut before the green. It is cut shorter than fairway, longer than greens, and longer than the typical apron. It adds a handsome country-club touch and is a good example of what Rich Alden can do with a mower.

No. 11, a par 3, has a hundred-foot drop from tee to green. But the green is still 239 yards away. Some golfers can't even *see* that far, let alone hit the green. Heavy trees line both sides and o.b. is on the right. The green was once half the size it is today. And it is not a large green. The right side was then protected by a tall pine. Back in the seventies, a disgruntled golfer slipped in under cover of darkness and chopped it down.

From the 18th tee, the stone clubhouse is visible in the distance. It is an especially pretty hole during the summer, when landing areas are trimmed and separated by rough.

Painesville Country Club is well worth the drive. Although it has provided challenge and delight for the better part of the 20th century, it is still largely undiscovered. And it is worth discovering.

Pine Brook Golf Club

☎ (440) 236-8689

Area: **Far West**   City: **North Eaton**   Cost: **$$$**$$ Difficulty: ●●●

Address: 11043 Durkee Rd., North Eaton

Tees	Ydg.	C/r	S/r	Pace
Back:	6162	68.3	113	3:38
Middle:	5741	66.8	110	
Forward:	5225	68.9	109	

	Weekdays	Weekends & hol.	Carts
Prices:	$9.50 / $17.00	$10.50 / $21.00	$10.00 / $18.00

Specials: Mon–Fri $46.00 for 2 players & cart; Seniors Mon–Fri before 11 a.m. $38.00 for 2 players w/cart

Season: Year-round **Hours:** 6 a.m.–10:30 p.m.; winter 7:30 a.m.–sunset **Tee times:** Not taken **Leagues:** Mon–Fri 5–6:30 p.m.; one 9 always open for public play **Ranger:** Most days **Practice facil:** Range, Putting Green, Chipping Green **Clubhouse:** Food, Beer, Dining room, Pavilion **Outings:** Available **Lessons:** Available

Directions: I-480 to Exit 1B for SR 10 (Lorain Rd.); west on Lorain (becomes Butternut Ridge Rd.); left (south) on Durkee Rd.; on left.

Description Interstate 480 makes Pine Brook Golf Club easily accessible. The clubhouse at this course was built in 1884. Of course, it wasn't built as a clubhouse, but as a barn. The course itself is young, having opened in 1964 with nine holes. The second nine was added a few years later. It is compact, beautifully maintained (when there is rain), and fun to play.

Highlights The front side features three par 3s, three par 4s, and three par 5s. No. 2, a short, 485-yard par 5, tempts big hitters. The green can be had in two, but only by avoiding water, o.b., and trees that protect the green. Plenty of players dreaming of eagles when lining up for their second shots walk away with bogies here. Prudence, perhaps an underrated virtue in public golf, is favored here.

No. 6, the second par 5 on the front side, measures 509 yards. It is a straightaway hole but unreachable in two for the overwhelming majority of golfers. By this hole, the dearth of sand becomes noticeable. Fink is mulling over the idea of additional grass bunkers, but not sand.

The back side measures a short 2,747 yards and has only one par 5, the 510-yard No. 11.

On No. 18 many players play from the blue tees. Then instead of a 300-yard par 4, it becomes 345 yards and much more challenging. The fairway slips down and away from the tee, then bends left around a lake, rising to an elevated green sitting in the shade of protective trees. A big drive to the right can go through the fairway; a big hook finds the lake and sleeps with the fish.

The specialty here is steak dinner outings.

PUBLIC 18+

Pine Hills Golf Club   ☎ (330) 225-4477
Area: **South**   City: **Hinckley**   Cost: **$$$**$$ Difficulty: ●●●

Address: 433 W. 130 St., Hinckley

Tees	Ydg.	C/r	S/r	Pace
Back:	6482	71.2	124	3:37
Middle:	6196	69.8	121	
Forward:	5685	74.3	126	

	Weekdays	Weekends & hol.	Carts
Prices:	$14.50 / $29.00	$14.50 / $29.00	$5.00 / $10.00

Specials: None

Season: Apr 1–Dec 25 **Hours:** Sunrise–sunset **Tee times:** Recommended **Leagues:** Mon–Fri from 4:00 p.m. **Ranger:** Daily **Practice facil:** Putting Green, Chipping Green, Sand, Practice area (use your own balls) **Clubhouse:** Food, Beer, Liquor, Dining room, Lockers, Showers **Outings:** Available **Lessons:** Available **Pro:** Steve Brzytwa

Directions: I-71 to Exit 226 for SR 303 (Center Rd.); east on SR 303 to W. 130 St.; left (north) on W. 130; on right.

Description There is no shortage of area players who argue that Pine Hills is the best public course in Northeast Ohio. There is plenty of competition for that mythical title, of course, but little doubt Pine Hills would be a contender. It is not the toughest course, but it is a beautiful and demanding layout, a golf course for people who love to golf. Beginners and slowpokes are not welcomed.

It is not an old course. Built in 1957, it was designed by Harold Paddock, Sr. (who also laid out Ironwood). The course record belongs to Joe Kruczek, who shot a 63 from the blue tees in 1989. It is tough to score well here without being adept with long irons and the putter. Kruczek's score is an eye-opener and his record will likely stand for a while.

Pine Hills is not a tight course, but it is compact. And it is often hilly.

The rough is not very rough, the fairways are cut short, and the greens are trimmed to be fast.

While it is always wise to get a tee time before setting out, getting one on weekend mornings is impossible. Permanent tee times belong to players who hold them more dearly than chili recipes or directions to a secret fishing hole.

Pine Hills Golf Club   (photo: Jonathan Wayne)

Highlights No. 6 is one of the prettiest tee boxes here. It's a straight par 4, 411 yards long, and it rises and falls—mostly falls—getting to the green. A line of trees runs down the left side and a deep forest is on the right. One of many dangerous greens on the course is found here. It is fairly large and pitched forward. Three-putting is made simple on greens like this.

No. 7 is the other par 5 on this side and, like No. 5, which plays to the left of it, has a blind tee shot. A stepladder at the tee provides a view of players ahead taking their second shots. The fairway on this 467-yard hole rises and slopes to the right. It parts company with No. 5 and goes its own way. Missing the fairway to the right sends the ball into a deep valley. About 175 yards from the green, the fairway suddenly drops, becoming part of the valley that lines the right side. The left side fills with trees and thick bushes. The valley bottoms out, then rises quickly and left to the green. It is not easy to hit in regulation or to hold. A player could shoot this hole six days in a row and play it well differently each day.

No. 11 offers a difficult tee shot. That's just one reason why it's the number three handicap hole. A valley sits in front of the tee on this 355-yard par 4. Deep, but not wide, it climbs quickly to a narrow fairway edged by trees, water, and deep rough. Missing the fairway means one

Little Thunder

Two years ago, Lake County developer Fred Slagle and his two boys, Darian, 6, and Damon, 5, were walking around the property adjacent to his Thunder Hill Golf Course. "What do you think we should do with this land?" he asked the kids. "Dad," Darian piped up, "we gotta build a kids' golf course." Slagle laughed and continued the hike.

Back in 1967, Slagle built the most fearsome course in Northeast Ohio: Thunder Hill GC, speckled with nearly 100 ponds and lakes, almost that many traps, and a topography that would challenge a tank. Players of the course often asked each other not for scores, but for number of balls lost.

On their way home, Darian tugged on his father's pant leg. "We could call it Little Thunder," he said. Slagle looked at the earnest eyes of his boy and laughed again.

At the supper table that night, it became clear Darian wasn't finished selling the idea of a golf course for kids. His mother, Eliette, suggested the boys could sneak out on Thunder Hill to play. Darian heaved an exaggerated sigh and turned to his father.

"Dad," he explained slowly, "we can't hit balls over the lakes, and those people don't want us there anyhow. Not only that, but where can our friends play?"

Slagle promised to look into the matter. Over the next week, he called the PGA, the USGA, and other golf organizations to ask where kids age 6 to 12 can play golf? The answer was always the same: nowhere.

Former President Gerald Ford had helped introduce First Tee, the program designed to bring kids to golf. "We immediately contacted them. They were going to cities and hoping to have a few acres donated and on that they would build a driving range and a three-hole course. It occurred to us kids still wouldn't have a place to play."

Part of the First Tee program is encouraging public courses to accommodate kids. "It's a well-known economic factor," Slagle said, "that it's very difficult to maintain any pace of play [with kids on the course.] We wish them the best, but it may be unrealistic to expect courses to accommodate kids."

The Slagle property measured 65 acres, roughly half of what was needed for a regulation–length course. He crunched numbers in his office and came up with a greens fee structure. Too bad it would prevent any kid from playing. "To build, maintain, and operate the course would mean greens fees of $25 to $35. There's no way a kid can afford that. So we looked into the possibility of a nonprofit golf foundation."

Over the winter, Slagle took topographical maps of the land to his winter residence in Costa Rica. It was there he designed the 18 holes. Little Thunder was underway.

When the family returned in spring, Slagle staked out the center lines. The routing plan was remarkably compatible with the 900 tagged trees; only seven had to be removed.

Five dozen sand traps and three lakes were incorporated into the design. Two of the lakes are for aesthetic purposes, one is for irrigation; none is a forced carry.

It was time for a few more angels to appear and they did.

"As we worked, we realized the cost would be substantial, that we didn't have the resources to do it all. At that point," Slagle said, "we thought, 'we haven't raised any money.' And that's the hardest thing to ask for. And none of us had any experience asking, either. So we wondered if people would help with raw materials and services."

Slagle's pitch was a simple one: He was building an 18-hole golf course for kids, a course where kids would be welcome, where they would learn the lessons golf offers all its students: honesty, fairness, consideration, respect. No other game teaches the lessons golf teaches.

The angels were legion; the course opens this year. Holes longer than 200 yards are par 5s; longer than 100 yards, they are par 4s; under 100 yards they are par 3s. A teaching academy is underway, as well.

—JHT

TIDYMAN'S TIDBITS #8

Most beautiful:
- Par 3: No. 18 at Berkshire Hills
- Par 4: No. 10 at Tam O'Shanter Dales Course
- Par 5: No. 3 at Skyland GC
- Opening Hole: Pine Valley
- Home Hole: Fowlers Mill
- Front Nine: Big Met
- Back Nine: Gleneagles

thing: trouble. Even hitting the fairway is no guarantee—there are some sand traps and tall hardwoods on the right side of the fairway, both within range of decent drivers.

No. 18, a 420-yard par 4, can create heroes and break hearts. It begins with a pretty tee box, flowers on the right, and a split-rail fence in the rear. On the left side is the backyard of a residential neighbor. Straight out a few hundred yards is a stand of tall pines, a good aiming point. Staying in the fairway is vital on this hole because the approach shot must clear a couple of lakes where the hole turns 10 or 15 degrees to the left. With a decent tee shot, getting over the water can be done with a mid-iron. But that is only to get over. To hit and hold the green calls for a long iron, and the lakes, often home to a few dozen Canada geese, provide a physical as well as psychological barrier. There is only one chance to make this shot. There is sand at the green, a large target that leans down towards the water.

Conditions are excellent here and play is brisk. For players, it's a great course. For hackers and beginners, the welcome mat is snatched away.

PUBLIC 18+

Pine Ridge Country Club   ☎ (440) 943-0293

Area: **East**   City: **Wickliffe**   Cost: **$$$$$**   Difficulty: ●●◦

Address: 30601 Ridge Rd., Wickliffe

Tees	Ydg.	C/r	S/r	Pace
Middle:	6132	68.7	116	4:15
Forward:	5330	72.2	121	

	Weekdays	Weekends & hol.	Carts
Prices:	$10.50 / $19.50	$12.00 / $22.25	$14.50 / $25.00

Specials: Seniors: 10% discount off golf fees

Season: Year-round **Hours:** Sunrise–sunset **Tee times:** Taken **Leagues:** Tue–Thu 3:30–4 p.m. start times; Tue–Thu Ladies League (mornings) **Ranger:** Daily **Practice facil:** Putting Green, Chipping Green, Sand **Clubhouse:** Food, Beer, Liquor, Dining room, Lockers, Showers, Pavilion, Club storage, Club rental **Outings:** Available **Lessons:** Available **Pro:** Tom Weiss, PGA

Directions: I-90 to Exit 189 for SR 91 (SOM Center Rd.); north on SR 91 to SR 84 (Ridge Rd.); left (west) on Ridge; on right.

Description The 1996 season was the last for the old Pine Ridge. It was a private club until a few years ago, when Lake Metroparks' management got taken for a ride with its purchase. Lack of maintenance had turned the homely course into a cow pasture. Weeds eight inches high on the first tee set the tone for the rest of the course.

In 1996, though, the park board allocated $540,000 for the course and another $1.6 million for the clubhouse and pro shop. Tom Weiss, PGA, brought superintendent Gordon Brail over from sister course Erie Shores and appointed him superintendent of golf maintenance operations for both courses. Weiss sat with a landscaper during the winter, and the two went over every hole as they decided on changes and improvements. "We'll have cart paths this fall," Weiss said. "And I just ordered 40 tons of rock (for landscaping). We decided what to do: split-rail fence, rock, new tees, and bunkers ..." The pond on holes 16 and 17 was enlarged and now drains 60 acres. It will mean better drainage and a better supply of water. The list goes on. It won't be long before the efforts of Weiss and his team bring Pine Ridge up to the same high standards adhered to at Erie Shores.

Pine Valley Golf Club ☎ (330) 335-3375

Area: **Far South**   City: **Wadsworth**   Cost: $$$$$ Difficulty: ●●●

Address: 469 Reimer Rd., Wadsworth

Tees	Ydg.	C/r	S/r	Pace
Middle:	6097	68.5	109	
Forward:	5268	67.9	107	

	Weekdays	Weekends & hol.	Carts
Prices:	$9.50 / $16.00	$12.00 / $22.00	$9.00 / $18.00

Specials: Mon–Fri before noon $34 for 2 players & cart; Seniors Mon–Fri before noon $7.50 / $12.00

Season: Mar–Nov **Hours:** 7 a.m.–sunset **Tee times:** Required **Leagues:** Mon–Fri, various times **Ranger:** None **Practice facil:** Putting Green **Clubhouse:** Food, Beer **Outings:** Available (for small groups) **Lessons:** Not available **Pro:** Garland Parsons

Directions: I-77 to Exit 136 for SR 21; south on SR 21 to I-76/US 224 west; west on I-76/US 224 to Exit 11 for Akron-Wadsworth Rd.; right (east) off highway; left (north) on Medina Line Rd.; left (west) on Reimer Rd.; on right.

Description   Pine Valley is an attractive little course tucked away in the farm country of Medina County and accessible from a two-lane blacktop. The Parsons family, who run it, draw on a great deal of experience in golf course maintenance. For many years, Garland Parsons ran the Good Park course near Akron. When he left, he purchased land and created the Bath Golf Club on Medina Line Road, which is now being developed for housing.

The Parsons sold Bath in 1978 to Jim McCartney, who was later shot to death by his former wife. The women who take Table 1 in Pine Valley's small clubhouse still enjoy talking about the murder.

When the bulldozers arrived a few years ago to turn McCartney's course into a housing development, the Bath Men's Golf League switched to Pine Valley, resuming the 30-year-old league's relationship with Garland Parsons.

Of her husband and son, Mrs. Parsons says, "They could grow grass on concrete." The father-son team looks after the course that was built in 1962 and designed by Cliff Deming. It is not a long course, 6,097 yards and par 72. Water and sand are minimal. The forward tees are well groomed and provide substantial advantage. The greens are manicured but not particularly fast. It is a nice, relaxed course.

There are plenty of pines at Pine Valley (and more going in every year), but they share space with sweet birch, pin oak, ash, dogwood, hickory, and witch hazel. The witch hazel, which blooms in the fall, has forked branches said to divine water in the right hands. If the right hands happen to be in the area between the No. 5, No. 6, and No. 7 greens, water will surely be found—there is a large pond there. The additional pines being planted are going in to provide both guidance on holes and protection from errant shots.

Highlights No. 1 is Gary Parsons' favorite hole because, he said, it's the prettiest. It is one of many pretty holes here. Not only the trees that line almost every fairway, but the gently rolling farmland of this deep green course make it a beautiful layout to walk and play. The opening hole is a straight par 4 of 416 yards.

Two rules help quicken play here: the continuous putting rule (unless the ball or your feet interfere with another player's line, you're obligated to putt out), and the stand-aside rule (which calls for waving the next group up on par 3s).

A trip to Pine Valley is not made by those hungry for heroic shots. The course is peaceful and encouraging—plenty of opportunities for pars and even a few birdies. It is easily accessible and offers good value.

Pleasant Hill Golf Course   ☎ (440) 285-2428
Area: **Far East**   City: **Chardon**   Cost: $$$$$ Difficulty:

Address: 13461 Aquilla Rd., Chardon *

Tees	Front & Middle 9s				Front & Back 9s				Middle & Back 9s			
	Ydg.	C/r	S/r	Pace	Ydg.	C/r	S/r	Pace	Ydg.	C/r	S/r	Pace
Middle:	6329				6295				6352			
Forward:	5447				5836				5599			

	Weekdays	Weekends & hol.	Carts
Prices:	$9.00 / $16.00	$10.00 / $19.00	$10.00 / $20.00

Specials: 27-hole special Mon–Fri $28.00 for greens fees, cart, lunch; Seniors $7.50 / $12.00; Seniors Mon–Fri $18.00 per player, 18 holes & cart

Season: Mar 15–Nov 15 **Hours:** Sunrise–sunset **Tee times:** Taken **Leagues:** Daily 5–6 p.m. **Ranger:** Most days **Practice facil:** Putting Green **Clubhouse:** Food, Beer, Lockers, Showers, Pavilion **Outings:** Available (banquet facilities for up to 300) **Lessons:** Available

Directions: I-271 to Exit 29 for Chagrin Blvd. (SR 87); east on SR 87; north on Ravenna Rd. (SR 44); right (east) on Butternut Rd.; left (north) on Aquilla Rd.; on right.

PUBLIC 18+

Description This layout has a few doglegs, a few hills, and some water. Many of the fairways here are wide and tempting. Sand is used judiciously, and the greens are kept in very good condition. It is a lovely course, and a good one to walk. Very playable, too, and many golfers finishing on the 18th green succumb to the temptation of another fresh nine holes.

Highlights No. 6, a long par 5 of 560 yards, is lined on the right side with woods. Just in front of the tee is a small lake with cattails filling the far shore. There are trees on the left side as well, but not so thick as to hide balls. The trees separate this fairway from the ninth fairway. This is a good birdie hole. Days probably go by without anyone getting on in two, but it's not difficult to get on in regulation, and there are no hazards in the way of the approach shot.

No. 9 is another long one, a par 5 of 603 yards. Reaching in four is no shame here. There is some water on the left side, the little lake that sits on the front of the sixth tee, but it is not a concern for straight hitters.

The finish is puzzling. Nos. 17 and 18 are par 3s, the former 165 yards and the latter 204 yards. Both tee shots go over water that should not come into play. No. 18 is the more difficult, not only for the length but because the hole plays uphill.

Pleasant Hill is a very nice stroll through the woods, a course that doesn't demand golf prowess—only that players stay up with the foursome before them. But 27 holes in a day is a dream (or a daydream) for a lot of players. Give them tee times, they will come.

Pleasant Valley Country Club ☎ (330) 225-2510

Area: **Southwest**   City: **Medina**   Cost: **$$$$**$ Difficulty: ●●●

Address: 3830 Hamilton Rd., Medina

Tees	Ydg.	C/r	S/r	Pace
Back:	6912	73.4	123	3:57
Middle:	6429	71.1	119	
Forward:	4984	68.9	113	

	Weekdays	Weekends & hol.	Carts
Prices:	$11.25 / $22.50	$13.50 / $27.00	$10.00 / $20.00

Specials: Seniors $1.50 off 9 holes

Season: Apr–until it snows **Hours:** 7 a.m.–7 p.m. **Tee times:** Taken weekends
Leagues: Mon–Fri evenings, Tue mornings **Ranger:** Some days **Practice facil:**
Putting Green **Clubhouse:** Food, Beer, Liquor **Outings:** Not available **Lessons:** Not available

Directions: I-71 to Exit 222 for SR 3; west off highway; right on Hamilton Rd. just after interstate; on left.

Description It is all golf here. There is no driving range and no lessons are offered. There are few price specials and outings are discouraged. The pro shop has little more than a few sleeves of balls. But for golfers seeking to test their skills, Pleasant Valley offers a great deal.

The layout, designed by Jack Kidwell (who also designed Punderson), rolls through Medina County farmland, presenting holes that reward thinking golfers and penalize the careless.

It's a long course, and it's a mix: tough and challenging holes along with straight and generous ones. The rolling terrain, the water, and the wealth of old and sturdy hardwoods provide the setting. The layout takes advantage of each virtue and presents a course for the thinking player. The fairways are trim and the rough is kept relatively short. Women are welcomed and provided a 1,500-yard advantage.

Highlights On No. 4, the course begins to show its personality. A 153-yard par 3 sounds easy, but this is not an easy hole to play. It is uphill, for starters, which makes club selection more important. Dense woods fill both sides, and a trap sits before the green.

At No. 5, a small lake and a weeping willow sit next to the tee. It's not unusual to find ducks paddling back and forth in the lake, especially early in the season. The fairway rolls a bit to another small lake, this one in front of the green. A bridge leads the way.

Nos. 16, 17, and 18 circle a large lake. The finishing hole, a 350-yard par 4, has the lake on the right side much of the way. The fairway bends sharply right; approach shots often have to carry the water's edge. That approach often adds drama and decides winners.

Pleasant Valley is a handsome and well-maintained course. Of course it's handsome—this is Medina County horse country. Good golf course management and rural beauty can co-exist very peacefully.

PUBLIC 18+

TIDYMAN'S TIDBITS #9

Toughest ...
- Par 3: No. 2 at Sleepy Hollow
- Par 4: No. 3 at Lorain CC
- Par 5: No. 17 Hinckley Hills
- Opening Hole: Powderhorn GC
- Home Hole: Orchard Hills
- Front Nine: Fowler's Mill
- Back Nine: Painesville

Pleasant View Golf Club ☎ (440) 564-7960

Area: **Far East**   City: **Newbury Township**   Cost: **$$$**$$ Difficulty: ●●●

Address: 14085 Ravenna Rd. (SR 44), Newbury Township

Tees	Ydg.	C/r	S/r	Pace
Back:	6439	71.8	125	
Middle:	6280	70.3	123	
Forward:	5140	69.8	118	

	Weekdays	Weekends & hol.	Carts
Prices:	$10.50 / $19.00	$11.50 / $22.00	$10.00 / $20.00

Specials: Seniors $8.00 / $13.00; Seniors Mon–Fri 18 holes & cart $19.00 per player

Season: Year-round **Hours:** Sunrise–sunset **Tee times:** Taken **Leagues:** Available
Ranger: Weekends **Practice facil:** Putting Green, Chipping Green, 2-hole practice
area **Clubhouse:** Food, Beer, Liquor, Dining room, Lockers, Showers **Outings:**
Available (weekdays & weekends, small groups) **Lessons:** Available **Pro:** Paul Tirpak

Directions: I-271 to Exit 29 for SR 87 (Chagrin Blvd.); east on SR 87; left (north) on
Ravenna Rd. (SR 44); on right, after Pekin Rd.

Description Pleasant View Golf Club was carved out of 180 acres of
dense woods in 1991 by Tucker Pfouts and sold to golf pro Paul Tirpak
in 1997. The layout assumes players can make a ball follow directions.
The hills assume walking players are in good condition.

There are eleven doglegs to contend with, and the only flat lies are on
the tees. The fairways are lined with woods, and trees often surround
greens. Colored stakes and fairway plates are at 200, 150, and 100 yards.
Tough greens here.

Recent work on the course includes one new green and a few
upgraded tees.

Highlights No. 4, a stunning 510-yard par 5, twists, rises, and falls. Much
of the way it is lined with old and beautiful trees. There is water on the
left and a big, sand-free green surrounded by mounds.

No. 9, a par 5 of 490 yards, is a dogleg left with the fairway sloping
right. Between tee and green there are ravines to carry, and the green on
this hole drops six feet from back to front.

TIDYMAN'S TIDBITS #10
The one thing missing:
- Hilliard Lakes: Tee times
- Pine Hills: Slice of Humble Pie
- Manakiki: Course Conditioning
- Big Met: Customer Relations training for
  staff

Powderhorn
☎ (440) 428-5951 or (800) T-OFF-PGC

Area: **Far East**   City: **Madison**   Cost: $$$$$$ Difficulty: ●●●

Address: 3991 Bates Rd., Madison

Tees	Ydg.	C/r	S/r	Pace
Back:	6004	68.5	117	
Middle:	5679	67.1	114	
Forward:	4881	67.6	113	

	Weekdays	Weekends & hol.	Carts
Prices:	$9.50 / $16.00	$10.50 / $18.00	$11.50 / $23.00

Specials: Several season pass options available; Daily specials; Seniors $6.00 / $9.50

Season: Year-round **Hours:** Sunrise–sunset **Tee times:** Taken **Leagues:** Mon–Fri 4:30–6 p.m. **Ranger:** Most days **Practice facil:** Putting Green **Clubhouse:** Food, Beer, Pavilion **Outings:** Available **Lessons:** Not available

Directions: I-90 to Exit 212 for SR 528 (River St.); north on SR 528; right (east) on SR 84; right (south) on Bates Rd.; on left.

PUBLIC 18+

Description The course starts a little herky-jerky with a very difficult 411-yard par 4 followed by a dinky little 254-yard par 4. But after this brush with schizophrenia, Powderhorn takes a wonderful tour through the Lake County countryside.

The boss here is Larry Knowles, and he admits the opening hole, the number one handicap hole, is too difficult to be an opening hole. But he notes that switching nines would not help; No. 10 is the number two handicap hole.

If this is criticism, it's about all there is here to be critical about. It is a well-maintained course that offers plenty of good golf.

A sign in the parking lot reads "No Hunting on Golf Course Property," which gives an idea of the rural setting of this course. It wasn't always Powderhorn. First a nine-hole course named Whispering Pines was here (none of the original holes exist today). In the late 1980s, Powderhorn was designed by the Detroit architectural firm of Anderson, Lesniak & Associates.

Highlights After playing the course a few times, players might look forward to the first hole. It begins with water and ends that way, too. It is a narrow fairway and a handsome hole, though it will pale by comparison a few holes later. The water in front of the tee won't come into play, but the sizable water in front of the green allows no mistakes on the long-iron approach. The greens here are big and can be treacherous—all the more reason to play here a few times before rendering judgment. The opening hole here has opportunities for players who know that course management is the 15th club in the bag.

Looking out from the No. 4 tee over the 492-yard par 5, first-time players are taken with the view. It is one of the most beautiful holes around—and there is no shortage of competition. Woods, sand, and a little bit of water make this the number seven handicap.

Walking the front side is a snap; walking the back nine is a workout. No. 10 brings memories of the first hole. It is longer, at 433 yards, and this par 4 has fairway sand and plenty of water near the green. Again, course management can carry the day (if not the water.)

The lone par 5 on the back side is No. 16, at 523 yards a beautiful and long straightaway with a manicured fairway and woods down both sides.

The course finishes with one of its short par 4s, only 257 yards. Par here is 35–35, and total yardage is only 5,679 from the whites. There are only two par 5s. On paper, that might sound like a pushover. It isn't. This layout calls for thoughtful play.

Punderson State Park Golf Course   ☎ (440) 564-5465

Area: **Far East**   City: **Newbury**   Cost: **$$**$$$ Difficulty: ●●●

Address: 11755 Kinsman Rd., Newbury

Tees	Ydg.	C/r	S/r	Pace
Back:	6815	72.9	119	3:55
Middle:	6600	72.0	114	
Forward:	6342	76.9	113	

	Weekdays	Weekends & hol.	Carts
Prices:	$17.00 / $32.00	$23.00 / $40.00	Prices include cart

Specials: Spring rates Apr–early May; Winter rates from late Sep until Nov; Senior rates w/ Buckeye card; discount after 3:00 p.m.

Season: Mar 1–Nov 1   **Hours:** Sunrise–sunset   **Tee times:** Taken weekends, starting previous Thursday   **Leagues:** Minimal   **Ranger:** Daily   **Practice facil:** Range, Putting Green, Use own balls on range   **Clubhouse:** Food, Beer, Pavilion, Punderson Manor available for overnight lodging; conference center also available.   **Outings:** Available   **Lessons:** Available   **Pro:** Kip Freeman

Directions: I-271 to Exit 29 for SR 87 (Chagrin Blvd.); east on SR 87 (becomes Kinsman Rd. in Geauga County); enter Punderson State Park (on right, in Newbury Twp.); right on second main road in park to golf course.

Description Ohio cities and Ohio counties own and operate golf courses, so why not the state? The Department of Natural Resources, in addition to scraping roadkill off park roads, runs a beautiful golf course designed by Jack Kidwell and built in the spring of 1969. Course and park are named after Lemuel Punderson, the first permanent settler of Newbury. He worked for the Connecticut Land Company during the latter part of the 18th century. A direct descendant with the same name still lives in Newbury.

Punderson is a lot of golf course: 6,600 yards, par 72. But that doesn't mean a slew of lengthy par 4s. Much of the yardage comes from the par

5s; four of them total 2,158 yards. And both par 3s on the back side measure close to 200 yards.

The clubhouse looks more like a ski lodge and has a large porch from which to sip a post-round beer, admire Mother Nature's woods, and watch players on the first tee. Special packages that include lodging in the Manor House or the cabins are delightful mini-vacations.

Highlights No. 3 is one of the big par 5s—this one 550 yards. The fairway is beautiful from the tee. The hole plays straight, but the greenskeeper, with light mower, puts a wavy edge on the right side of the fairway and a straight edge on the left. Out on the left is a huge and ancient willow. There is water farther to the left (but it belongs to another hole, and unless a powerful snap hook is in a player's bag, it should not come into play). There are hills and dales in this green, and four traps around its borders. Behind it is the next tee. That's a lot of golf on a single hole.

No. 6, another 550-yard par 5, has a small lake in front of the tee. It is an open fairway for the first 200 yards before trees appear on the edges. The first two shots here are blind because the slowly rising fairway doesn't crest until the 150-yard marker. This green is heavily bunkered.

On the back side, No. 11, a 390-yard par 4, is a magnificent hole. It is open but calls for an approach shot to clear a lake before the green. The lake is substantial and anchored on both sides by willows. This is another hole that gives pause to players when they stop to appreciate the fairways sculpted with light mowers.

The tee shot on No. 14, a 196-yard par 3, has to clear water covering much of the fairway and hold the green. There is fairway in front of the green for players unable to hit that shot. Among Punderson's many virtues are the challenging par 3s. None is easy; all are gorgeous.

No. 15, a 571-yard par 5, has a green virtually unreachable without three good shots. Deep woods line the right side, though that should not present problems because of a generous fairway here. A deep narrow valley opens up about 200 yards from the green. The valley is rough and cuts across the fairway. The second section of fairway picks up and heads straight to the green.

This is a first-class course and easy to get to. Too bad green fees, which used to be scandalously low, are now scandalously high. What used to be a value is no longer much of a deal.

PUBLIC 18+

TIDYMAN'S TIDBITS #11
Where the best-dressed players play:
- Windmill Lakes
- StoneWater
- Fowlers Mill

PUBLIC 18+

Punderson State Park Golf Course

Raccoon Hill Golf Club
☎ (330) 673-2111

Area: **Far South**   City: **Kent**   Cost: $$$$$ Difficulty: ●●●

Address: 485 Judson Rd., Kent

Tees	Ydg.	C/r	S/r	Pace
Middle:	6068	68.3	112	4:00
Forward:	4650	65.4	101	

	Weekdays	Weekends & hol.	Carts
Prices:	$11.00 / $19.00	$15.00 / $27.00	$10.00 / $20.00

Specials: Seniors Mon–Fri before 2 p.m. $9.00 / $16.00; senior special riding before 2 p.m. 12.00 / 20.00 (includes cart); Ladies get senior rates Tues and Fri

Season: Apr–Nov **Hours:** Sunrise–sunset **Tee times:** Recommended **Leagues:** Mon–Fri evenings **Ranger:** Daily **Practice facil:** Putting Green, Chipping Green **Clubhouse:** Food, Beer, Liquor, Lockers, Pavilion **Outings:** Available **Lessons:** Available **Pro:** Jim Beers

Directions: I-271 to Exit 18 for SR 8; south on SR 8 to SR 303; east on SR 303 (W. Streetsboro Rd.); right (south) on SR 91 (S. Main St.); left (east) on Norton Rd. (becomes Judson Rd.); on left, after Seasons Rd.

Description Purchased by Bill Snetsinger in 1989, this course has undergone a metamorphosis, including new cart paths, irrigation, and 2,500 new trees. It used to be Shawnee, and it used to be, as pro Chad Schraibman says, "a cow pasture."

Now, "It's a fun course," according to Solon resident Terry Uhl, whose regular foursome takes the first tee time every Saturday morning.

The course is meticulously maintained and features collars around the greens, which are themselves manicured and often, though not always, fast. There is lots of water here, but most of it won't come into play. There is sand here, too, though not so much as to slow you down. Women's tees are well maintained and give a substantial advantage—a difference of 1,418 yards.

Highlights No. 13 is the Z-hole, a par 5 of only 433 yards. It calls for three *very* accurate irons. It is followed by the L-hole, which demands a 200-yard drive and a sharp right turn. No. 18 is a heartbreaker, a par 3 of 187 yards with water in front.

PUBLIC 18+

Raintree Country Club   ☎ (330) 699-3232
Area: **Far South**   City: **Uniontown**   Cost: **$$$$$**   Difficulty: ●●○

Address: 4330 Mayfair Rd., Uniontown

Tees	Ydg.	C/r	S/r	Pace
Back:	6811	73.0	127	
Middle:	6358	70.6	121	
Forward:	5030	68.5	114	

	Weekdays	Weekends & hol.	Carts
Prices:	$13.00 / $23.00	$16.00 / $32.00	$10.00 / $20.00
	Carts mandatory on weekends; no 9-hole rates on weekends until 4 p.m.		

Specials: Mon–Thu 18 holes with cart before 9 a.m. $23.00

Season: Year-round **Hours:** Sunrise–sunset **Tee times:** Required **Leagues:** Mon–Fri 3:30 p.m. **Ranger:** Daily **Practice facil:** Range, Putting Green, Chipping Green **Clubhouse:** Food, Beer, Liquor, Dining room, Lockers, Showers, Pavilion **Outings:** Available **Lessons:** Available **Pro:** Don Olney

Directions: I-77 to Exit 118 for SR 241 (Massillon Rd.); south on SR 241; left (east) on Wise Rd.; left (north) on Mayfair Rd.; on left.

Description Owner-developer John Rainieri thinks Raintree will serve an emerging niche in the public player's market: golfers who want more than what the average public course offers, but less than the pricey amenities of a private club. There are some courses that serve that clientele now, such as Tam O'Shanter in Canton and Sleepy Hollow in Broadview Heights.

"It's a trend [upscale public courses] that started about four years ago in most parts of the country," Rainieri said. No debutante balls, of course, but amenities such as showers, locker rooms, bag-drop areas, and electric carts, as well as a first-rate course.

The clubhouse here is worthy of mention because few clubhouses measure 20,000 square feet and have room for 500 guests. Maybe no debutante balls, but wedding receptions will fill the calendar on Saturdays.

"I could have saved a quarter million dollars building this if we just built a public golf course, but we were looking for more than that," Rainieri said. "More" included 140 traps and seven lakes and meant moving 125,000 cubic yards of earth.

And it included the services of young course designer/architect Brian Huntley. Huntley was delighted with the property and the opportunity to create a course with both links-style and northern golf course–style holes. "That's what we have," Rainieri said, "about half and half. And I liked his layout, I liked the way he put his traffic patterns around the clubhouse, along with the driving range and the parking lot and so on."

This thoughtful design insists many golf shots be available for a round. Mid-iron play will make a difference and so will the short game. Greenside bunkers, both grass and sand, along with steep mounds, will present most players with the opportunity to show off the downhill-sidehill pitch shot.

Once on the green, it's no picnic, either. These greens are fast, and about as predictable as a teenager. Most are big, too. After a round or two on these greens, one cannot help but admire the golf skills of Mike Rosseti, who fired the current course record: 65 from the blue tees.

Highlights The challenge begins with a 371-yard par 4 that shoots out of a hallway of trees almost 100 yards deep, then opens up rising and bending a bit to the left. There is fairway sand on the right that can be reached from the tee and rough that is troublesome. The fairway narrows near the green; mounds and grass bunkers appear over the final 40 yards.

No. 2, a 465-yard par 5, is mildly shocking and thoroughly delightful. The fun, however, comes not on the first go-round, but on subsequent rounds when players know what to expect and where to place the ball. The fairway slopes left and descends slightly. At about 200 yards, it turns to the right and narrows. While trees on both sides help players concentrate, the water on the left side near the green gives them something to worry about. The creek runs across the fairway, and a tree sits almost centered in front of the green. There are also mounds and a huge grass bunker. One last challenge: the green has a hogback ridge running horizontally across its surface.

The tee at No. 4, the first of the par 3s, provides the first view of traffic on I-77, though the player had better concentrate on proper club selection for this 160-yard hole where the wind can make a difference. There is sand at the green that can't be seen from the tee.

No. 6, the number one handicap, doesn't look difficult. It's a par 4 of 403 yards from the blues and 378 yards from the whites. Straight and wide open, it doesn't always play like a low-handicap hole, either. But the prevailing wind out of the southwest can make a difference; it makes this hole (and many others on the course) play much longer.

One of the more fun holes, No. 7 is a 500-yard par 5. There is o.b. on the right side as the fairway rises straight out from the tee. The fairway crests, then drops left toward the green, which is reached over a lake. Flying the green can send the ball onto private property and o.b. This hole looks as simple as arithmetic but has hazards, especially near the green, that will quickly sober the overconfident player.

The real signature hole here is No. 18, where most players will thank the Gods of Golf for a par and hustle to the clubhouse. Others, carding double and triple bogies on this short, 459-yard par 5, will question their future in the game. Water bisects the fairway. Pick one side or the other at the tee and go for it. The next shots must cover all sorts of water and fairway traps. The water gets more troublesome as the fairway narrows. The green slopes sharply forward. With the pin in front, putting off the green suddenly becomes a realistic fear. It is a great finishing hole because two (or more) stroke swings make for memorable matches.

For all that Raintree offers, the price is surprising. When it was suggested to Rainieri that his greens fees provide an excellent value, he said, "The people in this community don't believe that. They think we're holding them up." We should have more stick-up artists like Rainieri.

PUBLIC 18+

Red Tail Golf Club   ☎ 440-327-1277

Area: **West**   City: **Avon**   Cost: **NA**   Difficulty: **NA**

Address: 4400 Lear Nagle Rd., Avon, OH

Tees	Ydg.	C/r	S/r	Pace
Middle:	6542			

	Weekdays	Weekends & hol.	Carts
Prices:	New course: call for prices		

Specials: Call for specials

Season: NA **Hours:** NA **Tee times:** NA **Leagues:** None **Ranger:** NA **Practice facil:** None **Clubhouse:** None **Outings:** NA **Lessons:** NA

Directions: I-90 to exit 156 for Crocker Rd./Bassett Rd.; west on Detroit Rd.; south on Lear Nagle Rd. to main entrance (St. Francis Dr.).

Description   Red Tail is scheduled to open for play in mid- to late-1999. Play it while you can. The course will be open to the public for the first couple of years (so they can show the place off); after that it will be private, open only to members.

This golfing community, developed by Carnegie Residential Development Corporation, has been a five-year labor of love for project director Pete Restivo, whose handicap hovers around 15. There is room for nearly 500 homes in this sleepy Lorain County town, and at present five different builders are putting up homes costing from $275,000 to more than $500,000. Residents will automatically enjoy social memberships. Private club memberships will be additional. But for the first season or two, the course will be available for daily fee play.

This marketing strategy makes sense. "We want to have a lot of people come out and play," Restivo says. "First, it builds the reputation of the course. You can have the finest course in the world, but if no one plays it … Second, it exposes the course to potential home buyers."

It was designed by veteran Robert Von Hagge, whose domestic and international design credentials are impeccable. Especially around here, where he was the designer of the Quail Hollow track used every season by the Nike Tour.

Von Hagge was selected for more than his golf course design experience, substantial as it is. "He's done more than five dozen golf course communities and he owns and operates about nine of them, so he has real hands-on experience," Restivo says. "[Von Hagge] is truly world class and we wanted something special. One of the things that struck us is his longevity. He's been around forever. He's the connection to the old and classic courses. And he's down to earth."

Anxious as Restivo is to tee it up, he knows that new courses are often damaged by opening before the grass has taken strong enough root. At development seminars across the country, he hears the same message: Let the professionals decide on opening day and amount of play. His agronomist will have a major influence in the decision.

The Reserve at Thunder Hill   ☎ (440) 298-3474

Area: **Far East**   City: **South Madison**   Cost: **$$$$$**   Difficulty: ●●●

Address: 7050 Griswold Rd., South Madison

Tees	Ydg.	C/r	S/r	Pace
Back:	7504	78.5	152	
Middle:	6437	72.5	137	
Forward:	4769	68.5	121	

	Weekdays	Weekends & hol.	Carts
Prices:	NA / $45.00	NA / $55.00	Prices include cart

Specials: $35.00 after 2:00 p.m.; $25.00 after 4 p.m.; Mon–Fri Juniors (17 & under) $20.00, Sat–Sun $25.00; after 4 p.m. Juniors play free when accompanied by paying adults; carts included in all fees.

Season: Mar 1–Nov 30   **Hours:** Sunrise–sunset   **Tee times:** Recommended   **Leagues:** Few, Mon–Fri   **Ranger:** Daily   **Practice facil:** Range, Putting Green, Chipping Green   **Clubhouse:** Food, Beer, Liquor, Dining room, Showers, Patio, Facilities for parties   **Outings:** Available   **Lessons:** Available   **Pro:** Bryan Huff

Directions: I-90 to Exit 212 for SR 528; south on SR 528; left (east) on Griswold Rd.; on right.

Description It started in 1976 when developer Fred Slagle fired up the bulldozer and took the first giant bite out of this rich Ashtabula County soil. He created a course that wended its way between an apple orchard and trout ponds, over hill and dale, and around stands of pine. Thunder Hill. A course of mythical proportions. Slope rating of 150, four-wheel-drive carts, a canine corps to find players lost in the rough, and with nearly 100 lakes and ponds, a bonanza for a golf ball salesman.

The name was truly delivered from the heavens. Slagle was on the bulldozer one day when a thunderstorm rolled across the property. A couple lightning bolts were followed by thunder close enough to bounce him around a bit.

After a few incarnations, the course is managed today by the Meadowbrook Golf Group, which just dumped $3.3 million into improvements.

The renovation includes installation of cement cart paths throughout; irrigation improvements in the bunker areas; clubhouse/parking/grounds renovation; fairway conversion to bent grass (formerly bluegrass). That's on the course. In the clubhouse nearly $600,000 is being spent on new washrooms, showers, new carpeting, a full service pro shop, a new banquet room, and a sports/snack bar combination.

A nice touch is the complimentary bucket of balls. The driving range, while small, is new and a good idea. There are five sets of tees here. The Thunder tees play more than 7,500 yards; the Champion plays 6,866; Reserve plays 6,437 yards; Challenge tees go 5,754 and the Sanctuary tees are 4,769.

Greens are large, undulating, and well maintained. A hole-by-hole booklet is attached to each cart, with drawings and yardage figures from various points.

Highlights For all its reputation, the front side here is not worthy of myth. It is a very challenging nine holes, but divine intervention is not necessary to score well.

The first hole looks out over a couple of ponds and runs straight until it meets a pine grove. The fairway then veers right. There are plenty of trees on the course, but very little underbrush. The rough is minimal, and chipping out from the woods is usually a simple matter. The last 150 yards of No. 1 are lined with hardwoods on the right and pines on the left. The green is surrounded by four sand traps.

No. 12, a 497-yard par 5, lets players stumble directly into harm's way. The fairway on this hole is filled with ambushes: one big tree, four ponds, four sand traps. Woods close in around the edges. It calls for remarkable accuracy and sound shot planning. Lady Luck can be a valuable partner here, as well.

And No. 13, an even 400 yards long, suggests strongly that there is brutal golf ahead. As it nears the 150-yard marker, a narrow fairway suddenly drops down and sharply to the right, then zooms up again to the green. About seven ponds can come into play on this hole. Thick groves of trees here are omnivorous, swallowing hooks and slices alike.

At No. 14, a 377-yard par 4, vestiges of the orchard remain and the rich smell of apples fills the summer air. This is no tee for a lapse in concentration. There is a valley in front of the tee, and beyond it the fairway is closely guarded on both sides by trees. The opening for the drive is only about 35 yards wide. Just a slight draw will send the ball into a pine grove.

The green on No. 16 is most unusual. Long and narrow, it has a huge hump near the rear. It's not likely the flag would be placed behind it (one would hope not, anyway). But putting from back there will be unimaginably difficult. Next to the green is a beautiful beech tree. Its bark is filled with what appear to be scars in the shape of putter heads.

Ridge Top Golf Course ☎ (330) 725-5500; (800) 679-9839

Area: **Far South**   City: **Medina**   Cost: $$$$$ Difficulty: ●●●

Address: 7441 Tower Rd., Medina

Tees	Ydg.	C/r	S/r	Pace
Back:	6211	69.5	114	3:34
Middle:	5893	67.4	109	
Forward:	4968	67.9	107	

	Weekdays	Weekends & hol.	Carts
Prices:	$10.00 / $18.00	$13.00 / $23.00	$10.00 / $20.00

Specials: Mon–Fri $48.00 for 2 players 18 holes & cart; Seniors Mon–Fri $42.00 for 2 players 18 holes & cart

Season: Mar–Dec **Hours:** Sunrise–sunset **Tee times:** Taken **Leagues:** Mon–Thu 4–6 p.m. **Ranger:** Daily **Practice facil:** Putting Green **Clubhouse:** Food, Beer, Liquor, Dining room **Outings:** Available **Lessons:** Not available **Pro:** Larry Miksch

Directions: I-71 to Exit 218 for SR 18; west on SR 18; left (south) on River Styx Rd.; right (west) on Poe Rd.; left (south) on SR 57 (Wadsworth Rd.); bear right (south) on Tower Rd.; on left.

Description   There are only two types of golfers, according to owner Bob Emery: considerate and inconsiderate. "Fifty percent of your golfers will repair the greens where the others will not." Like many other owner/operators, he takes great pride in those layered sand-and-soil gardens so fragile, yet so important to the game.

Ridge Top was Medina County farmland until the 1970s. Across Tower Road is a farm; its silo provides an aiming point on one of the tees. The course was designed by Bob Pennington and plays a surprisingly short 5,893 yards, par 71.

Highlights   The front side is much more interesting than the back. It starts with a 360-yard par 4 that is not, despite its length, an easy warm-up hole. White o.b. stakes line the right side, and on the left the terrain drops to a valley where the next hole is played. The fairway is not narrow, though, and a decent drive (one that misses the big oak on the right edge of the fairway at the 150-yard marker) will suffice. Overshooting the green will send the ball into deep rough and nearly off the course. These greens are fast.

No. 3 is the first of several tough doglegs. It is a 384-yard par 4 with a sharp right turn about 200 yards out. The elbow is filled with trees and uneven ground; only very big hitters will succeed in cutting this corner. After the turn, the hole falls slightly to a narrow creek bed.

The back side begins with one of the more difficult and challenging holes on the course. No. 10 is a 425-yard par 4 that calls for two very good shots. From the tee, players look across a deep valley to the fairway, which bends left and slopes down to the green. All along the right side it is wide open. But all along the left are deep woods. Behind the green are tall hardwoods. It is the number four handicap hole and a real challenge to par.

There is a nasty little gorge just in front of the No. 11 tee, but unless players top the ball it is only decorative. This hole was recently rebuilt into a 320-yard dogleg par 4. The left side is filled with deep woods; the right side is open, though playing to the right lengthens the approach. The green is nestled in thick woods, which were cleared to fit it—an expensive but valuable change.

Ridge Top is off the beaten path but worth the effort it takes to find. It has a great variety of holes, good prices, and enlightened management.

PUBLIC 18+

Ridgewood Golf Course   ☎ (440) 888-1057

Area: **South**   City: **Parma**   Cost: **$$**$$$ Difficulty: ●●●

Address: 6505 Ridge Rd., Parma

Tees	Ydg.	C/r	S/r	Pace
Back:	6299	70.3	115	3:54
Middle:	5825	67.9	110	
Forward:	5090	69.1	113	

	Weekdays	Weekends & hol.	Carts
Prices:	$8.75 / $15.75	$9.25 / $16.25	$10.00 / $20.00

Specials: Seniors $5.25 (Parma residents), $6.00 (non-residents)

Season: Mar 1–Nov 30 **Hours:** Sunrise–sunset **Tee times:** Not taken **Leagues:** Various times **Ranger:** Daily **Practice facil:** Putting Green **Clubhouse:** Food, Beer, Liquor **Outings:** Available **Lessons:** Available **Pro:** Danny Panek

Directions: I-480 to Exit 15 for Ridge Rd. (SR 3); south on Ridge; on left.

Description There is an ancient oak next to the practice green here, and at the base of it is a plaque. It is inscribed "In memory of Howard A. Stahl, 1875–1930. A pioneer in the development of the City of Parma and builder of Ridgewood Golf Course."

Clearly this course has been around a while. It has not always been owned and operated by City Hall, however—Parma did not assume ownership until the mid-1950s. By that time, the original layout of the course had been sacrificed for some new homes. Instead of its original 6,306 yards, it now plays 5,825. What was a great course is now just a fair course.

LPGA player (and four-time Tour winner) Barb Mucha prepped here; so did Walker Team player Chris Wollman, who won the National Public Links Championship in 1996. Other players of note who have teed it up here include Arnold Palmer, Walter Hagen, Romeo Palumbo, Byron Nelson, Patty Berg, and Babe Didrikson Zaharias. In May 1950, Zaharias won the Weathervane Women's Open here.

Highlights Ridgewood's tees are well cared for and adorned with flower boxes. The flowers, like the greens, are watered by hand. During dry weather the greens are watered three times a day. This hand grooming produces healthy greens of average speed.

No. 5 is a very short par 5, only 435 yards. It's a beautiful hole from the tee, though the green is not visible. The fairway drops off from the tee and rumbles along for a few hundred yards. About 200 yards from the green, it begins rising and bending to the right. It's especially easy to measure length on this course because the yardage markers appear to be hewn from telephone poles. They are placed on the edges of the fairway.

No. 12 is a 260-yard par 4 that appears to have been designed as an afterthought. The fairway is lined with trees and rises slightly to a green that appears jacked up four or five feet. Approaching from the left side puts the ball at odds with a tall tree near the green. There is plenty of sand at the hole.

Then it's through the W. 54th Street tunnel to No. 13, a brutal and exciting par 5 that covers hill and dale, woods and plain, and 575 yards. The first few hundred yards go straight out from the tee and up. At its crest, the fairway suddenly turns 90 degrees to the right and falls to a green marked by two sand traps on the left and one on the right. The length, the dogleg, and the hills on this hole give bragging rights to any birdie.

Most of the fairways here are generous; playing and staying on the short grass is not as difficult as it is on other public courses. Many Ridgewood veterans tell visitors, "You should have seen it before they chopped it up." Such is the price of progress.

Riverside Golf Club

☎ (440) 235-8006

Area: **Southwest**   City: **Olmsted Falls**   Cost: **$$$**$$ Difficulty: ●●●

PUBLIC 18+

Address: Sprague & Columbia Rds., Olmsted Falls

Tees	Ydg.	C/r	S/r	Pace
Middle:	5498	65.9	106	
Forward:	5162	68.9	111	

	Weekdays	Weekends & hol.	Carts
Prices:	$9.25 / $18.50	$9.75 / $19.50	$10.00 / $20.00

Specials: None

Season: Year-round **Hours:** Sunrise–sunset **Tee times:** Required **Leagues:** Mon–Fri 4–6 p.m. **Ranger:** Most days **Practice facil:** Putting Green, Chipping Green **Clubhouse:** Food, Beer, Liquor, Lockers, Showers, Pavilion **Outings:** Available **Lessons:** Available **Pro:** Ray Reid

Directions: I-480 to Exit 6 for SR 252 (Great Northern Blvd.); south on SR 252 (becomes Columbia Rd.); left (east) on Sprague; on right.

Description Riverside has a lot of golf history. Managing pro Ray Reid has shares of stock issued in 1928 for the Berea Golf & Country Club, the original name of the club. "We nestle in Nature," reads the prospectus (a quote from Ralph Waldo Emerson). The club got its current name from the west branch of the Rocky River. Baker and Robinson creeks also cut around and through the course.

More unusual than water is the small graveyard that rests next to the fairway on No. 9. Reid calls it the Baker Graveyard for the frequent appearance of that name on tombstones there. He guesses an influenza epidemic swept through the area because there are so many headstones for children. The graveyard is o.b.

Riverside is not a long course, but the top three handicap holes are anything but short. It is very walkable. League play has been regular here since the Riverside Golf Association scheduled tee times in 1937. The RGA continues today.

Highlights No. 2 is in the corner of the course. A 309-yard par 4, it begins from an elevated tee and falls into a shallow valley. Trees are a factor on this hole, especially close to the creek that cuts across close to the green. Down the right side is o.b., and a few trees stand in the left rough. But near the water woods grow thick and close in suddenly, making the approach shot more demanding. Markers at 150 yards are 4 x 4s and easy to find.

No. 3 is an unusual hole, a par 3 of only 101 yards (and depending where the tee is located, often less than 100.) The tee is shaded by an old triple-trunked sycamore. It is virtually a blind tee shot, because 10 or 15 yards in front of the green the terrain suddenly shoots straight up. None of the green can be seen. There is a large sand trap on the right front, and the green leans from back to front. Missing the green short means a steep uphill lie in deep rough, not the average player's favorite shot.

No. 9 is a 471-yard par 5 that begins with a wide and level fairway. All the way down the right side are deep woods, but to get a ball in there calls for a super slice. After 200 yards, the fairway bends left and the wooded area on the right falls away into a valley. At 120 yards from the green, a large grass bunker sits on the right side of the fairway. There are a couple of fairway traps and, at the green, three more traps. Off to the right of the green is the graveyard (whence lies the body of Uraniam Hickox, who threw off his mortal coil in 1860). This resting place is o.b. The green itself encourages careful play; one of the penalties easily meted out here is putting right off the green. The green is high in back, low in the front. It drops three feet very quickly. And it all falls to the right front corner, where a pine tree sits.

The back side here begins and ends with gorgeous par 3s. One in, and one over, a valley. No. 10 is 141 yards from an elevated tee to a generous green. The green is on the other side of a creek and is stuck in the corner of the valley. The terrain rises behind it. It's a climb out of the valley to the next tee.

Riverside is a particularly good course for beginners and groups; it's also a good layout for women who don't hit the ball far. It would be a good choice, too, for mixed foursomes seeking an alternative to the usual Friday night routine.

Royal Crest Golf Club   ☎ (440) 236-5644

Area: **Southwest**   City: **Columbia Station**   Cost: **$$$**$$ Difficulty: ●●●

Address: 23310 SR 82, Columbia Station

Tees	Ydg.	C/r	S/r	Pace
Back:	6746	70.5	108	
Middle:	6205	68.0	108	
Forward:	5903	72.0	112	

	Weekdays	Weekends & hol.	Carts
Prices:	$10.00 / $19.00	$10.50 / $20.00	$10.00 / $20.00

Specials: Seniors and Juniors weekdays $9.00 / $17.00

Season: Apr 1–Oct 31 **Hours:** Sunrise–sunset **Tee times:** Not taken **Leagues:** Every morning and evening **Ranger:** Most days **Practice facil:** Putting Green **Clubhouse:** Food, Beer, Showers, Pavilion **Outings:** Available (small groups; 16–72 players) **Lessons:** Available **Pro:** Trummie J. Hudson

Directions: I-71 to Exit 231 for SR 82 (Royalton Rd.); west on SR 82; on right.

Description This property has been in the Madak family since the turn of the century. The family farm was developed into a golf course in the late 1960s, and the barn into the clubhouse, which seats about three dozen players. More than 40 leagues play every week at Royal Crest.

It's a little longer than the average area course at 6,205, par 71, and the forward tees don't provide much relief. The number one and two handicap holes on the women's course are par 3s measuring 195 and 192 yards; many members of the LPGA would find those holes difficult. The terrain is generally level, and the course is well cared for. Clearly, the Madak family plans to keep this course for generations.

Highlights The layout is not fancy, but it is often challenging. No. 4 is the only par 5 on the front side, a 544-yard dogleg left. The hole is played in the corner of the course; much of the right side is o.b. But it's a wide fairway until the last hundred yards. Cutting the corner of the dogleg is impossible. Another tee is near the elbow, and the area is marked with white stakes. It also has a stand of tall pines that would challenge even the biggest hitters. This is not a hole for risk taking. Three good shots will get the ball on the green.

The last hole on the front side is pure Royal Crest: long, straight, and lined with trees. No. 9 is a par 4 of 396 yards. The green is slightly elevated and behind it is a sand trap.

No. 16 is a fun par 5. A wide fairway and generous landing area tempt players to swing for the long ball. Big hitters not yet in control of their fades, however, might find either drive or second shot o.b. on the right.

Like many area courses, this is a family operation and likely to stay that way. Here, that's reassuring.

PUBLIC 18+

Seneca Golf Course ☎ (216) 348-7274

Area: **South**   City: **Broadview Hts.**   Cost: **$$**$$$ Difficulty: ●●◉

Address: 975 Metro Valley Pkwy., Broadview Hts.

Tees	A Course Ydg.	C/r	S/r	Pace	B Course Ydg.	C/r	S/r	Pace
Middle:	6559	71.2	118		6639	71.6	121	
Forward:	6387	74.6			6476	75.1		

Prices:	Weekdays	Weekends & hol.	Carts
	$8.00 / $15.00	$8.50 / $16.00	$9.00 / $18.00

Specials: Seniors Mon–Fri until 3 p.m. $5.00 / $9.00; Seniors Sat–Sun after 3 p.m. $5.00 / $9.00; single carts $6.50 / $13.00

Season: Mid-Mar–mid-Dec **Hours:** 6 a.m.–8 p.m. Mon–Fri, 5:30 a.m.–dusk Sat, Sun **Tee times:** Taken weekends **Leagues:** Mon–Fri 4–6 p.m. **Ranger:** Daily **Practice facil:** Range, Putting Green, Use own balls on range **Clubhouse:** Food, Beer, Dining room, Lockers, Showers **Outings:** Available (tent rental avail.) **Lessons:** Not available

Directions: I-77 to Exit 149 for SR 82; west on SR 82 (E. Royalton Rd.); left (south) on SR 176 (Broadview Rd.); left (east) on Metro Valley Pkwy.; on right.

Description In recent years, the mayor of Cleveland had threatened to privatize some city functions, including the operation of its two golf courses, Highland and Seneca. The sooner the better. Seneca doesn't have any of the essentials: manpower, equipment, or incentive. And that's a shame, because it could be a premier course. And it's a course with some history. Seneca was built under the Works Progress Administration during the mid-1930s and opened for play in 1940.

Highlights The number one handicap on B Course is No. 3. The 582-yard par 5 plays along a wide fairway with little trouble on either side. The tee shot is blind, as the terrain rises from the tee. A lake in front of the green is about 40 yards deep and easily 100 yards wide. B Course has only one par 5 and one par 3 per nine.

A few holes into the first nine, one gets used to the groundskeeping. The rough here is not long but is often filled with weeds. It has an unkempt look to it. The greens are sometimes in good shape. The sand traps look as if they were never raked or filled with any new sand.

No. 6 is a 380-yard par 4 that rolls softly downhill toward a lake at the 150-yard marker. Often filled with more mud and cattails than water, the lake is as wide as the fairway. From the other side of the water the fairway rises slightly to a generous green.

Some of the trees on this old course are more than 100 years old and measure 15 to 20 feet around. Many of the holes are defined by trees, but woods don't become a problem except around the perimeter of the course.

The front side is unusually long for having no par 4s over 400 yards. The back is longer and has two monster par 4s.

No. 13, a 452-yard par 4, is another blind tee shot to a rising fairway. There is a fairway trap on the right and sand on the left side of the green as well. It's a long, long way for the average player to reach in regulation. No. 16 has a generous fairway, and it should. This par 4 is a long 449 yards to a green with sand on both sides.

All of B Course and the back side of A Course are played in an area east of the clubhouse. The front side of A Course is to the west. Unlike the other three nines, it does not have a wealth of century oaks; it plays a bit more open and is the side used for winter golf.

Sitting between the east and west sides of the clubhouse is a practice range and huge practice green. The clubhouse porch overlooks the practice areas and provides a good view of the 18th hole of A Course.

The back side of A Course is the only side here with two par 5s and two par 3s.

No. 17 is awfully long: straightaway 608 yards from tee to green. The fairway is wide and the green only slightly elevated. Except for the length, it's almost hazard free. But the length of this hole pushes many players to swing much harder than they normally might. The results rarely match one's hopes. A par on this hole is worth talking about.

The underlying features that once made Seneca a fine course are not lost. But the course's present owner has neither the resources nor the drive to make it playable again. It's time to let somebody else try.

Shawnee Hills Golf Course   *(photo: Casey Batule/courtesy of Cleveland Metroparks)*

Shawnee Hills Golf Course   ☎ (440) 232-7184

Area: **South**   City: **Bedford**   Cost: **$$**$$ Difficulty: ●●●

Address: 18753 Egbert Rd., Bedford

Tees	Regulation Course				Par 3 Course			
	Ydg.	C/r	S/r	Pace	Ydg.	C/r	S/r	Pace
Back:	6366	69.9	114	3:50				1:48
Middle:	6175	68.7	112		1293			
Forward:	5884	72.5	116					

	Weekdays	Weekends & hol.	Carts
Prices:	$9.00 / $16.00	$10.00 / $18.00	$9.00 / $18.00

Specials: Golfer's Dozen: 12 rounds for the price of 10; Seniors (62+) & Juniors $7.00 / $12.00; Par 3 prices: Mon–Fri $6.50, Sat–Sun $7.50, Sr. & Jr. $5.00.

Season: Mid-Mar–Dec 31 **Hours:** Sunrise–sunset **Tee times:** Taken, 1 out of 4 tee times kept open for walk-on players. **Leagues:** Mon–Fri, various times **Ranger:** Daily **Practice facil:** Range, Putting Green, Chipping Green, Lighted driving range **Clubhouse:** Food, Beer, Porch **Outings:** Available (Mon, Wed, Fri; call Golf Services at 440-232-2722.) **Lessons:** Available **Pro:** Jeff Staker

Directions: I-77 to Exit 153 for Pleasant Valley Pkwy.; east on Pleasant Valley (becomes Alexander Rd.); left (north) on Dunham Rd; right (east) on Egbert Rd.; on left.

Description The amenities offered at this 32-year-old Cleveland Metroparks course include a lighted driving range, a 40-seat clubhouse, and a four-minute response time from the Bedford Fire Department— especially valuable if players are prone to (or prone from) heart attacks.

In addition to the 6,160-yard, par 71 course, Shawnee Hills also offers a 9-hole par 3 layout.

The grounds are very well tended here. Even driving to the course, if one drives from downtown, is a delight, because the road through the Metroparks Bedford Reservation is filled with beautiful woods, horse trails, picnic spots, and the picturesque Bridal Veil Falls, where wise newlyweds might pose for their wedding photos before changing clothes and heading to the first tee.

The deep woods are along the perimeter of the course, but the designers of Shawnee Hills kept as many of the old, tall, stately hardwoods on the course as they could. The trees provide guidance, protection, and hazards. Their stature gives the course a mature look.

Highlights No. 3 is a 347-yard par 4, a beautiful hole with a fairway that rises and falls a few times before it arrives at the green. Near the 150-yard marker it falls precipitously, and water cuts across at the bottom of the little valley. (Unusual note: this hole is one of three 347-yard holes on the course. A lucky number? The others are No. 5 and No. 15.)

The back nine starts next to the driving range. The 364-yard No. 10 is a straight par 4 and its fairway is littered with practice balls. Fortunately, the club uses yellow balls at the range. There is a lake behind this green, but it will have much more influence later.

No. 16 is the only par 5 on this side, 525 yards. It dips at the tee then rises to the right. The entire left side is filled with pines, and on the right a few trees separate this fairway from the adjacent 17th. The fairway slowly rises to the green.

It's a quiet course. A lovely, simple, and beautifully groomed course that doesn't present challenges so much as it offers players the pleasures of the game.

TIDYMAN'S TIDBITS #12
Best conditioned courses:

• Painesville
• StoneWater
• Hawks Nest
• Mallard Creek
• Fowlers Mill

Skyland Golf Course   ☎ (330) 225-5698

Area: **South**   City: **Hinckley**   Cost: **$$$**$$ Difficulty: ●●●

PUBLIC 18+

Address: 2085 Center Rd. (SR 303), Hinckley

Tees	Ydg.	C/r	S/r	Pace
Middle:	6239	68.9	113	
Forward:	5563	70.7	112	

	Weekdays	Weekends & hol.	Carts
Prices:	$11.00 / $17.50	$12.50 / $22.50	$10.00 / $20.00

Specials: Mon–Thu until 1 p.m. 2 players 18 holes & cart $50.00; Seniors Mon–Fri $9.50 / $15.50, Sat–Sun $20.00 (18 holes)

Season: Apr–Nov 15 **Hours:** Sunrise–sunset **Tee times:** Recommended **Leagues:** Heavy play Tue–Fri 8–9:30 a.m., Mon–Fri 4–6:15 p.m. **Ranger:** Most days **Practice facil:** Putting Green **Clubhouse:** Food, Beer, Liquor, Dining room, 2 pavilions **Outings:** Available **Lessons:** Available **Pro:** Tim Monroe

Directions: I-71 to Exit 226 for SR 303 (Center Rd.); east on SR 303; on left.

Description Across the street from the clubhouse is a dairy farm, a pastoral reminder of how close rural Ohio still is to Cleveland. Just down the street is an apple and cider market. At the course entrance is a big, blooming flower box built of railroad ties. This is a beautiful old layout, thought by some to be the oldest course in Medina County.

It brings with it some history. It was the first course in the area, owner Tim Rhodes said, to discard the "Women After Eleven a.m. Only" rule. "We thought that rule was one of the most arrogant things around. We were the first to break it. We didn't see any sense to it, and I have women with permanent tee times on Sunday mornings, as well as women's leagues."

Skyland was built by the father of owners Tim and Tom Rhodes. Every April, Tom leaves Hinckley to visit his favorite course: Augusta. He returns home inspired.

The first nine was built in the early thirties and the course was known as Hinckley Golf Course. When the second nine was added, in 1940, the name was changed to Skyland for the views available from some tees. "During the Depression, my mom and dad would charge 25 cents a round. Plenty of people would come out, five and six to a car, and play all day," Tim Rhodes said. The prices have changed, but the value remains.

Plenty of people still come out: 30 leagues play at Skyland. The oldest is the Hinckley Skyland Men's League, which first scheduled tee times in 1957. St. Bridget's Holy Name Society started playing in 1960. Both continue today.

The clubhouse, a large and airy brick one-story building, was erected in 1968. A brisk trade is done in outings. Tee times are available, but permanent weekend tee times are in the clutches of longtime regulars.

PUBLIC 18+

"Some of these go back to 1956, when we first gave out tee times. Even if they move from the area, they find a way to move their friends into those tee times so they don't lose the slot."

Highlights The front side is much longer than the back. No. 3 is a par 5 with a hilly fairway that is straight and tree lined. The tee box on this 480-yard hole is the site of one of the stranger golf stories picked up during the research for this book.

A regular foursome was making ready to tee off when one member began complaining about chest pains. He thought he was suffering a heart attack. His playing partners accused him of malingering and refused to do anything about his complaints. When he grew more frantic, his partners offered him a deal: they would walk him over to the rough on the adjacent No. 7 and lay him gently down. They would then play holes 4, 5, and 6. When they again reached him on the adjacent No. 7, they would inquire as to his health and, if he still feared he was dying, would take him in. So they resumed play as a threesome. A player from another group came across the heart-attack victim, and, after inquiring how he came to be prone in the rough on No. 7, rushed the man back to the clubhouse and medical assistance.

No. 18 is a long, 449-yard par 4, perfect for settling the match when players are tied. It rises a bit and bends a bit, but is essentially just a long hole.

Skyland is well into its second half century. It has long offered the golfing public a most wonderful walk in the woods. Management takes care of the big things, such as greens and fairways, and the little things, such as flower gardens and a warm welcome to the course. Just as it should be.

TIDYMAN'S TIDBITS #13

Great short par 4s:

- No. 3 Pine Hills
- No. 7 Forest Hills
- No. 10 Berkshire Hills
- No. 17 Sleepy Hollow
- No. 18 Springvale

More Excessories . . .
Have a Hole in Your Head? Stick Your Cigar in It.

Here are a few more products offered to golfers who have more money than common sense and more blind hope than vision.

The Kestrel 1000 pocket wind meter goes for $89—unless you find value in the deluxe version, which has temperature and wind-chill meters, as well. That one is $119. The only feature missing is a device to measure the sound of the wind whistling through the hole in the head of anyone showing up with one.

For $5, you can screw the Smoker's Caddy on to your bag. If keeping the stogie in your mouth or hands is too difficult, now you have a place to stick it. It has been rated, the ad says, "the most versatile cigar holder today." The competition is doubtless intense.

Butch Harmon has a new piece of software called "Golf Manager," and it is said to be the "world's first graphical golf analyzer." Geez, how did we ever play without one? I think Harmon, whose record on the PGA Tour is only slightly more impressive than mine, probably left out his best advice: Get a superstar like Tiger Woods as a student and ride it for all it's worth, including junk such as this.

A Precept ad featuring Nick Price notes that Mr. Price is the winningest player in the 1990s. "And this is his new ball," the ad crows. How nice and so what? He *became* the winningest player of the '90s using his *old* ball.

Here's a short list of equipment manufacturers whose advertisements brag about players using their equipment to win tournaments: Ping Putters (Lee Westwood), Innovative Comp Tour LT shafts (John Cook), Griptec grips (Phil Mickleson), Sensicore shafts (Davis Love III), Rifle shafts (Lee Janzen), Foot Joy gloves (Brad Faxon, Curtis Strange, and Steve Jones), Cleveland Golf irons (Frank Nobilo and Andrew Magee), Taylor Made drivers (Lee Janzen), Graffalloy shafts (John Huston and Gary Player). Clearly this is a matter of serendipity, not product excellence. I mean, players have to use *somebody's* sticks, right?

I picked up a golf ad the other day. The advertiser said that after 25 years of research had led to the creation of clubs "with centers of gravity in absolutely coordinated sequence. It's never been done before! It gives you amazing new ease of shot control!" As if that were not enough, the manufacturer bragged about handing these new clubs to hundreds of players. "Results were spectacular," the ad read, "almost unbelievable. Lower scores in every instance." Then it begins smearing it on even thicker: "Professionals report that, in case after case, members' handicaps were reduced by one-third and more!" Now that caught my eye. Who wouldn't buy if it meant lowering a handicap by a third? From an 18 to a 12? From a 12 to an 8? The advertiser was Spalding; the magazine was the *Saturday Evening Post* and the date was February 23, 1953.

My own tested-and-found-reliable advice for hitting a tee shot farther is this: Get a longer stick. My tee shots with a 48-inch driver go substantially farther than shots hit with a 43- or 44-inch driver. With this equipment change, instead of hitting the ball into the deep rough, I hit it into the deep woods.

Veteran teaching pro Mike Mural, PGA, is probably right: "I don't care what you put in the hands of a bogey golfer, he's going to shoot bogey."—*JHT*

Sleepy Hollow Golf Course ☎ (440) 526-4285

Area: **South**　City: **Brecksville**　Cost: $$$$$　Difficulty:

Address: 9445 Brecksville Rd., Brecksville

Tees	Ydg.	C/r	S/r	Pace
Back:	6630	71.9	124	3:43
Middle:	6295	70.5	123	
Forward:	5715	73.5	128	

	Weekdays	Weekends & hol.	Carts
Prices:	$13.00 / $22.00	$15.00 / $25.00	$12.00 / $20.00

Specials: Golfer's Dozen: 12 rounds for the price of 10; Seniors (62+) & Juniors $8.50 / $15.00

Season: Mid-Mar–Dec 31　**Hours:** Sunrise–sunset　**Tee times:** Taken　**Leagues:** Mon–Fri 4:30–6:30 p.m.　**Ranger:** Daily　**Practice facil:** Range, Putting Green, Chipping Green　**Clubhouse:** Food, Beer, Liquor, Dining room, Lockers, Showers　**Outings:** Available (Mon, Wed, Fri)　**Lessons:** Available　**Pro:** John Fiander

Directions: I-77 to Exit 149 for SR 82 (E. Royalton Rd.); east on SR 82; right (south) on SR 21 (Brecksville Rd.); on left.

Description With its polished clubhouse, bag drop, showers, phones, and hair dryers, Sleepy Hollow feels much more like a private club than a Metroparks layout. It is also one of the toughest tracks in town. Not for beginners or players who are easily frustrated, this difficult and challenging layout has greens that are among the fastest and trickiest in Northeast Ohio public golf. Now if management could only speed play.

Highlights No. 2, the Par Three From Hell, is 220 yards to a two-tiered green. Along the right side is a shallow valley filled with dense underbrush and golf balls. The tee is elevated. Once over a small valley in front, the fairway rises slightly. There is sand to the right and near the green, which is long and rather narrow.

No. 3 is rated the number one handicap hole on the course, and with good reason. It is a 450-yard par 4, slightly downhill at first before the fairway drops more severely. A big drive has to stay left in order to see the green for the approach. Coming in from the right leaves a couple of tall trees in the way. In front of the green is a small but severe valley. On the left side, deep woods angle in, making the hole more narrow as it progresses. The generous green has sand to the left and right. A tournament hole.

On the front side, it's generally clear where the ball should go. Not so on the back, which has a number of blind tees and very sharp doglegs. Taken as a whole, the two sides combine to present a sort of golfing trip through the Fun House—around every corner is a surprise.

No. 10 was shortened a bit when the tee box was rebuilt and moved as part of the driving range construction. The range now runs down its right side. The number two handicap, it's a 437-yard par 4. An unrestricted fairway bends a bit to the right at the 150-yard marker. More troublesome than the bend is the grass valley that cuts across the fairway there. And sand surrounds the hole.

No. 14 begins by racing up the first 80 yards. It is a very blind tee shot—almost like shooting over a wall of grass—to a wide fairway that stretches out a couple of hundred yards before falling into a steep, small valley. On the right side of this 490-yard par 5 are deep woods. And when the fairway climbs up from the valley it takes a severe dogleg right; trees fill the elbow. The green can be reached in two great shots, the second a blind shot over tall trees to a smallish green. There is sand at the flat green. From any angle, this is a lot of golf hole.

No. 17 is the rare tee here that does not require length, only accuracy. Well, that's not always true. For lack of length, Paul Rowland, a retired librarian at *The Plain Dealer*, once hit eight consecutive tee shots into the small lake in front of the tee. Rowland saved himself an ignominious 30 by dropping a long putt, penciling in a 29. He still answers when people ask for the Legend of Sleepy Hollow. Once over the pretty lake on this 265-yard par 4, the fairway takes a 90-degree left turn. In the elbow of the dogleg are tall trees, so cutting the corner is virtually impossible.

No. 18 is a 364-yard par 4, a straight hole with few difficulties. A couple of trees mark the rough on the sides, and the fairway dips a bit before the green. At the sloped green are sand traps. Like many of the holes at Sleepy Hollow, this one calls for big hitting and fearless putting.

On any ranking of area courses, Sleepy Hollow will rank very high. With the new clubhouse and related amenities, it has been transformed from just a very tough course to a glamorous one. It is easy to forget that this course and facility are owned and operated by the government. It sets a standard for all public courses.

PUBLIC 18+

Sleepy Hollow Golf Course   *(photo: Casey Batule/courtesy of Cleveland Metroparks)*

PUBLIC 18+

Springvale Golf Course

☎ (440) 777-0678

Area: **West**   City: **North Olmsted**   Cost: $$$$$ Difficulty: ●●●

Address: 5873 Canterbury Rd., North Olmsted

	Men's Tees				Women's Tees			
Tees	Ydg.	C/r	S/r	Pace	Ydg.	C/r	S/r	Pace
Back:	6303	69.0	112	3:35	6303	73.4	123	
Middle:	6033	67.8	110		5586	71.4	118	
Forward:	5586	66.4	108		5077	67.7	110	

| | Weekdays | Weekends & hol. | Carts |
| Prices: | $9.75 / $18.50 | $11.00 / $21.00 | $10.00 / $20.00 |

Specials: Cart Special Mon–Tue, Thu, 6 a.m.–12:30 p.m. $40.00 for two 18-hole tickets and cart; Sat–Sun walkers after 3:30 p.m. $9.50 for one 9-hole ticket; Sat–Sun riders after 3:30 p.m. $27.00 for two 9-hole tickets and cart

Season: Year-round **Hours:** Sunrise–sunset **Tee times:** Taken weekends, holidays **Leagues:** Mon–Fri 4–6 p.m. **Ranger:** Daily **Practice facil:** Range, Putting Green, Chipping Green, Sand, Six target greens **Clubhouse:** Food, Beer, Liquor, Dining room, Lockers, Patio, Ballroom dancing Wed, Fri, Sun nights **Outings:** Available **Lessons:** Available **Pro:** Jerry Ludvik

Directions: I-480 to Exit 6 for SR 252 (Great Northern Blvd.); south on SR 252; right (west) on Butternut Ridge Rd.; left (south) on Canterbury Rd.; on left.

Description Built in the early part of this century, this club is still influenced by the 1930s: in addition to serving the passion for golf, it is also home of the Springvale Ballroom, where big bands still play.

The clubhouse is old-fashioned and very comfortable. The dark woodwork is handsome, and the card room downstairs is a wonderful throwback to another era. A long bar dominates the room, and stuffed fish and game trophies cover the walls. A screened-in porch almost the width of the clubhouse provides a view of the first tee.

Springvale Golf Course, Banquet, Dance and Meeting Facility. What a name for a golf course! While the name is fancier than the amenities here, the course provides a few noteworthy holes and a good challenge to area players. It also provides big band music for people who appreciate the box step. A most elegant combination.

Highlights A local rule is often invoked on No. 1, a 323-yard par 4. Just in front of the tee is a lake. Players dribbling their balls into the water have to shoot from the forward tee on the other side of the water hazard. It speeds play. Once over the water, the hole is straight with some fairway sand on the left side and more sand at the green. The greens here are fast.

No. 5, a 334-yard par 4, bends to the right. An Eisenhower tree is in the fairway near the bend, favoring left-to-right players. On this end of the course it is not unusual to halt play, especially in the evening or early morning, to let deer trot across the fairway.

No. 11, a 476-yard par 5, is the signature hole on this course. The fairway is wide and flat to begin with, but drops near the 150-yard marker to a crossing valley and creek. Beyond the water, the green is jammed in the side of a hill, sloping forward. An interesting hole, a very different hole. Some players find it an unfair hole because the average player has to hit a drive, a wedge to the edge of the valley, then a 6- or 7-iron over the valley and the water to a green that is very difficult.

St. Denis Golf Club   ☎ (440) 285-2183

Area: **Far East**   City: **Chardon**   Cost: $$$$$ Difficulty: ●●●

Address: 10660 Chardon Rd. (US 6), Chardon

Tees	Ydg.	C/r	S/r	Pace
Back:	6640	71.7	117	
Middle:	6375	69.9	115	
Forward:	5800	72.5	117	

	Weekdays	Weekends & hol.	Carts
Prices:	$9.50 / $19.00	$12.00 / $24.00	$10.00 / $20.00

Specials: 2 golfers with cart $52.00 for 18 holes; Seniors Mon–Fri $8.25 / $16.50

Season: Mid-Apr–mid-Nov **Hours:** 7 a.m.–9 p.m. **Tee times:** Taken **Leagues:** Mon-Thu 3:30-6:30 p.m. **Ranger:** Most days **Practice facil:** Putting Green, Chipping Green **Clubhouse:** Food, Beer **Outings:** Available **Lessons:** Not available

Directions: I-90 to Exit 189 for SR 91 (SOM Center Rd.); south on SR 91 to Chardon Rd. (US 6); left (east) on Chardon Rd; on left.

Description There are many reasons to visit this quiet town in Geauga county: maple syrup in the spring, the town square with the opera house on one end . . . but visiting Chardon's St. Denis is right up there.

Course superintendent Bill Griesmer and his father, Scotty Foecking, have built and manage a course that is an absolute delight. Father and son had the design done by Harry Burkhart, the veteran who designed Astorhurst, Shawnee, and Thunderbird.

Foecking purchased 135 acres for the course in 1966. His orders to the designer were simple: "We just wanted a regulation 18-hole golf course that the average golfer could really enjoy."

That is just what he has today. A big, comfortable one-story clubhouse contains pro shop and snack bar. Flowers are everywhere. Flower pots hang from the ceiling and fill tee boxes. The fairways are meticulously manicured. The holes roll with the terrain. It is gently hilly. It is not short, at 6,375 yards, but it often looks more challenging than it plays. Walking these 18 is a fine cardiovascular workout.

Highlights No. 5, one of two holes favored by Foecking as signature holes, is a 400-yard par 4 with a narrow landing area. It is largely downhill until 80 yards before the green when it zooms up and right.

Between the No. 7 green and the No. 8 tee is a small grove of apple trees. When the trees are producing, a garbage can is set out for cores.

No. 14, the number one handicap hole, is Foecking's other great hole. The challenge on this 410-yard par 4 is at the tee. An inability to land the drive accurately means fishing the ball from the stream that gurgles diagonally across the fairway. Missing here can tarnish an otherwise good round.

No outings here, and that's fitting. This course is far too nice for the boorish behavior that marks most outings.

StoneWater Golf Club   ☎ (440) 461-4653

Area: **East**   City: **Highland Hts.**   Cost: **$$$$$**   Difficulty: ●●●

Address: One Club Dr., Highland Hts.

Tees	Black/Gold/White				Green/Green/Silver			
	Ydg.	C/r	S/r	Pace	Ydg.	C/r	S/r	Pace
Back:	7100	75.2	139	4:30	5661	68.5	123	4:30
Middle:	6750	73.4	133		5661	73.3	133	
Forward:	6260	71.0	128		5062	70.0	124	

	(Non-peak)	(Peak)	Carts
Prices:	$29.00 / $55.00	$39.00 / $75.00	$9.50 / $19.00 *per person
	Peak and Non-peak times change—call ahead for times and rates.		

Specials: Seasonal rates available. Players may carry clubs after 4 p.m. or anytime during off-season.

Season: Apr 1–Dec 1 **Hours:** Tues–Sun: 7 a.m.–7 p.m.; Mon: 11 a.m.–7 p.m. **Tee times:** Recommended; Non-members may call 1 week in advance; tee times more than 1 week in advance subject to privilege fee. **Leagues:** None **Ranger:** Daily **Practice facil:** Range, Putting Green, Chipping Green, Sand, (available for warming up prior to round) **Clubhouse:** Food, Beer, Liquor, Lockers, Patio service; clubhouse to open for the 2000 season **Outings:** Available (member-sponsored only) **Lessons:** Available **Pro:** Rob Karnes

Directions: I-90 to Exit 187 for Bishop Rd.; south on Bishop; left (east) on Aberdeen Blvd. for ½ mile; on left. OR, I-271 to Exit 36 for Wilson Mills Rd.; west on Wilson Mills; right (north) on Bishop Rd.; right (east) on Aberdeen Blvd. for ½ mile; on left.

Description When you arrive, the bag boy takes your sticks for you. He straps them onto a cart that has your name on it. Freshly laundered towels are on board. On the dashboard is a small beige box; on its screen will appear information about the hole you're playing, including the yardage from the cart to the cup. Within three feet. It is satellite technology that is also used to provide updates on World Series scores, weather alerts, and the leaders playing the majors. That's the global positioning system.

StoneWater Golf Club   *(photo: Henebry Photography)*

PUBLIC 18+

The driving range is all grass, 300 yards deep, and stocked with Pro Staff balls. The starter arrives at the range to lead your foursome to the first tee. Starting times are every ten minutes.

That's the way a round begins at this singular upscale club, honored by *Golf Digest* as one of the top four new courses in 1997 and featured in *Golf Magazine*. Designed by Dana Fry of the Fry/Hurdzan Design Group, this course takes stonework to a level not seen before. Bridges, sand taps, tee boxes and lakes are lined with sandstone, quarried on site as the course was being built.

Craig Immel, PGA, and Jim Skoch are partners in this remarkable enterprise. Construction has started on the clubhouse, which will open in 2000 and feature food service by Hyde Park Restaurant Group, the premier steak and chop house.

Business entertaining suddenly is available to executives who need the private club amenities but don't have a private club membership.

As a semi-private club, StoneWater will fill a niche created by three forces: tax laws, traditional club life, and a growing number of players who seek and are willing to pay for excellent facilities. Initiation fees and dues are no longer tax deductible, so businesses no longer automatically provide private club membership as an executive perk. Club life is not what it once was, when virtually all a member family's socializing was done there.

Highlights The front side is open and suggests to players that the path to par is without difficulty. While the landing areas for tee shots are generous, the challenges to par are both subtle and obvious.

The opening hole is 397 yards and water plays an important role. It begins next to the green and gurgles down the right side until it cuts across the fairway and continues down the left side.

No. 3 is the signature hole on this side, a gorgeous par 3 over water and marsh to a stonewalled green. Mallards often dine here and the big egret from No. 7 drops in on occasion.

The cottage at the turn provides food and drink, but players are encouraged to eat and run. The back side is far different from the front, marked by drama, high adventure and great challenge. These nine holes were carved from woods and it will be on the last four holes that matches are decided.

The home hole is the signature hole on this side, though No. 16 provides competition. Each has water and distinct landing areas. Each calls for excellent iron play, and par on either hole is satisfying.

Along the way, players often see Cody, the border collie whose job it is to keep the Canada geese off the course. At the end of a match, the bag boy utters a line never heard on public courses: "Clean your clubs, sir?"

Sunny Hill Golf & Recreation   ☎ (330) 673-1785

Area: **Far South**   City: **Kent**   Cost: $$$$$ Difficulty: ●●●

Address: 3734 Sunny Brook Rd., Kent

Tees	1st & 2nd nines				3rd nine			
	Ydg.	C/r	S/r	Pace	Ydg.	C/r	S/r	Pace
Back:	6224	68.4	110					
Middle:	5919	66.8	107		2273	30.7		
Forward:	5083	68.4	107		2084	31.5		

	Weekdays	Weekends & hol.	Carts
Prices:	$10.00 / $18.00	$15.00 / $25.00	$10.00 / $20.00

Specials: Seniors Mon–Fri $7.50 / $12.50; Guys & Dolls Sat–Sun after 3 p.m. 2 players, 9 holes & cart $22.00; 18 holes w/cart, sandwich, and drink $21.00 ($18.00 Senior)

Season: Apr 1–Dec 31 **Hours:** Sunrise–9 p.m. **Tee times:** Taken **Leagues:** Various times **Ranger:** Daily **Practice facil:** Range, Putting Green, Chipping Green **Clubhouse:** Food, Beer, Liquor, Pavilion **Outings:** Available **Lessons:** Not available

Directions: I-77 to I-76; east on I-76 to Exit 31 for Tallmadge Rd.; east on Tallmadge; right (south) on Sunny Brook Rd.; on left.

Description The front side here is the tough side. It's short and very, very, tight and its greens are all elevated. Little room for error. Lots of short holes; if you're good with short irons you can chew it up. The back side is more open, and greens are more amenable to play: flatter and more forgiving.

Sweetbriar Golf & Pro Shop

☎ (440) 871-0822

Area: **West**   City: **Avon Lake**   Cost: **$$$**$$ Difficulty: ●●●

Address: 750 Jaycox Rd., Avon Lake

Tees	Courses 1&2				Courses 1&3				Courses 2&3			
	Ydg.	C/r	S/r	Pace	Ydg.	C/r	S/r	Pace	Ydg.	C/r	S/r	Pace
Back:	6491	68.7	106		6075	66.3	100		6292	67.5	104	
Middle:	6311	67.8	105		5895	65.5	99		6112	66.7	102	
Forward:	5612	68.9	105		5505	68.0	105		5411	68.3	104	

	Weekdays	Weekends & hol.	Carts
Prices:	$9.75 / $18.50	$12.50 / $24.00	$10.00 / $20.00

Specials: Mon–Fri $24.95 for 18 holes and ½ golf cart

Season: Year-round **Hours:** Sunrise–sunset **Tee times:** Taken weekends **Leagues:** Daily **Ranger:** Daily **Practice facil:** Range, Putting Green **Clubhouse:** Food, Beer, Pavilion **Outings:** Available **Lessons:** Available **Pro:** Kevin Krysty

Directions: I-90 to Exit 153 for SR 83; north on SR 83 (Center Rd.); SR 83 briefly joins Chester Rd. then turns north; continue east on Chester; left (north) on Jaycox Rd.; on left.

PUBLIC 18+

Description There is a lot of golf to be had at Sweetbriar, where 27 holes lie in wait just a driver and mid-iron from Interstate 90. There are also two well-kept practice greens, a driving range, and a nice clubhouse. The course is open year round and has especially attractive decorations at Christmas, when a sleigh by the bag rack is filled with brightly wrapped boxes and plenty of golf equipment.

Lessons are offered, and the teaching staff includes two members of the LPGA. Do men or women make better teachers? Pro Joe Lombardi, PGA, said, "Our women pros have a lot of students and a lot of repeat business, so they must be doing something right."

Highlights The strengths of Sweetbriar begin on No. 3, a 449-yard par 4—not beautiful, but tough. O.B. down the left side. The hole starts out to the right and then bends back to the left. It's a wide fairway, but a long way in to the elevated green. Not a gorgeous hole, but a real challenge to par.

No. 6 is a blind tee shot, a par 4 of 386 yards and a dogleg right. There is plenty of room on the left side to land a drive. Drivers with "lazy wrists" or slices will find themselves between trees and mounds, unable to go for the green. A wide creek passes in front of the green.

The second nine opens with a 349-yard dogleg left. This par 4 requires a drive to the right side of the fairway for a clear approach. Trees make the hole more narrow at the dogleg. On the left side of the fairway is the driving range. Many players will break a Rule of Golf here by hitting stray practice balls back to the range.

No. 17, a 522-yard par 5, has some water in front of the tee that is merely decorative. The fairway begins bending to the left after 120 yards or so. From 300 yards in to the green, stands of trees line the rough on both sides.

The first two nines were built in 1964. The third nine was built in 1981. It is substantially shorter and has only one par 4 longer than 400 yards—No. 26. Yes, 26. On the scorecard, the holes are not listed 1 through 9, but 19 through 27. Somehow, it doesn't feel right to refer to a hole as No. 26. And most players look to the clubhouse for the 19th hole. But Sweetbriar runs a good course and a fine clubhouse, so they can call the holes whatever they like.

Management here understands that golf is not a seasonal malady but an addiction that must be sated year round. If the snow is not deep, there is play here. And then the clubhouse provides all the coffee needed to warm up—on the house.

Valleaire Golf Club   ☎ (440) 237-9191
Area: **South**   City: **Hinckley**   Cost: $$$$$ Difficulty: ●●●

Address: 6969 Boston Rd., Hinckley

Tees	Ydg.	C/r	S/r	Pace
Back:	6442	70.2	117	
Middle:	6067	68.4	113	
Forward:	5552	70.9	116	

	Weekdays	Weekends & hol.	Carts
Prices:	$12.00 / $18.00	$14.00 / $23.00	$12.00 / $22.00

Specials: Seniors Mon–Fri $8.25 / $11.50

Season: Apr–Nov **Hours:** Sunrise–sunset **Tee times:** Required weekends **Leagues:** Mon–Fri 4–4:30 p.m. **Ranger:** Daily **Practice facil:** Putting Green **Clubhouse:** Food, Beer, Liquor, Lockers, Showers, Pavilion **Outings:** Available **Lessons:** Not available

Directions: I-71 to Exit 226 for SR 303; east on SR 303; left (north) on SR 3 (Ridge Rd.); right (east) on Boston Rd.; on right.

Description Golf courses are built for all sorts of reasons: as a family business, for a land bank, to fill a market niche. Here the course was built because the Knights of Columbus were having difficulty securing tee times for their traveling league. Members purchased property in the north of Medina County and built a gorgeous little course.

Valleaire is very playable, a course where average golfers will find themselves looking at a few birdie putts. Only one hole is longer than 500 yards. It's a beautiful layout, cut from softly hilly forest and manicured with a professional touch. Recent improvements include a computerized watering system and paved cart paths.

Highlights Representative of the holes to follow is No. 2. At the tee of this 447-yard par 4, civilization is suddenly left behind. Getting on this green in regulation is very difficult for reasons of distance alone. The fairway narrows as it heads toward an elevated green, one of the trademarks of this course. The 150-yard markers are the best in the area: wooden planks hanging from pipes in the rough. In addition to being elevated, this long and narrow green also has a stand of pines behind it.

No. 9 is a par 3 of 148 yards, much of it over water. Shade is provided at the tee by an old and stately oak tree, and the lake separating the tee from the green has a fountain. Some Canada geese regularly lounge about, close to water's edge and unaffected by the spouting from the fountain or the occasional curses from the tee.

Water is much more important on the back side than on the front. The course takes advantage of the land, especially the beautiful old hardwoods, and offers players a slightly hilly round of golf. The greens, most of them elevated, are kept in good shape, and few have sand around them. The two-story clubhouse is comfortable, like an old K of C hall.

PUBLIC 18+

Valley View Golf Club ☎ (330) 928-9034

Area: **Far South**   City: **Akron**   Cost: **$$$**$$ Difficulty: ●●●

Address: 1212 Cuyahoga St., Akron

	Valley-River				Lakes-River			
Tees	Ydg.	C/r	S/r	Pace	Ydg.	C/r	S/r	Pace
Back:	6293	68.8	111		6183	68.2	110	
Middle:	6006	67.4	109		5871	66.2	102	
Forward:	5322	69.1	113		5277	68.6	112	

	Weekdays	Weekends & hol.	Carts
Prices:	$10.00 / $18.00	$10.00 / $20.00	$9.00 / $18.00

Specials: Seniors Mon–Fri before 11 a.m. $8.00 / $14.00

Season: Mar–Dec **Hours:** 6 a.m.–10 p.m. **Tee times:** Required weekends, Recommended for weekdays. **Leagues:** Mon–Fri 4:30 p.m. **Ranger:** Weekends **Practice facil:** Putting Green, Chipping Green **Clubhouse:** Food, Beer, Pavilion **Outings:** Not available **Lessons:** Not available

Directions: I-271 to Exit 18 for SR 8; south on SR 8 to exit for Cuyahoga Falls Ave.; southwest on Cuyahoga Falls; right (west) on W. Tallmadge Rd.; right (north) on Cuyahoga St.; on left.

Description It was Carl Springer and his family who started building these 27 holes known as the Valley, River, and Lake nines 40 years ago, and the course will likely stay a family operation. Maintenance and course conditioning are hallmarks here. The course is playable; the hosts are gracious.

Highlights On the Valley nine, it's No. 2 that confounds players. It is only a 370-yard par 4, but the green sits on a hill. This nine has rolling terrain, and sand shows up on only a half dozen holes. Pines here are 30

years old and oaks are 35 to 40, but this nine is largely open.

The River nine is the flattest of the three, and it is hole No. 7 that provides a noteworthy challenge. It's a short par 5, only 459 yards from the whites, but the river floats through about 320 yards out. On the Lake nine, No. 2, another short par 5, gets the nod. It plays along the river to an elevated green and is a bit of a dogleg right.

PUBLIC 18+

Western Reserve Golf & Country Club   ☎ (330) 239-9902

Area: **Far South**   City: **Sharon Center**   Cost: **$$$**$$ Difficulty: ●●●

Address: 1543 Fixler Rd., Sharon Center

Tees	Ydg.	C/r	S/r	Pace
Back:	5923	68.1	108	
Middle:	5545	66.1	104	
Forward:	4516	64.7	101	

	Weekdays	Weekends & hol.	Carts
Prices:	$10.00 / $16.00	$12.00 / $22.00	$10.00 / $20.00

Specials: Seniors: $2.00 off all golf rates; Senior special Mon–Fri: $18.00 for 18 holes, cart included

Season: Year-round **Hours:** 6 a.m.–10 p.m. in summer **Tee times:** Taken **Leagues:** Available (various schedules) **Ranger:** Weekends **Practice facil.:** Putting Green **Clubhouse:** Food, Beer, Lockers, Showers, Pavilion **Outings:** Available (up to 150 people) **Lessons:** Available **Pro:** Bill Giles, USGTF

Directions: I-71 to Exit 218 for SR 18; east on SR 18; right (south) on Boneta Rd.; left (east) on Fixler Rd.; on left.

Description The clubhouse sits above the practice green and looks down on the course. It's a wide building with an equally wide porch in front. The course and the clubhouse have an old-fashioned informality about them that is fun. Clearly, the mortgage doesn't rest on a game of golf here. Golf is played for the pleasure of it.

This course used to be a farm. It is a short and tight layout with a couple of holes that make little sense, but who's to criticize? Plenty of league play fills the tees from Monday through Friday. Between a growing (and laudable) juniors program, the league play, and the regulars, the first tee here can be a busy spot.

Highlights Play opens on the number one handicap hole, a 394-yard par 4 and big dogleg right. Neither short nor tight, this hole makes plenty of sense. In the elbow of the dogleg a stream meanders between the first and 10th fairways. Over on the left side of the bend there is deep rough and a small pond. About 180 yards from the green there are two fairway traps on the left side. A nicely trimmed apron leads up to a large green. A tough opening hole.

At 415 yards, No. 5 is one of the shortest par 5s around. It is a straight hole with water near the green. Just before the apron, a small pond cuts into the fairway. There are some mounds at the green but no sand here. A real birdie opportunity.

No. 8, a 352-yard par 4, is straight 100 yards before it bends sharply left. In the corner are trees, deep rough, and o.b. It's a hole of questionable design. The right side—the edge of the course—is o.b. as well. Pines and an occasional oak tree line the hole on the left side, and the green, with a large sand trap on the front left, is slightly elevated.

No. 9 is a difficult hole for club selection. This third par 3 on the front is only 162 yards, but all of them steeply uphill. It is virtually a blind tee shot. In front of the tee is a small pond, and over to the right is a trash dump. Missing the green short and left can send the ball into a valley filled with trees and thick underbrush.

Like many area courses, Western Reserve was transformed from farmland to fairway. It is reached via a couple of two-lane blacktops and rarely promotes itself. A good little hideaway for the salesperson who keeps sticks in the trunk. While not especially notable, neither is it pretentious. And it has a great front porch.

PUBLIC 18+

Windmill Lakes Golf Club   ☎ (330) 297-0440

Area: **Far South**   City: **Ravenna**   Cost: **$$$$$**   Difficulty: ●●●

Address: 6544 SR 14, Ravenna

					Tournament tees			
Tees	Ydg.	C/r	S/r	Pace	Ydg.	C/r	S/r	Pace
Back:	6503	71.8	124	3:48	6936	73.8	128	
Middle:	6132	69.7	118					
Forward:	5368	70.4	115					

	Weekdays	Weekends & hol.	Carts
Prices:	$12.50 / $25.00	$12.50 / $33.00	$10.00 / $20.00

Specials: Seniors Mon–Tue $25.00 for 18 holes & ½ cart; Seniors Wed–Fri $32.00 for 18 holes & ½ cart; Sat–Sun before 2 p.m. $47.00 (includes cart)

Season: Late Mar–late Oct (pro shop open all year) **Hours:** 7 a.m.–9 p.m. **Tee times:** Taken, credit card guarantee for advance booking **Leagues:** Various times **Ranger:** Daily **Practice facil:** Range, Putting Green, Chipping Green **Clubhouse:** Food, Beer, Liquor, Dining room, Lockers, Showers, Pavilion, Cipriano's restaurant, Banquet facilities **Outings:** Available **Lessons:** Available **Pro:** Herb Page

Directions: I-271 to Exit 27 for US 422; east on US 422 to SR 44; right (south) on SR 44 (Painesville-Ravenna Rd.); left (east) on SR 14 (merges with SR 44); on left.

Description This home course of the Kent State University golf team, opened in 1970, was designed by Maryland golf architect Edward Ault. Sr. Herb Page, manager at Windmill Lakes, describes the style of the layout as "typical of that period, with big, rolling greens. Ours average 7,000–8,000 square feet. Three sets of men's tees, big tee boxes. Fifty-four greenside bunkers. It's a big maintenance style."

The tournament tees (Windmill Lakes host qualifying matches for the USGA Public Links Championship), play 6,936 yards—a lot of golf course. The course record, 63, is held by Hogan Tour pro Karl Zoller, who helps Page coach at KSU. Page says that the typical player at Windmill is an above-average golfer. That could be. Ravenna is off the beaten path, and many players consider the trip to be more than a round at the closest public course. It is one well worth planning.

Highlights The first hole is a 398-yard par 4 (from the tournament tees it measures 450 yards). The slight dogleg right slopes down from the tee and then bends right. Near the 150-yard marker on the left is a small lake. Oak trees fill the right side of the fairway and traps mark the green. The green on No. 1 is indicative of the rest: fast, true, and undulating. And the fairway on No. 1 has features that will become familiar as the round goes on. The turf is thick and healthy, grass cut to about half an inch. It is beautifully manicured, and the difference between fairway and rough is substantial. The rough is not of U.S. Open length, but it is rough. The value of staying in the fairway is at a premium. Such grooming also adds to the physical beauty of the game and can best be appreciated with a view from the tee.

No. 8 is a beautiful par 3. A big pond lies in front of the green, the largest on the front side. Behind the green is dense underbrush. Along the right side of the hole are tall trees that can be troublesome.

The experienced player, reflecting on the difficult greens of the front side, will likely opt for simply chipping the ball directly into each cup on the back side, dispensing with even trying to read them. That only slows play.

The only par 5 on the back side is No. 16, a 495-yard hole with a fairway that rises ever so slightly and bends as slightly to the right. From the tee, an average player hitting a good shot will clear the soft turn and save a few yards. A particularly troublesome sand trap yawns right in front of this green.

Many of the tees at Windmill Lakes have flower boxes; No. 17 is one. Beside gorgeous flowers is a sign: "Any person seen to be hitting golf balls at the tower will be lawfully prosecuted to the fullest extent of the law." The warning refers to a tower, off the course to the left, that is about three stories high and resembles a water tower. It is pockmarked by hundreds of dents from outlaw golf balls. Likely the sign and its stern warning incite this tempting crime.

There are amenities here not found at other clubs—the best known is Cipriano's, a restaurant and lounge frequented by area residents as well as players. Herb Page also runs one of the best pro shops in Northeast Ohio. The PGA once named him "Merchandiser of the Year." Tee times are not so important during the week but are very important on weekends and holidays, when the course offers a credit-card guarantee.

Public Courses

FARTHER AWAY BUT
WORTH THE DRIVE

Avalon Lakes Golf   ☎ (330) 856-8898

Area: **Farther East**   City: **Warren**   Cost: $$$$$ Difficulty: ●●◉

Address: One American Way, Warren

Tees	Ydg.	C/r	S/r	Pace
Back:	7001	74.3	127	
Middle:	6453	71.7	122	
Forward:	5324	70.1	116	

	Weekdays	Weekends & hol.	Carts
Prices:	$35.00 / $55.00	$35.00 / $55.00	Prices include cart
	Prices include use of range		

Specials: Twilight rates after 4 p.m. $35.00 w/ cart

Season: Apr–Oct **Hours:** Sunrise–sunset **Tee times:** Required, taken up to 1 year in advance **Leagues:** None **Ranger:** Daily **Practice facil:** Range, Putting Green **Clubhouse:** Food, Beer, Liquor, Dining room, Lockers, Showers, Pavilion, Tavern by the Green restaurant & banquet facility; Gazebo Grill avail. on course **Outings:** (Avalon Travel, Inc. offers full-service travel agency; restaurant seats 200; Grand Pavilion available for outings or banquets, seats 300.) **Lessons:** Available **Pro:** John Diana

Directions: I-271 to Exit 27 for US 422; east on US 422; east on SR 82 for 9 miles; left (north) on Howland Wilson Rd.; right (east) on E. Market Rd.; ½ mile on left.

Description We are blessed to have bragging rights to a couple of Pete Dye courses, and this one, built in 1967, is a gem. Dye had not yet developed his penchant for railroad ties, but he built courses that demanded a great deal from players. He built one of those in Avalon Lakes.

It looks and acts like a resort course. But it is also open to the public, and greens fees are lower than at other resorts. American Golf Corporation bought the course in 1988 from the Chamber of Commerce. The purchase covered the course and equipment only. The Avalon Inn, the adjacent resort, leases space for the pro shop. In 1995, the course became a subsidiary of American Waste Services, Inc.

The layout is long, powerful, and demanding. The record is held by John Diana, PGA, who shot a 67 from the blue tees (6,825, par 71). He was 17 at the time, and in a tournament.

His affection and regard for the course have not faded since then. "I love it," he said. "The strong points are the finishing holes, the size of the greens, and the length; it can be stretched out to seven thousand yards."

There was league play at one time, but the course is too expensive for that now. There are no special rates for seniors or juniors. The outings held here are corporate outings.

Highlights The front side opens with everything ordered up by Mr. Dye: narrow driving areas, length, big and subtle greens (that don't putt fast, but do putt tough), big sand (often figure-8 bunkers), and enough water to drown a golf cart. And trees. Gorgeous stands of oak and maple line a great many holes here. They have no underbrush, though, and being able to see through the stands suggests that they are not as dangerous as they might be. Just the opposite is true. The woods are easy to enter and difficult to leave except by chipping back to the fairway.

The tee boxes are huge and often have brightly filled flower boxes. Barb Myers, who prepped at Trumbull CC, is one of those responsible for the flowers. "We have geraniums, impatiens, New Guinea impatiens (that can grow in direct sunlight), red and blue salvia, and we've been putting in some foxglove," she said. (Foxglove is the plant that provides heart patients with digitalis.)

No. 5 is only 310 yards, but this par 4 has a lot of challenge to it. Two well-struck irons can leave a player looking at a birdie putt, but those well-struck irons have to clear a few obstacles first. The hole is a dogleg to the left, and the elbow is filled with trees tall enough to prevent anyone without a mortar in the bag from clearing them. To the right of the trees is a series of fairway sand traps. The landing area, then, is small.

No. 12, a long par 3, is 191 yards over a great deal of water. There is plenty of sand at the green. At the tee, a wooden bucket filled with grass seed has a golf ball for a handle on top. A range ball? Not here. An Ultra.

No. 17 is a 429-yard par 4, essentially a straight hole, but with water lining much of the right side, big hitters have to think twice at the tee. A slice at this point will be costly. Yardage markers include red maples at 150 yards, blue discs at 200, and yellow discs at 100. In addition, many sprinkler heads have yardage marked on them. (But the one in front of the 17th green, the one marked 41 yards—that's going a bit overboard.) The green at No. 17 is surrounded by sand.

It takes a big drive to score well here. It also takes a bit of a drive from Cleveland to get here. But the drive is worth it. Where else will staff pick you up in the parking lot, load your clubs, and give you free rein on a big and powerful Pete Dye course?

Chippewa Golf Club   ☎ (330) 658-6126

Area: **Farther South**   City: **Doylestown**   Cost: $$$$$ Difficulty: ●●●

Address: 12147 Shank Rd., Doylestown

Tees	Ydg.	C/r	S/r	Pace
Back:	6273	69.1	109	
Middle:	5933	67.4	107	
Forward:	4877	67.0	103	

	Weekdays	Weekends & hol.	Carts
Prices:	$11.00 / $18.00	$16.00 / $27.00	$10.00 / $20.00

Specials: Mon–Thu Seasonal Breakfast Special, call for prices; Sat–Sun after 2 p.m. 18 holes and cart $28.00

Season: Year-round **Hours:** Dawn–dusk **Tee times:** Required **Leagues:** Weekday evenings **Ranger:** Most days **Practice facil:** Range, Putting Green, Chipping Green **Clubhouse:** Food, Beer, Liquor, Pavilion **Outings:** Available **Lessons:** Available **Pro:** Dan Dauk

Directions: I-77 to Exit 136 for SR 21; south on SR 21; left (east) on Clinton Rd.; left (north) on Shank Rd.; on right.

Description How could a relatively short course play so tough? Answer—the Bermuda Triangle is here: Nos. 14 (364 yards, par 4), 15 (381 yards, par 4), and 16 (383 yards, par 4). No. 14 is on the cover of the scorecard. This dogleg right has a clearly defined landing area, and missing the fairway means no shot to the green. Oh, there's a shot, but launching one from the rough to a green fronted by water is risky business.

Furthermore, as Bob Gainer says, "all the Triangle greens are two-tiered and slick as ice." Gainer, who runs a hair salon in nearby Barberton, didn't take up golf until his three kids were old enough to fend for themselves. Today he is among the game's most passionate proselytizers. He is, of course, a student of the Triangle. "If you're even through the Triangle, you have some skins coming," he says.

Lots of matches are determined at No. 18, a 408-yard par 4 that plays into a westerly breeze and finishes on a two-tiered green.

Owner Kevin Larizza keeps the rest of the greens here reasonably slick and keeps rangers on the course to maintain fast play. With the ups and downs, the fast greens and the troublesome rough, this is not a course for hackers or beginners.

Hawks Nest

☎ **(330) 435-4611**

Area: **Farther South**   City: **Creston**   Cost: **$$$$$**   Difficulty: ●●●

Address: 2800 E. Pleasant Home Rd., Creston

Tees	Ydg.	C/r	S/r	Pace
Back:	6680	71.5	124	4:10
Middle:	6200	69.2	121	
Forward:	4767	67.9	110	

	Weekdays	Weekends & hol.	Carts
Prices:	$12.00 / $22.00	$14.00 / $27.00	$12.00 / $22.00

Specials: Seniors Mon 7–11 a.m. $25.00 for 18 holes & cart; Women: Thu 7 –11 a.m. $25.00 for 18 holes & cart

Season: Apr–Nov **Hours:** 7 a.m.–sunset **Tee times:** Recommended **Leagues:** Weekdays after 4:30 p.m. **Ranger:** Daily **Practice facil:** Range, Putting Green **Clubhouse:** Food, Dining room, Pavilion **Outings:** Available **Lessons:** Available **Pro:** Chris McCormack

Directions: I-71 to Exit 204 for SR 83; south on SR 83 to New Canaan; east on SR 604; right (south) on SR 3 for 3 miles; on left.

Description Chris McCormack, PGA, former assistant at Wooster CC, is the pro here.

Betty Hawkins built the course. It was designed by Steve Burns, who clearly had a ball transforming 200 acres of rolling farmland into 18 holes of rolling golf course. Burns also designed Fox Meadows, and there are some players who think the Hawk got the better of the Fox.

Ms. Hawkins, an avid golfer, always wanted a golf course. She had been looking for land and had been playing at Hillcrest, but that course was sold and the property developed. This land came up at auction one day, and she and her husband came out and bought it.

The first round was played in July 1993; the next year the back nine was opened. Four sets of tees here, and "ready golf" is the norm.

The prevailing wind comes out of the southwest and is always a factor. When it's blowing, it makes the long par 4s play longer.

Eighty percent of the trade comes from towns north of here. From Cleveland to the first tee it's one stop sign and one stoplight. The trip takes about 45 minutes and is well worth it.

Golf Digest magazine gave Hawks Nest a four-star rating and also ranked the course among Ohio's top five public courses.

Highlights The only homely hole is the first one, a straightaway par 4 of 365 yards; two-lane blacktop is the left-side border. But once that's out of the way, this course provides one of the great rides in public golf.

At 522 yards, No. 7 begins with an uphill drive, then a blind second shot that sets up an approach over a lake and creek to the green. It's one of those holes that should be played a half dozen times in order to play it best.

No. 13, par 5, 520 yards. One of the toughest holes in the county. A dogleg left, players have to be long and straight; woods follow the curve of the fairway to an elevated green.

No. 14 is another hole that is surprising and delightful. Only 323 yards, the drive on this par 4 heads toward the edge of a cliff. The flag and the green are at the bottom, and the flat is 12 feet long, the better to see it from a distance.

Hemlock Springs Golf Club   ☎ (800) 436-5625

Area: **Farther East**   City: **Geneva**   Cost: **$$$$**$ Difficulty: ●●●

Address: 4654 Cold Springs Rd., Geneva

Tees	Ydg.	C/r	S/r	Pace
Back:	6812	72.8	123	3:46
Middle:	6520	72.0	121	
Forward:	5453	73.8	115	

	Weekdays	Weekends & hol.	Carts
Prices:	$10.00 / $19.00	$13.00 / $25.00	$10.00 / $20.00

Specials: Mon–Fri $33 for 27 holes (with hot dog & pop), $37 for 36 holes, $40 all day; Seniors, Juniors Mon–Fri $7.00 / $12.00

Season: Mar–Nov **Hours:** Mon–Fri 7 a.m–7 p.m.; Sat–Sun 5:30 a.m.–7 p.m. **Tee times:** Recommended **Leagues:** None **Ranger:** Daily **Practice facil.:** Range, Putting Green **Clubhouse:** Food, Beer, Liquor, Lockers, Pavilion **Outings:** Available **Lessons:** Not available **Pro:** Bill Crawford, PGA

Directions: I-90 to Exit 218 for SR 534; south on SR 534 for 3 miles; left (east) on Cold Springs Rd.; ½ mile on right.

Description Nestled in the heart of Ohio wine country is this course built in the early sixties. Without sounding like a shill for the Ashtabula County Chamber of Commerce, can we suggest a day of golf followed by dinner? In this part of the state, they go together.

In its December 1997 issue, *Golf Digest* magazine had high praise for the course: "The championship bent grass greens are a pure joy to putt."

Good marketing spoken here. Rangers will present discount coupons to players replacing divots or repairing ball marks. The coupon is good for 15 percent off in the pro shop. For every $100 spent in the shop, a round of golf is included in the change. And I never saw a golf course so clean, so free from litter, cigarette butts, ball sleeves, soda cups . . .

Highlights This is a lot of course, and it has everything it needs: woods, water, changes in elevation, and good design. The Stimpmeter usually reads 8.5, so the greens can be quick. No. 11, a par 3, 186 yards, takes all those virtues into account. It's the signature hole. An elevated tee overlooks a lake and a narrow tree-lined fairway. The elevated green is guarded in front by two sand traps. In the past 20 years it has been aced only once. Great home hole: 530-yard par 5 is a dogleg right with a lake to the right of the fairway and in the landing area.

Hemlock Springs is one of golf's better values.

PUBLIC 18+
WORTH the DRIVE

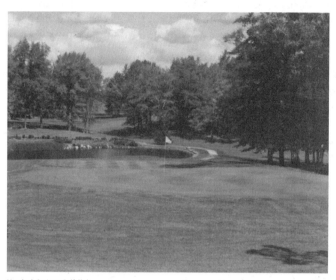

Hemlock Springs Golf Club

Legends of Massillon

☎ (330) 830-4653

Area: **Farther South**   City: **Massillon**   Cost: **$$$$$**   Difficulty: ●●●

Address: 2700 Augusta Dr., Massillon

Tees	Ydg.	C/r	S/r	Pace
Back:	7002	73.7	121	
Middle:	6390	70.9	116	
Forward:	5627	72.3	108	

	Weekdays	Weekends & hol.	Carts
Prices:	$12.00 / $22.00	NA / $34.00	$10.00 / $20.00

Specials: Fri $25 for 18 holes; May–Sep Mon–Thu before 1 p.m. $60 for 2 players 18 holes & cart

Season: Apr–Nov **Hours:** Dawn to dusk **Tee times:** Required **Leagues:** Mon–Fri 3–6 p.m. **Ranger:** Daily **Practice facil:** Range, Putting Green, Chipping Green, Sand **Clubhouse:** Food, Beer, Liquor, Dining room **Outings:** Available **Lessons:** Available **Pro:** Ray Bush

Directions: I-77 to exit for SR 21; south on SR 21; east on US 30; left (north) on SR 627; left (west) on Nave St. (adjacent to US 30); right (north) on Veterans Blvd.; left (west) on Augusta Dr.; on left.

From the Pro's Lips to Your Ears

Golf Talk with Charlie Stone, Master PGA Professional

Charlie Stone, head pro at Beechmont Country Club and one of the youngest PGA members with Master Professional status, is interviewed by John H. Tidyman.

Q: When does someone decide to become a club pro?

A: I think it begins in junior high or high school. It does in the best ones. If a guy gets out of college and is a player, maybe he'll think about becoming a club pro. But the long hours, the low pay, and the hard work turn most of them away. If you have a degree in your hip pocket and your job at the club only pays $1,500 a month, reality has a way of cooling the desire. Your friends are starting jobs making twice that much. When I started, I saw my apprenticeship as just that: an apprenticeship. If you see the work as your lifelong goal and career, the apprenticeship makes sense. But in our society, apprenticeships are a thing of the past. Not many guys are willing to work hard for three to five years at the low salary. They just are not.

Q: What sort of education is required to succeed as a club pro?

A: It used to be a high-school diploma, but the PGA now requires an associate degree or a bachelor's degree. Back in the days when a club pro only had two responsibilities—play the game with members and hang around the bar—not much education was necessary. But that was then and this is now. The head pro today is a businessman, a human resources department, a teacher as well as a student of the game, and a public-relations executive for his club. In each area, situations constantly change, so the pro has to be able to learn. Nothing teaches us like education. I'm constantly learning—from members, or books, or the Association ... it doesn't stop.

Q: How important is teaching to the club professional?

A: If you teach well, you pass on to other players the joy of golf. But more than that, you make sure golf's future is bright. When you teach, you become part-owner of the swing. If done properly, it's a source of satisfaction unlike any other. And like a lot of the work in golf, teaching can be fun. Watching a young kid go from whiffing the ball to hitting it solidly is a journey I never tire of. When the kid hits the ball solidly and the ball goes just where he imagined it would go, that kid knows the difficulty of properly striking the ball and he knows the rewards golf offers.

Q: What's the difference between teaching juniors and teaching adults?

A: With young players, first I teach distance, then I teach accuracy. But with adults, the average player is more concerned with accuracy and less concerned with distance. When accuracy is your primary goal, you become a short hitter. So with adult students, I have to work from another angle. With juniors, I try to make it fun for them. Kids learn by watching. You demonstrate, they learn. Every game you ever learned, you learned by watching. Michael Jordan is a good example. He probably taught a million kids to play basketball without giving a single lecture. But adults don't learn that way and that's a shame. If you're the student, it's much easier and much more pleasurable if I show you, not tell you.

Q: What makes a good outing?

A: There's only one mistake you can make with an outing and that's treating it as an outing. I think an outing is a golf tournament, so I want all the amenities to be perfect. Remember, the guests coming have paid a pretty penny to be there, and they're excited about playing your course. So the carts are spotless, the announcements are professional, the names on the scorecards are legible, the scoring is accurate and timely ... there are lots of details. I like to think that every winter, there are players sitting around while the snow is swirling, and they say something like "Remember that outing at Beechmont?"

Q: Why do members come to you instead of going to other golf equipment stores?

A: Lots of it goes back to teaching. If I've helped a player create confidence, he is going to trust my expertise when it comes to equipment selection. It's always my hope that our relationship is for the long term. And then the price. The smart businessman has to set up his store according to the competition. I don't care if you're a millionaire or not, everyone wants value in what they purchase. The price has a great deal to do with that. I can't compete with a megastore using equipment as loss leaders, but I have some advantages, thanks to the club, that the stores don't have. I don't have the overhead, for one thing, and the help here is dedicated to the customer. Customer loyalty is important, too. For every great store, there's a version of it at the outlet mall. So I have to offer personal service that really is personal. I know my customers and I know what they like. If I have equipment they want to try, I make it easy for them.

Q: What's the future for caddy programs?

A: They're dying, but I think the classic clubs that have always had them will always have them. For the younger, private clubs it's tough because carts produce between $100,000 and $125,000 in revenue. Younger clubs need that cart revenue. An even bigger problem is the work ethic. There is none. A caddy here can carry two bags for 18 holes and walk away with $50 in his pocket. But too many people look down on this work. Beechmont has always supported the caddy program and I think we'll always have it, but again, the problem is not with the club, but with the lack of hard workers.

Q: What's the job pool for assistant pros?

A: Lots has changed in the job pool. It went from a market that had a million assistant pros, but only a half million jobs. In recent years, the PGA tried to make the apprentice program tougher. For a kid coming out of college, the program is tough to get in and tough to stay in. Lots of them wash out, so the market is really changed now. There are more jobs than there are assistant pros to fill them. I'm not sure it means we'll get better head professionals, but I know it means assistant pros can move up much faster.

Description Now there are two Legends of Massillon. Paul Brown, of course, is the first; this course is the second. Recently, the starter took a player's arm on the way to the first tee and asked, "Ever play here before?" When the player said he had not, the starter's face brightened and he said, "You're going to love it!" All courses should have staff that committed to the club. The starter was right. The course is worthy of a golfer's love. At least it is now. But housing tracts are going up fast, and that development will take away from the beauty of the course.

No. 1, a straightaway 400-yard par 4, is a good opening hole. No surprises and a large landing area for the tee shot. The greens here are often contoured and give pause to good players. Water shows up on lots of holes and it is more than a hazard to carry; it is often a hazard to accurately lay up to. Worth the trip? Yes.

PUBLIC 18+
WORTH THE DRIVE

Mill Creek Park Golf Course   ☎ (330) 758-2729

Area: **Farther East**   City: **Boardman**   Cost: **$$**$$$ Difficulty: ●●●

Address: West Golf Dr., Boardman

	South Course				North Course			
Tees	Ydg.	C/r	S/r	Pace	Ydg.	C/r	S/r	Pace
Back:	6511	71.8	129	3:44	6412	71.9	124	3:46
Middle:	6302	70.7	122		6173	70.7	122	
Forward:	6102	74.9	118		5889	74.4	117	

	Weekdays	Weekends & hol.	Carts
Prices:	$8.25 / $16.50	$8.25 / $16.50	$9.50 / $19.00
	Nonresidents of Mahoning County: $10.75 / $21.50		

Specials: Coupon books avail.; Seniors $6.50 for 9 holes; Autumn rates after Sept 30

Season: Apr–Dec **Hours:** Sunrise–sunset **Tee times:** Taken weekends, holidays **Leagues:** Weekdays **Ranger:** Daily **Practice facil:** Putting Green, Chipping Green, Sand **Clubhouse:** Food, Lockers, Showers, Pavilion **Outings:** Available **Lessons:** Available **Pro:** Dennis Miller

Directions: I-80 to exit for SR 11; south on SR 11 to exit for SR 224 (Boardman); east on SR 224; left (north) on West Golf Drive at park entrance.

Description Just a couple years before the Depression, Donald Ross finished work on a pair of courses at Mill Creek Park. The North and South courses are owned and maintained by the Mill Creek Metropolitan Park District.

Highlights Pro Andy Santor says most players think the South course is more challenging than the North, but the North, he points out, has two great finishing holes, 9 and 18 and the North better reflects the style of the Scotsman from Dornach: small greens, mounding, and a demand for accurate iron play. Number 9 is a 440-yard par 4 with a creek in the middle of a fairway, a narrow landing area and a green, the pro says, "about the size of your desk." Pure Ross. And it is on the home hole on the South course, a 450-yard dog leg par 4, that many matches are settled. Par is 70 on both courses.

Sawmill Creek ☎ (419) 433-3789

Area: **Farther West**   City: **Huron**   Cost: **$$$$$**   Difficulty: ●●●

Address: 600 Mariner Village, Huron

Tees	Ydg.	C/r	S/r	Pace
Back:	6702	72.3	128	
Middle:	6321	70.3	125	
Forward:	5124	69.4	115	

	Weekdays	Weekends & hol.	Carts
Prices:	$30.00 / $59.00	$29.00 / $54.00	$15.00 / $30.00

Specials: None

Season: Apr 1–Nov 1 **Hours:** 7 a.m.–10 p.m. **Tee times:** Taken **Leagues:** Mon–Fri evenings on one 9 only, varied times **Ranger:** Daily **Practice facil:** Putting Green, Intermediate pitching area **Clubhouse:** Food, Beer, Liquor, Dining room **Outings:** Available **Lessons:** Available

Directions: SR 2 to exit for Rye Beach Rd.; right (north) on Rye Beach; left (west) on Cleveland Rd. W.; on right.

Description Few courses are as well cared for as this resort in Huron, hard by Lake Erie. Your lawn should look like the rough here. It is a great neighborhood for golf, as well. In the vacation villages that line the lake are a number of good fish houses. This means 18 holes at a Tom Fazio course followed by fresh walleye or a big plate of fresh perch. It's like the commercials featuring a bunch of guys standing around a campfire saying "It doesn't get any better than this." Except in this case it would be true.

This course is eminently playable but by no means a pushover. It's a resort course, so it is not supposed to overwhelm players. But good scores here only come from very good play. Most of the greens are elevated and have sand on both sides. The greens are the most demanding feature here; getting on in regulation hardly means an automatic par. The greens are very big, quite fast, and full of undulation. While the rough is manicured, make no mistake—it is rough. Leaving the comfort of the fairway rarely means losing a ball, but once the ball nestles down in the thick grass, the possibility of par drifts away.

Highlights Play begins with two straightaway par 4s: the opening hole of 340 yards and No. 2, which stretches out 425 yards. Both have fairway bunkers. Properly warmed up, players then face a series of doglegs and holes that flirt with the marshes and inlets. Fazio took every advantage of the local physical beauty, which is augmented by a nearby bird sanctuary. There is nothing unusual here about watching a hawk circle above, or a cardinal or barn swallow work for dinner. When the Canada geese are arguing and a train is murmuring in the distance, the game becomes a delight for all the senses.

Holes 12 and 13 are the signature holes here. Both have water, both call for exacting tee shots, and both are noteworthy for their views from the tee box. They are the Big Brother and Little Brother of the Back Side. No. 12 is a par 5 of 566 yards and features a narrow landing area and marsh on the left and water on the right. No. 13 is a short par 3, only 142 yards, but it carries water the entire ride.

Sawmill Creek has a reasonable pro shop, and a very good lounge called A. Mulligan's Pub.

Tam O'Shanter Public Golf Course   ☎ (800) 462-9964

Area: **Farther South**   City: **Canton**   Cost: $$$$$ Difficulty: ●●●

Address: 5055 Hills and Dales Rd. NW, Canton

	Hills Course				Dales Course			
Tees	Ydg.	C/r	S/r	Pace	Ydg.	C/r	S/r	Pace
Back:	6385	69.1	104	4:10	6509	70.4	110	4:10
Middle:	6054	67.6	103		6184	68.9	107	
Forward:	5076	67.4	102		5317	69.7	100	

	Weekdays	Weekends & hol.	Carts
Prices:	$12.00 / $22.00	$14.00 / $27.00	$10.00 / $20.00

Specials: Season golf and cart passes available; Hotel packages available; Seniors Mon–Fri before noon 18 holes $14.00

Season: Year-round **Hours:** Sunrise–sunset **Tee times:** Recommended, as far in advance as requested; credit card guarantee Sat, Sun **Leagues:** Mon–Fri 8:30–9 a.m., 4–6:30 p.m. **Ranger:** Daily **Practice facil:** Range, Putting Green, Chipping Green, Sand, 8 covered tees **Clubhouse:** Food, Beer, Liquor, Dining room, Lockers, Showers, Pavilion **Outings:** Available (up to 150 people) **Lessons:** Available **Pro:** Martin Roesink, PGA

Directions: I-77 to Exit 109 for Everhard Rd./Whipple Ave.; west on Everhard; left (south) on Dressler Rd.; right (west) on Hills and Dales Rd. NW; on right.

Description Management at Tam O'Shanter works hard to stand out from the crowd. Here, aspiring professionals play under tournament pressure, golf vacationers come from as far away as Boston, and the dining room and pro shop are first rate. It is the only course taking a billboard on Interstate 77 to brag about itself.

Tam O'Shanter boasts a pair of distinctly different 18-hole layouts, classic golf course architecture, and a country-club atmosphere. The clubhouse should be surrounded by magnolias; it is an old-fashioned, three-story house with a half-dozen tall columns supporting the broad porch roof.

The courses were built as part of a housing development, the Hills and Dales project, which is just across the street. Had the project been successful and a building boom continued, backyards and basements would today be where a driving range and practice green are. Development was slowed first by the Depression, then by World War II.

"The Dales course opened in 1928," former general manager Chuck Bennell said, "and the Hills course opened in 1931. When Hills opened, Mr. T. K. Harris, the developer, added some hoopla because of the Depression. He brought Walter Hagen and Gene Sarazen in from the Western Open to play the dedication round. And a Massillon bootlegger made sure the refreshments were spirited."

Bennell pointed out the style of golf architecture that marks these 60-year-old layouts. "They say the old-time architects didn't design courses so much as they found them." The Dales Course was designed by Leonard Maycomber, the construction superintendent for Donald Ross when Ross created Canton Brookside in the early twenties. The Hills Course was designed by Merle Paul.

Highlights Holes 4 and 5 are good examples of what the Dales course is like. No. 4 is a straight 411-yard par 4. The last few hundred yards of fairway are lined on both sides with pine trees. The old hardwoods to the right of the green should not be a hazard—they protect the next tee. To the right of the green is a new staircase built of wood pieces the size of railroad ties. It leads to the No. 5 tee.

There, the drive is a blind shot. This 348-yard par 4 can delight as well as confound. The fairway does more than rise—it has a steep hill in the middle of it. Hitting over the hill is not difficult and provides an easy shot to the green, but missing a tee shot can be costly. This is one of many holes that plays better with practice.

The back side starts off with a very challenging par 4; No. 10 is 439 yards bending to the right almost off the tee. Players grateful for the opportunity to use their slices learn quickly that accuracy does not lose its value here. It is a narrow, hilly fairway and landing area. There is fairway sand to the right front of the green and more sand on the right side of the green. The green is elevated and calls for a most difficult approach: a high, long iron.

No. 15, a 405-yard par 4, tumbles down into a valley, turns right, and climbs the side of a hill. This is a blind tee shot (make sure the players in front of you have cleared the landing area!) with o.b. on the left. The green has sand on the right side. This is certainly one of the holes that the course architect "found."

After Dales, real golfers relax over lunch and maybe take a brief nap before heading out to the first tee on the Hills Course. It is more open than Dales, and shorter, too. No. 1 is a 381-yard par 4 that plays straight, though not level. Even in the heart of the fairway, unlevel lies are to be expected. Near the green is sand on the right front; getting out of it is a matter of lofting the ball eight feet.

No. 5 is only 434 yards, a very short par 5. But the fairway narrows on this dogleg right and there are o.b. stakes all the way down the right side. In the last 150 yards, the rough on both sides rises, giving the hole a riverbed look. Tall trees close in as golfers near the green, and hardwoods form a backdrop for the approach.

It's a bit of a drive to Canton, but the only regret of most players making the trip is not playing both layouts the same day. Counting clubhouse, courses, and history, Tam O'Shanter would have to be considered one of the top public courses in northern Ohio.

Tannenhauf Golf Club   ☎ (800) 533-5140
Area: **Farther South**   City: **Alliance**   Cost: $$$$$ Difficulty: ●●●

Address: 11411 McCallum Ave. NE, Alliance

Tees	Ydg.	C/r	S/r	Pace
Back:	6666	72.0	111	
Middle:	6290	70.2	108	
Forward:	5455	70.8	100	

	Weekdays	Weekends & hol.	Carts
Prices:	$13.50 / $23.00	$15.50 / $25.00	$10.00 / $20.00

Specials: Breakfast special Mon–Fri before 11 a.m. (non-holidays): 18 holes & cart $26.00; Sat–Sun after 2:00 p.m.; Mon–Fri Junior & Senior rates available

Season: Apr–Oct **Hours:** Sunrise–sunset **Tee times:** Recommended **Leagues:** Mon–Thu 4–6 p.m.; Women's League Thu 8–9 a.m. **Ranger:** Weekends **Practice facil:** Range, Putting Green, Chipping Green **Clubhouse:** Food, Showers, Pavilion **Outings:** Available **Lessons:** Available **Pro:** Jim Goodwin, PGA

Directions: I-77 to Exit 188 for SR 241; north on SR 241; right (east) on SR 619 (becomes Edison St.); right (south) on McCallum Ave.; on right.

Description The name comes from the Swiss word for pine trees; it refers specifically to a pair of pines in front of the old farmhouse. Manager Rick Snode's father, uncle, and aunt created the course on what was once a family dairy farm. That was in 1957, and the layout designed by James Harrison and Fred Garbin is aging well. The course has grown a bit tighter, as trees planted a couple decades ago are now big enough to knock down errant shots.

Twilight golf on Friday nights, when there is no league play, is delightful. The course is a good one for walking, and course conditions are excellent. Soft spikes are encouraged though not mandatory. Every August, when the Alliance Carnation Festival is in full swing, the course hosts the Carnation Scramble event; during play, the Queen of the

Court tours the course. That's the sort of stuff that makes small towns special (though Alliance is fast moving away from small-town status).

Highlights The first and tenth holes are parallel, separated by the home hole. No. 1 features a lake 240 yards out. Most players lay up (most players can *only* lay up) on this 501-yard straightaway par 5. It's during Carnation Week, when the Scramble is on, that many players try to fly the water, which means 280 yards of carry. No. 3, usually the number one handicap hole, is a long one from the blues at 605 yards and 545 from the whites. When the wind is out of the north, this dogleg plays much longer.

PUBLIC 18+
WORTH THE DRIVE

Thunderbird Hills   ☎ (419) 433-4552
Area: **Farther West**   City: **Huron**   Cost: $$$$$ Difficulty: ●●●

Address: 1316 Mud Brook Rd., Huron

Tees	North Course Ydg.	C/r	S/r	Pace	South Course Ydg.	C/r	S/r	Pace
Back:	6347	70.3	109		6534			
Middle:	5973	74.0	121		6368			
Forward:	5008							

	Weekdays	Weekends & hol.	Carts
Prices:	$10.00 / $19.50	$12.00 / $22.00	$10.60 / $21.20

Specials: Couples: gentleman pays regular rate, lady pays $3.00 per 9 holes; Seniors $14.25 for 18 holes (north course only)

Season: Year-round **Hours:** Seasonal **Tee times:** Required **Leagues:** Weekdays: various times mornings and afternoons **Ranger:** Most days **Practice facil:** Range, Putting Green, Chipping Green **Clubhouse:** Food, Beer, Pavilion **Outings:** Available (catering avail.) **Lessons:** Available **Pro:** Ryan Spicer

Directions: SR 2 to exit for Huron/Mud Brook Rd.; right on Mud Brook; on right.

Description Owner Bruce Palmer was so pleased with the operation of one course that he had a second created. They are now called North and South. South is the new layout, opened just a few seasons ago and still wrestling with growing pains. It is not as hilly as North and features bent grass on tee boxes, fairways, and greens. In its former life it was farmland.

North, the older sibling, is known for pine trees and irrigation. The trees help define the holes here. There is no sand and very little water—just some feeder streams from the Huron River. Fairways are generous. Greens are medium to small and will play faster than in recent years thanks to a new superintendent. North is open year round.

Nice and playable as these layouts are, the claim to fame here comes from the pro shop, named every year for the last decade as one of the

CLEVELAND GOLFER'S BIBLE • 4TH EDITION

best 100 pro shops in the country by *Golf Digest*. Manager Will Spence makes it sound easy: "Customer service is the key. We can get anything for anybody. We have 4,000 square feet filled with 1,500 pairs of shoes and 400 bags. We have a full line of clothing and clubs and there's no hassle on returns. We take care of you."

Willow Creek Golf Club   ☎ (440) 967-4101

Area: **Farther West**   City: **Vermilion**   Cost: **$$**$$$ Difficulty: ●●●

Address: 15905 Darrow Rd., Vermilion

Tees	Ydg.	C/r	S/r	Pace
Back:	6356	68.1	108	
Middle:	5957	66.2	105	
Forward:	5419	68.0	111	

	Weekdays	Weekends & hol.	Carts
Prices:	$8.00 / $15.00	$9.00 / $17.00	$9.00 / $18.00

Specials: Mon–Fri before 2 p.m. $18.50 for 18 holes with ½ cart; Seniors $5.00 / $9.50

Season: Mar–Dec **Hours:** Sunrise–sunset **Tee times:** Taken weekends **Leagues:** Mon–Fri early mornings, evenings until 6 p.m. **Ranger:** Most days **Practice facil:** Range, Putting Green, Chipping Green **Clubhouse:** Food, Beer, Pavilion **Outings:** Available (catering avail.) **Lessons:** Available **Pro:** Frank Cisterino, PGA

Directions: I-90 to SR 2; SR 2 to SR 60; south on SR 60 (Vermilion Rd.); left (east) on Darrow Rd.; on left.

Description Century oaks provide dramatic and beautiful scenery here, whether budding in spring, providing deep shade in the summer, or lining the forest floor with golden leaves in autumn. Owner Frank Cisterino calls the trees his greatest asset here. In addition to the oaks and willows there are a half dozen apple trees. In the late summer and fall, they produce a sweet and crisp fruit, favored by a few golfers as well as families of deer that live around the course.

The course is nearly an antique; the first nine was carved out of the woods at the end of World War II. Twenty years later, a second nine was created.

Eighteen leagues call Willow Creek home, and outings regularly use the pavilion. There are both driving range and practice green. The pro shop is moderately well stocked, and the snack bar offers all that players need. Tee times are taken for league play, and Cisterino is available for players needing lessons.

Highlights From the first hole on, it is a beautiful course to walk. No. 1 is a long par 4, 396 yards with a leftward bend. It plays into a setting sun in the early evening. But most of the course is laid out north-and-south, adding a distinct measure of comfort to the round. The green is small at the first hole, but lush and of average speed. Getting down in two should be routine.

No. 9 is the signature hole here, but not for its length or difficulty, though a par 4 of 440 yards is no piece of cake. It's a dogleg left crossed diagonally in front of the tee by a creek, which continues up the left side near the green. An old willow squats next to it there. Players don't get to see the green until the second shot.

No. 12 is a very tough par 4 of 315 yards. About halfway, the hole turns right. That can't be seen from the tee. A maple sits almost in the middle of the fairway and forces tough choices on the tee. Most players leave the driver in the bag and opt for a more controlled shot.

No. 18 is a par 4 of 413 yards. It is a straight hole, with woods continuing down its left side. On the right are more apple trees—they produce quite a crop. A creek cuts across the fairway in front of the green, which is slightly elevated, and a willow rests on the left side.

Willow Creek is an attractive old course in good hands. It will likely provide great golf for another half century.

TIDYMAN'S TIDBITS #14

Home holes of note:

- Orchard Hills. Designed by Sisyphus.
- Skyland. Par 4s don't get much longer.
- Pine Hills. Drama spoken here.
- Manakiki. Drive into a narrow valley; approach to an elevated green with sand front left and right. Smallest green on this Donald Ross course.
- Gleneagles. Lots of matches will be settled on this demanding par 4.
- Fowlers Mill. A big, beautiful, classic, sand-studded, dog-legged par 5.

Public Courses

9-HOLE, PAR-3 AND EXECUTIVE-LENGTH

Aqua Marine Resort & Country Club
9 holes, par 3

Area: **Far West**   City: **Avon Lake**   Cost: **$**$$$$ ☎ **(440) 933-2000**

Address: 216 Miller Rd., Avon Lake

	Weekdays	Weekends & hol.	Carts
Price:	$6.50 / $10.00	$8.00 / $12.00	$10.00 / $15.00

Specials: Seniors & Juniors Mon–Fri $5.00 / $7.00; rental $3.00

Season: Year-round **Hours:** Sunrise–sunset **Tee times:** Taken **Leagues:** Various times **Ranger:** Weekends **Practice facil:** Putting Green, Chipping Green **Clubhouse:** Food, Beer, Liquor, Dining room, Lockers, Showers, Pavilion **Lessons:** Available **Pro:** John Martin

Directions: I-90 to Exit 151 for SR 611 (Colorado Ave.); west on Colorado; right (north) on Miller Rd. for 2 miles; on left.

Casement Club
9 holes

Area: **Far East**   City: **Painesville**   Cost: **$$**$$$ ☎ **(440) 354-4443**

Address: 349 Casement Ave., Painesville

Tees	Ydg.	C/r	S/r	Pace
Middle:	3047	69.8	119	
Forward:	3047	74.0	127	

	Weekdays	Weekends & hol.	Carts
Price:	$10.00 / $17.00	$11.00 / $18.50	$10.00 / $18.00

Specials: Seniors & Students Mon–Fri before 3 p.m. $6.00 / $11.00

Season: Year-round **Hours:** 6 a.m.–sunset **Tee times:** Recommended **Leagues:** Daily 3:30–6 p.m. **Ranger:** Some days **Practice facil:** Range, Putting Green **Clubhouse:** Food, Beer, Liquor, Dining room, Lockers, Showers **Lessons:** Available

Directions: SR 2 to Painesville exit for Richmond St.; south on Richmond; left (east) on E. Erie St. across Grand River; right (south) on Casement Ave.; on right.

Cherry Ridge Golf Course   9 holes

Area: **Far West**   City: **Elyria**   Cost: $$$$$ ☎ **(440) 324-3713**

Address: 1211 W. River Rd., Elyria

	Weekdays	Weekends & hol.	Carts
Price:	$9.00 / $16.00	$10.00 / $19.00	$10.00 / $10.00

Specials: Seniors Mon–Fri $5.50 all day; club rental $5.00

Season: Mid-Mar–Oct **Hours:** Sunrise–sunset **Tee times:** Taken weekends **Leagues:** Mornings and evenings **Ranger:** Weekends **Practice facil:** Putting Green **Clubhouse:** Food, Beer, Enclosed patio **Lessons:** Not available

Directions: I-90 to Exit 145 for SR 57; south on SR 57; left (east) on SR 113/SR 57 (Northeast Bypass); left (north) on W. River Rd.; on right.

Emerald Valley Golf Course   9 holes

Area: **Far West**   City: **Lorain**   Cost: $$$$$ ☎ **(440) 282-5663**

Address: 4397 Leavitt Rd., Lorain

	Weekdays	Weekends & hol.	Carts
Price:	$7.00 / $13.00	$7.50 / $14.00	$9.00 / $17.00

Specials: Seniors before 5 p.m. $4.00; club rental $5.00 / $8.00

Season: Year-round **Hours:** Sunrise–sunset **Tee times:** , Not required **Leagues:** Mon–Fri 5:00 p.m. **Ranger:** Weekends **Practice facil:** Putting Green, Chipping Green **Clubhouse:** Food, Beer, Liquor, Dining room, Nightclub open noon–2:30 a.m. **Lessons:** Available **Pro:** Joe Kucirek

Directions: I-90 to SR 2 west (I-90 splits off to merge with the Ohio Turnpike); north on Leavitt Rd. (SR 58); on right, after Jaeger Rd.

Firestone Golf Course (9-hole layout)   9 holes

Area: **Far South**   City: **Akron**   Cost: $$$$$ ☎ **(330) 724-4444**

Address: 600 Swartz Rd., Akron

Tees	Ydg.	C/r	S/r	Pace
Back:	3008	67.8	109	
Middle:	2880	66.6	107	
Forward:	2386	66.2	105	

	Weekdays	Weekends & hol.	Carts
Price:	$11.00 / $20.00	$11.00 / $20.00	$11.00 / $22.00

Specials: Seniors Mon–Sat $11.00 for 9 holes, cart included

Season: Year-round **Hours:** Summer: 7 a.m.–10 p.m.; winter: 10 a.m.–8 p.m. **Tee times:** Taken **Leagues:** Available **Ranger:** Daily **Practice facil:** Range, Putting Green **Clubhouse:** Food, Beer, Liquor, Dining room, Pavilion, Hackers Bar & Grill to open in Spring 1999 **Lessons:** Available **Pro:** Rick Schmidt

Directions: I-277 to Exit 3 for S. Main St.; south on S. Main; east on Swartz Rd. (Swartz is directly opposite eastbound exit for S. Main); on right.

Geauga Hidden Valley Golf Course   9 holes

Area: **Far East**   City: **Thompson**   Cost: $$$$$ ☎ **(440) 298-3912**

Address: 17261 Thompson Rd., Thompson

Tees	Ydg.	C/r	S/r	Pace
Middle:	3206	35.1		
Forward:	2600	35.9		

	Weekdays	Weekends & hol.	Carts
Price:	$7.00 / $12.00	$7.50 / $13.00	$8.50 / $17.00

Specials: Seniors & Juniors Mon–Fri $6.00 / $11.00, Sat–Sun $7.50 / $12.50

Season: Mar–Nov **Hours:** Sunrise–sunset **Tee times:** Not taken **Leagues:** Wed 5 p.m. **Ranger:** Some days **Practice facil:** Putting Green **Clubhouse:** Food **Lessons:** Not available

Directions: I-90 to Exit 212 for SR 528; south on SR 528 to Thompson Rd.; east on Thompson Rd.; on right.

Green Hills Golf Course   9 holes

Area: **Far South**   City: **Kent**   Cost: $$$$$ ☎ **(330) 678-2601**

Address: 1105 Tallmadge Rd., Kent

	Weekdays	Weekends & hol.	Carts
Price:	$8.00 / $13.00	$8.00 / $13.00	$8.50 / $17.00

Specials: Seniors before 2 p.m. $5.75

Season: Apr–Nov **Hours:** Sunrise–sunset **Tee times:** Recommended **Leagues:** Mon–Fri 4 p.m. **Ranger:** Weekends **Practice facil:** Putting Green, Chipping Green **Clubhouse:** Food, Beer, Dining room, Pavilion **Lessons:** Not available

Directions: I-271 to Exit 18 for SR 8; south on SR 8 to exit for Hudson/SR 303; left (east) on SR 303 (W. Streetsboro Rd) to Hudson; right (south) on SR 91; left (east) on SR 59 to Kent; right (south) on Middlebury Rd.; right (west) on Tallmadge Rd.; on right.

Green Ridge Public Golf Course   9 holes, exec

Area: **East**   City: **Wickliffe**   Cost: $$$$$ ☎ **(440) 943-0007**

Address: 29150 Ridge Rd., Wickliffe

	Weekdays	Weekends & hol.	Carts
Price:	$10.00 / $19.00	$10.00 / $19.00	$11.00 / $21.00

Specials: Seniors Mon–Fri $8.00 first round, $7.00 second round; club rental $5.00

Season: Year-round **Hours:** Sunrise–sunset **Tee times:** Not taken **Leagues:** Various times **Ranger:** Most days **Practice facil:** Putting Green **Clubhouse:** Food, Pavilion **Lessons:** Not available **Pro:** Ralph Bond

Directions: I-90 to Exit 187 (Bishop Rd.); north on Bishop; right (east) on Ridge Rd.; on right.

PUBLIC 9, EXEC, PAR 3

Johnny Cake Ridge Golf Course

9 holes, exec

Area: **East**   City: **Willoughby**   Cost: **$$**$$$ ☎ **(440) 946-3154**

Address: 7134 Mentor Ave., Willoughby

Tees	Ydg.	C/r	S/r	Pace
Back:	1888			2:00
Middle:	1724	28.5	90	
Forward:	1586	29.2	89	

	Weekdays	Weekends & hol.	Carts
Price:	$8.50 / $14.00	$9.25 / $15.50	$10.00 / $20.00

Specials: Seniors Mon–Fri $6.50, Sat–Sun $8.00

Season: Year-round **Hours:** Sunrise–sunset **Tee times:** Taken **Leagues:** Various times **Ranger:** Some days **Practice facil:** Putting Green, Chipping Green **Clubhouse:** Food, Covered deck **Lessons:** Available **Pro:** James Bukovec

Directions: I-90 to Exit 190 for SR 306; north on SR 306 to US 20 (Mentor Ave.); left (west) on Mentor Ave. for 1 mile; on left.

Leaning Tree Golf Course

9 holes, exec

Area: **South**   City: **Richfield**   Cost: **$**$$$$ ☎ **(330) 659-4900**

Address: 3770 Broadview Rd., Richfield

	Weekdays	Weekends & hol.	Carts
Price:	$5.00 / $8.00	$5.00 / $8.00	No power carts

Specials: None

Season: Apr 1–1st Sun in Nov **Hours:** Sunrise–sunset **Tee times:** Not taken **Leagues:** Available **Ranger:** None **Practice facil:** Putting Green **Clubhouse:** Food **Lessons:** Not available

Directions: I-77 to Exit 143 for Wheatley Rd.; west on Wheatley (becomes Broadview Rd./SR 176 after Brecksville Rd.); on left.

Leisure Time Recreation

9 holes, exec

Area: **Far South**   City: **Stow**   Cost: **$**$$$$ ☎ **(330) 688-4162**

Address: 4561 Darrow Rd., Stow

	Weekdays	Weekends & hol.	Carts
Price:	$7.50 / $12.50	$7.50 / $12.50	No power carts

Specials: Seniors & students Mon–Fri before 5 p.m. $6.50 / $10.50

Season: Mar–Nov **Hours:** 8 a.m.–10 p.m. **Tee times:** Not taken **Leagues:** Mon–Fri 6–6:30 p.m. **Ranger:** None **Practice facil:** Putting Green, Chipping Green **Clubhouse:** Food, Beer, Dining room, Showers, Restaurant, Motel **Lessons:** Available **Pro:** Ken Miller

Directions: I-271 to Exit 18 for SR 8; south on SR 8 to exit for SR 303/Hudson; left (east) on SR 303 (W. Streetsboro Rd) to Hudson; right (south) on SR 91 (becomes Darrow Rd. in Stow); on left.

The Tornado Tour

Slices…

Russ Jeske enjoys gambling on golf. Not Nassaus or skins, but entire tournaments. He produces them. In its inaugural season, 1995, the Tornado Tour included 21 events, 149 players, and a total purse of $80,000. In 1999, the Medical Mutual Tornado Tour, with support from Mullinax Ford and Coca-Cola, will offer 21 events for 450 players and a total purse of $400,000.

A player of some repute in his salad days, Jeske realized that his game was not improving despite playing in local tournaments such as the Tiger Town Open in Massillon and the Canton Open. "I wondered what effect the absence of tournament play was having on my game. Tournament golf is to league play or mixed foursomes what Bengal tigers are to house cats: a different breed. Tournament golf gives the good player the opportunity to take the game to a higher level. It's something that's just not available playing with your friends."

As he watched other players, he wondered if their games were stunted because of lack of tournament opportunity. What if, he wondered, area players could compete against each other for money on a weekly basis.

He got his answer. "Joe Ogilvy played with us for three years. Last year he won twice on the Nike Tour. This year he's playing the PGA Tour. That's why people come out to watch Tornado players. The quality of play is awesome."

Of course, Jeske's own playing time has been slashed. "Like any new business," he said, "it's a tough road. The scheduling and everything that goes into it, plus the constant search for sponsors, means it's a 12-month project." He sometimes wonders where the Tour would be without the support of his dad, Ralph, a retired electrician. "My dad is to the Tornado what a great caddy is to a player: The best partner of all."

Some of the courses he's taken the Tour to have treated players like members of an outing. Other courses treat them as aspiring golf champions. This season three tournaments will be played at Chippewa GC in Doylestown. "It's important that the courses lend a hand," Jeske said. "River Greens in Coshocton treats us like family, and the same with Chippewa. The season opener is at Aurora Country Club, where Gary Trivisonno is the pro, and he's been behind us since Day One."

"In the final analysis," Jeske said, "the Tornado Tour doesn't exist to make touring professionals. It exists to provide the opportunity good players need to fulfill their potential, to become the players they can be. So if you ask me if running the Tour is satisfying, I guess that's my answer."

—JHT

Little Met Golf Course
9 holes, exec

Area: **West**   City: **Cleveland**   Cost: $$$$$ ☎ **(216) 941-9672**

Address: 18599 Old Lorain Rd., Cleveland

	Weekdays	Weekends & hol.	Carts
Price:	$7.00 / $14.00	$8.00 / $16.00	$11.00 / $16.00

Specials: Golfer's Dozen: 12 rounds for the price of 10; Seniors (62+) & Juniors $5.00; Single-rider cart $5.50

Season: Mid-Mar–mid-Dec   **Hours:** Sunrise–sunset   **Tee times:** Taken weekends
Leagues: Mon–Fri, various times   **Ranger:** Daily   **Practice facil:** Putting Green, Club rental   **Clubhouse:** Food, Beer   **Lessons:** Available

Directions: I-480 to Exit 9 for Grayton Rd.; north on Grayton; left (west) on Puritas Rd. into Rocky River Reservation; right (north) on Valley Pkwy. past Big Met Golf Course; right (east) on Old Lorain Rd.; on right.

Little Met Golf Course   *(photo: Casey Batule/courtesy of Cleveland Metroparks)*

Locust Grove Par Three Golf Course
9 holes, par 3

Area: **East**   City: **Mayfield Hts.**   Cost: $$$$$ ☎ **(440) 442-0991**

Address: 2153 Lander Rd., Mayfield Hts.

	Weekdays	Weekends & hol.	Carts
Price:	$6.75 / $10.75	$8.00 / $12.00	No power carts

Specials: Seniors any time $5.75 / $9.00; club rental $3.00

Season: Apr 1–Oct 31   **Hours:** Sunrise–sunset   **Tee times:** Not taken   **Leagues:** Thursdays   **Ranger:** None   **Practice facil:** None   **Clubhouse:** Food, Snacks only
Lessons: Not available

Directions: I-271 to Exit 32 for Cedar Rd.; east on Cedar; left (north) on Lander Rd.; on right.

Mastick Woods Golf Course

9 holes, exec

Area: **West**   City: **Cleveland**   Cost: ☎ **(216) 267-5626**

Address: 19900 Puritas Ave., Cleveland

	Weekdays	**Weekends & hol.**	**Carts**
Price:	$6.50 / NA	$7.50 / NA	No power carts

Specials: Golfer's Dozen: 12 rounds for the price of 10; Seniors (62+) & Juniors Mon–Fri $5.00; pull carts available

Season: Mid-Mar–mid-Dec **Hours:** Sunrise–sunset **Tee times:** Taken weekends, until noon **Leagues:** Mon–Fri, various times **Ranger:** Most days **Practice facil:** Putting Green **Clubhouse:** Food, Beer **Lessons:** Not available

Directions: I-480 to Exit 9 for Grayton Rd.; north on Grayton; left (west) on Puritas Rd. into Rocky River Reservation; on left.

Mastick Woods Golf Course

photo: Casey Batule/courtesy of Cleveland Metroparks)

PUBLIC 9, EXEC, PAR 3

North Olmsted Golf Club

9 holes, exec

Area: **West**   City: **North Olmsted**   Cost: $$$$$ ☎ **(440) 777-0220**

Address: 5840 Canterbury Rd., North Olmsted

	Weekdays	**Weekends & hol.**	**Carts**
Price:	$6.50 / $12.50	$7.00 / $13.00	$7.00 / $14.00

Specials: Seniors Mon–Fri noon–4 p.m. $4.75

Season: Apr 1–Dec 1 **Hours:** Sunrise–sunset **Tee times:** Required weekends **Leagues:** Mon–Fri 7:30–10 a.m.; 4–5:30 p.m.; other times vary **Ranger:** Weekends **Practice facil:** Putting Green **Clubhouse:** Food, Beer **Lessons:** Available **Pro:** Steve Steinhilber

Directions: I-480 to Exit 6 for SR 252 (Great Northern Blvd.); south on SR 252; right (west) on Butternut Ridge Rd.; left (south) on Canterbury Rd.; on right.

Pepperidge Tree Golf Course   9 holes

Area: **Far East**   City: **N. Madison**   Cost: **$$**$$$ ☎ **(440) 428-1398**

Address: 6825 N. Ridge Rd., N. Madison

	Weekdays	Weekends & hol.	Carts
Price:	$8.50 / $14.00	$9.50 / $16.00	$10.00 / $20.00

Specials: Senior specials available

Season: Year-round **Hours:** Sunrise–sunset **Tee times:** Taken **Leagues:** Mon–Fri 5 p.m. **Ranger:** Some days **Practice facil:** Putting Green **Clubhouse:** Food, Beer, Pavilion **Lessons:** Not available

Directions: I-90 to Exit 212 for SR 528 (River St.); north on SR 528; right (east) on N. Ridge Rd. (SR 20); on left.

Riverwoods Golf Course/Pine Valley Sports   9 holes, exec

Area: **Far South**   City: **Akron**   Cost: **$**$$$ ☎ **(330) 928-2669**

Address: 1870 Akron-Peninsula Rd., Akron

	Weekdays	Weekends & hol.	Carts
Price:	$6.50 / $13.00	$6.50 / $13.00	$7.00 / $14.00

Specials: Seniors (62+) Mon–Fri before 2 p.m. $5.00

Season: Mar–Dec **Hours:** Sunrise–sunset **Tee times:** Not taken **Leagues:** Mon–Fri, various times **Ranger:** Daily **Practice facil:** Range, Putting Green, Chipping Green, Sand, Lighted range, Grass tees, Covered tees **Clubhouse:** Food, Beer, Pro Shop open year round **Lessons:** Available

Directions: I-77 to Exit 138 for Ghent Rd.; west on Ghent; right (east) on Yellow Creek Rd. under I-77; right (east) on W. Bath Rd.; right (south) on Akron-Peninsula Rd.; on right.

Sycamore Valley Golf Course   9 holes, exec

Area: **Far South**   City: **Akron**   Cost: **$**$$$ ☎ **(330) 928-3329**

Address: 1651 Akron-Peninsula Rd., Akron

	Weekdays	Weekends & hol.	Carts
Price:	$6.50 / $13.00	$6.50 / $13.00	$7.00 / $14.00

Specials: Seniors (65+) Mon–Fri before noon $6.00 / $12.00

Season: Year-round **Hours:** Sunrise–sunset **Tee times:** Not taken **Leagues:** Ladies league only **Ranger:** Some days **Practice facil:** Putting Green **Clubhouse:** Food, Beer **Lessons:** Not available

Directions: I-77 to Exit 138 for Ghent Rd.; west on Ghent; right (east) on Yellow Creek Rd. under I-77; right (east) on W. Bath Rd.; right (south) on Akron-Peninsula Rd.; on left.

Westlake Meadowood Golf Course 18 par-3 holes; 9 exec holes

Area: West   City: Westlake   Cost: $$$$$ ☎ (440) 835-6442

Address: 29800 Center Ridge Rd., Westlake

Tees	Ydg.	C/r	S/r	Pace	Ydg.	C/r	S/r	Pace
Middle:	2635	66.8	118		2845	56.2	80	

	Weekdays	Weekends & hol.	Carts	
Price:	$7.00 / $11.00	$8.00 / $12.00	$8.00 / $16.00	(Par-3 course)
Price:	$6.50 / $9.50	$8.00 / $12.00	$8.00 / $16.00	(9-hole course)

Specials: Seniors & Juniors Mon–Fri: Exec. 18 is $5.00 / 8.00; Reg 9 is $5.50 / 8.50

Season: Year-round **Hours:** Sunrise–sundown **Tee times:** Not taken **Leagues:** Mon–Thu afternoons **Ranger:** Some days **Practice facil:** Putting Green **Clubhouse:** Food, Beer, Pavilion **Lessons:** Not available

Directions: I-90 to Exit 156 for Crocker Rd./Bassett Rd.; south on Crocker; right (west) on Center Ridge Rd.; on right.

TIDYMAN'S TIDBITS #15

Eagle-proof par 5s:
- No. 9 Hinckley Hills
- No. 11 Springvale
- No. 12 Thunder Hill
- No. 16 Brandywine
- No. 17 Seneca B Course

PUBLIC 9, EXEC, PAR 3

Private Courses

Acacia Country Club

☎ (440) 442-2686

Area: **East**   City: **Lyndhurst**   Difficulty: ●●●

Address: 26899 Cedar Rd., Lyndhurst   **Pro:** Chris Wagner, PGA

Tees	Ydg.	C/r	S/r	Pace
Back:	6701	72.5	129	3:40
Middle:	6395	71.1	126	
Forward:	5736	73.3	129	

Directions: I-271 to Exit 32 for Cedar Rd.; west on Cedar; on right.

Description "The Anniversary Waltz" was played at Acacia in 1996, when 75 candles were lit. And as soon as the plates were cleared, plans were finalized for some renovation. There had been some speculation that this storied course would be sacrificed to retail development. That's not the case; Acacia will be here for a long, long time.

A good thing, too. This Donald Ross design challenges and rewards finesse players as it rolls up and down 6,400 yards from the blues.

Of course, not everyone who played here was known for finesse. Brawny baseball slugger Babe Ruth played his one and only pro match here on August 17, 1937, in the True Temper Open.

And talk about a foursome! Tris Speaker, Billy Burke, and Tommy Armour rounded out the group.

Ashtabula Country Club

☎ (440) 964-2800

Area: **Far East**   City: **Ashtabula**   Difficulty: ●●●

Address: 4338 Lake Rd. W., Ashtabula   **Pro:** Brad Ruminski

Tees	Ydg.	C/r	S/r	Pace
Back:	5971	68.6	120	3:43
Middle:	5805	67.9	119	
Forward:	5378	71.1	118	

Directions: I-90 to Exit 223 for SR 45; north on SR 45 (becomes Center Rd.); right (east) on Lake Rd.; on right.

Description This is a short track at 5,805 from the whites, but par is only 70. The club was founded in 1923 and has 220 members.

Highlights The number one handicap hole is No. 6, a par 4 of 407 yards, best played down the right side. On the back side, No. 12 is the number 2 handicap hole, a powerful par 4 of 420 yards, a dogleg left that calls, of course, for a magnificent tee shot.

Aurora Country Club

☎ (330) 562-5300

Area: **Southeast**   City: **Aurora**   Difficulty: ●●●

Address: 50 Trails End Rd., Aurora   **Pro:** Gary Trivisonno, PGA

Tees	Ydg.	C/r	S/r	Pace
Back:	6658	72.5	133	4:10
Middle:	6315	71.1	130	
Forward:	5544	72.7	128	

Directions: I-271 to Exit 27 for US 422; east on US 422; right (south) on SR 306 (Chillicothe Rd.); left (east) on SR 82 (Garfield East Rd.); right (south) on Hudson Rd.; left (west) on Trails End Rd. to entrance.

Description The course record here, 64, is shared by a trio of out-of-towners: Arnold Palmer, Bruce Devlin, and Charles Coody. When the Cleveland Open was a tour stop, Aurora CC was the site three times. Glancing at the scorecard, you may think this course looks easy, at only 6,200 yards. That's until you realize there are only three par 5s and three par 3s on this course; there are plenty of long par 4s.

On No. 1, players meet for the first time a creek that will meander through a half dozen or so holes as the match proceeds. Lots of bunkers near the greens, too. Head pro Gary Trivisonno describes his course as "sporty, tight and somewhat hilly. It has small greens and it plays longer than 6,200 yards." Trivisonno is one of the longest-hitting pros in the area. His reputation for being genuinely nice is well deserved, as well.

TIDYMAN'S TIDBITS #16

The Donald Ross courses in Greater Cleveland:

- Shaker Country Club (1913)
- The Oakwood Club (1915)
- Acacia Country Club (1920)
- Hawthorne Valley Country Club (1926)
- Manakiki Golf Course (1928)

PRIVATE

Avon Oaks Country Club

☎ **(440) 871-4638**

Area: **West**   City: **Avon**   Difficulty: ●●●

Address: 32300 Detroit Rd. (SR 254), Avon   **Pro:** Judd Stephenson, PGA

Tees	Ydg.	C/r	S/r	Pace
Back:	6720	72.7	128	3:53
Middle:	6402	71.0	125	
Forward:	5671	72.6	125	

Directions: I-90 westbound to Exit 156 for Crocker Rd./Bassett Rd.; left (south) on Crocker to SR 254 (Detroit Rd.); right (west) on Detroit; on right.
I-90 eastbound to Exit 153 for SR 83 (Center Rd.); south on SR 83; left (east) on Detroit Rd. (SR 254); on left.

Description   Avon Oaks plays 6,402 from the member tees, so this is no short layout. In addition, the demands on tee shots are substantial. Fairways and landing areas are narrow. Making the course play longer is the prevalence of elevated greens. A few years ago, the course added gold tees. From these new championship tees, Parma resident Rob Moss fired a 66 for the course record. From the blue tees, the record of 63 is shared by a small group of players.

New head pro Judd Stephenson, PGA, picks No. 12 as his favorite hole. From the back of the box, it stretches 170 yards and has water and bunkers. Reaching it is not easy, and once there you're putting on the layout's most undulating green.

Barrington Golf Club

☎ **(330) 995-0667**

Area: **Southeast**   City: **Aurora**   Difficulty: ●●●

Address: 350 N. Aurora Rd., Aurora   **Pro:** Rich DeLaat

Tees	Ydg.	C/r	S/r	Pace
Back:	7138	74.6	135	3:54
Middle:	6595	71.3	125	
Forward:	5272	69.8	117	

Directions: I-271 to Exit 27 for US 422; east on US 422; right (south) on SR 306 (Chillicothe Rd.); right (west) on Treat Rd.; left (south) on N. Aurora Rd. (SR 43); on left.

Description   The dedication round at this Jack Nicklaus course was a foursome composed of Nicklaus and the developers who built this housing development/country club. Playing for $1,000 a stroke, Bart Wolstein ended up donating two grand to the Nicklaus Scholarship Fund at Ohio State University. Barrington was built in 1994 and named by *Golf Digest* as one of the top 10 new courses.

PRIVATE

Bob Fazio, chairman of the golf committee, is also a member at Canterbury Country Club, Cleveland's host to PGA and USGA tournaments. When he compared the two courses, he was looking at the antique and the modern. "Barrington is modern course design," he said. "The fairways are much larger, and it has state-of-the-art conditioning, which means four-row irrigation."

Former head pro Joel Piekaraski played his first round at the height of the autumn color explosion. "I was overwhelmed," he said. "It's unique in this area to have a course cutting right through the woods." To score here, he suggests a short game. "Most Nicklaus courses are heavily bunkered and they're severe around the greens."

Beechmont Country Club ☎ (216) 831-9100
Area: **East**   City: **Beachwood**   Difficulty: ●●●

Address: 29600 Chagrin Blvd., Beachwood   **Pro:** Charlie Stone, Master PGA

Tees	Ydg.	C/r	S/r	Pace
Back:	6648	72.3	131	3:40
Middle:	6359	70.8	128	
Forward:	5845	73.4	130	

Directions: I-271 to Exit 27 for SR 87 (Chagrin Blvd.); east on Chagrin; on right.

Description First things first. Try hard to get Ed Preisler, the skinny octogenarian, in your foursome. He is older than many of the hardwoods that line the fairways here and just as resilient. Every club should have a member like him.

Two tips should always be kept in mind here. First, this is not a course for aggressive putting. In most cases, the smart play is to lag putt. Getting down in two is nothing to be ashamed of here. Preisler counsels, "A guest here would be wise to ask where the ball should be putted." Second, at one point or another, you will find yourself behind one of the gorgeous oaks or yews. Ignore what your ego says and chip back to the short grass.

"There are more shots wasted because you think you're going to make that shot over the tree," Preisler cautions. Wasted shots count, too.

Club pro Charlie Stone has good advice as well. "The first few holes are very difficult," he says. "No. 1 is long (412 yards), No. 2 is tight, No. 3 is a long par 3 (184 yards), and No. 4 (at 440 yards) is the longest par 4 on the course. It would be easier if you could play the back nine first."

A powerful ego is no match for this course; good judgment is probably the best ally.

Beechmont Country Club

Canterbury Golf Club

☎ (216) 561-1000

Area: **East**   City: **Shaker Hts.**   Difficulty: ●●●

Address: 22000 S. Woodland Rd., Shaker Hts.   **Pro:** Craig Murray

Tees	Ydg.	C/r	S/r	Pace
Back:	6942	73.9	138	3:54
Middle:	6471	71.7	130	
Forward:	5890	74.5	133	

Directions: I-271 to Exit 27 for SR 87 (Chagrin Blvd.); west on Chagrin; right (north) on Green Rd.; left (west) on S. Woodland Rd.; on left.

Description   This is the course where Jack Nicklaus won his 14th major, one of many records in his trophy case. It is here that the PGA and the USGA have come for championship play. This is not a country club; it is a golf club. An example of that could be seen in the 1996 U.S. Senior Open. The best senior professionals played the course just as it is played every day by its members. It is a big and powerful course, with three finishing holes that try the souls of the best players in the game. To be a guest here is quite an honor. Strict dress code: pants with drawstrings are not allowed. It goes without saying that jeans are forbidden.

Chagrin Valley Country Club ☎ (440) 248-4314

Area: **Southeast**   City: **Chagrin Falls**   Difficulty: ●●●

Address: 4700 SOM Center Rd. (SR 91), Chagrin Falls   **Pro:** Michael Heisterkamp

Tees	Ydg.	C/r	S/r	Pace
Back:	6614	72.9	131	3:53
Middle:	6410	72.1	130	
Forward:	5211	69.3	120	

Directions: I-271 to Exit 27 for US 422 (east) to SR 91 (SOM Center Rd.); north on SR 91; on left.

Description When 19-year member Phil Kish thinks about the joys of golf, his mind's eye focuses on No. 4, the 170-yard par 3. The green is elevated and surrounded by shelf rock. Flowers brighten the stone and trees provide the background. "It's a well-defined hole, easy to see the challenge. It's a beautiful hole, too, and playing No. 4 is memorable. Finally, it's a satisfying hole. Most players who walk away with par are smiling." He birdies it a few times every season.

This club, nestled in heavy woods, began in 1921 when the Chagrin Valley Country Club Company built its first nine holes on the former Mapes family farm. That course later become the Moreland Hills Golf Course, a public track on the east side of SOM Center Road. The club built a course and clubhouse on the west side of SOM Center in 1928.

PRIVATE

Columbia Hills Country Club ☎ (440) 236-5051

Area: **Southwest**   City: **Columbia Station**   Difficulty: ●●●

Address: 16200 E. River Rd., Columbia Station   **Pro:** Jim Wise

Tees	Ydg.	C/r	S/r	Pace
Back:	6432	70.9	134	3:59
Middle:	6045	69.0	130	
Forward:	5471	72.6	130	

Directions: I-71 to Exit 231 for SR 82 (Royalton Rd.); west on SR 82 for 5 miles; right (south) on E. River Rd. (SR 252); 1 mile, on right.

Description One of many virtues here is the landscaping. Few other clubs can match the incredible size, variety, color, or quality of the flower and plant displays throughout this course. This is a hilly layout and a fairly short one, only 6,068 yards from the members' tees. The steep inclines make it play lots longer than it measures, though. Much work has been done on the severe flooding problem, including the installation of an irrigation system. The clubhouse has been renovated and carts are now electric.

Sand Ridge: Pure Golf

Bill Conway has a regal air about him: tall, weathered, trim, gray hair thinning precipitously, electric blue eyes. Smiles easily. Doesn't look like a czar. He sits on a plastic chair on a temporary deck attached to the temporary pro shop at Sand Ridge Golf Club in Munson Township, a quiet town in Northeast Ohio. He works his way through a sandwich and root beer, recounting the last few years, from the day he decided this patch of land was not suitable for sand quarrying to today. Today he is the czar of the golf club that sets an unattainable standard for new courses in this area.

Sand Ridge is the result of the stars being perfectly aligned: a vision and the leadership to carry out the vision, a market anxious for just such a venture and willing to pay for it, a big and rangy piece of property natural for golf, and a designer with the time and energy to take on this project.

Sand Ridge is pure golf. No debutante balls (no ballroom), no tennis or swimming lessons, no outings. No houses lining fairways. Instead, it offers (and encourages the use of) caddies, and the course itself—designed by Tom Fazio and spread over 380 acres of Geauga County maple forests so naturally and powerfully beautiful that the emotional dimension of golf is drawn out.

Conway's company, Fairmount Minerals, Inc., has nearby quarrying operations. In 1995, the company purchased adjoining property to quarry. After testing the full range of the property, they found insufficient sandstone to justify development.

Conway wondered about a golf club. He ordered a market study. "We knew the concept: an equity club open to a variety of individual members. We knew there would be members from other clubs, that this would be a second club, or in some cases, a third club."

The results of the study were interesting. Yes, there was interest in a new golf club, but only if it was "absolutely first rate." If there was any question who would design the new course, it was settled right then: it had to be Fazio, the half-Italian/half-Irish designer who cut his teeth in the employ of his uncle George, the successful PGA touring pro and designer. At age 19, Tom was driving the bulldozer, shaping holes for his uncle, and learning from the ground up.

Fazio and Conway shared a mutual friend: Dusty Murdock, who knows golf. At Murdock's request, Fazio flew north to meet Conway. "Anyone who knows Bill [Conway] says, 'Oh, he's a prince,' and he is," Fazio said. "Sand Ridge is as good as it is because of Bill Conway and the quality of his commitment. It's no accident."

Fazio studied the aerial photographs and topo map. He started by creating eight distinct routings (later expanded to 20).

Ecologist and teacher Edward Hauser was hired to conduct an environmental study. There were five wetlands areas, totaling 104 acres on the property. They would have to first be protected and then incorporated into the design. The largest of the five totals nearly 90 acres and runs diagonally across the course from southeast to northwest. On the course are the headwaters of both the Chagrin and Cuyahoga Rivers.

A great deal of work went into a comprehensive environmental and ecological land–management program. For example, all the water used at the course is reused and recycled within the golf course and never reaches streams or wetlands. More than 50 bat, owl, and bird houses have been strategically placed. Eleven wooden bridges allow players to walk over wetlands. From the green at No. 11 to the tee at No. 12, a bridge crosses Butternut Creek, flowing into the Cuyahoga River. The bridge at No. 15 spans the East Branch, which flows into the Chagrin River. Both rivers are designated Scenic Rivers and support endangered species such as brook trout.

As a result of these efforts, Sand Ridge is the first firm in Ohio (there are only 10 in the world) to receive Audubon International Signature Program status.

The course has four tee boxes—not red, white, blue, and gold but double diamond, diamond, square, and circle, taken from downhill skiing markers. Double diamond, the longest, is 3,565 yards going out, 3,523 coming in, par 72. The diamond plays 6,502, the square 5,925 and the circle 5,078. All are par 72.

For the czar, it has been a wonderful couple of years. From slogging through the wetlands with Hauser, to strategizing with Murdock, to meeting and working with Fazio, to watching the course take shape, to playing the first round on May 18, 1998. With his wife, Mary. No string quartet, no speeches, no nothing. Just a mixed foursome on the first tee and off they went, followed by other foursomes. The czar says, "I spent a lot of time going around the course as it was being built. It's entirely different when you have a club in your hand and you're hitting the ball. The first round was just a wonderful experience."

The first of many.

—JHT

TIDYMAN'S TIDBITS #17

Big names in local course design:
- Pete Dye—Avalon, Fowler's Mill
- Tom Weiskopf and Jay Parrish— Quail Hollow
- Jack Nicklaus—Barrington
- Tom Fazio—Sawmill Creek, Sand Ridge
- Dana Fry—StoneWater, Little Mountain
- Robert Von Hagge—Quail Hollow, Red Tail

The Country Club   ☎ (216) 831-9252
Area: **East**   City: **Pepper Pike**   Difficulty: ●●●

Address: 2825 Lander Rd., Pepper Pike   **Pro:** Jack McKelvey

Tees	Ydg.	C/r	S/r	Pace
Back:	6908	73.5	130	3:51
Middle:	6558	71.9	125	
Forward:	5684	72.2	123	

Directions: I-271 to Exit 29 for Chagrin Blvd.; east on Chagrin to Lander Circle; north on Lander Rd.; on right.

Description This ancient (for these parts) club and course (1889) is joined at the hip with Pepper Pike Club, and each serves a distinct purpose: Pepper is the course for Cleveland corporate executives; Country is truly a country club, with a wonderful course and all the amenities, including facilities for debutante balls. A walk through the locker room reveals an impressive representation of WASP royalty.

Country Club of Hudson   ☎ (330) 342-1193
Area: **Southeast**   City: **Hudson**   Difficulty: ●●●

Address: 2155 Middleton Rd., Hudson   **Pro:** Jim and Jeff Camp

Tees	Ydg.	C/r	S/r	Pace
Back:	6732	71.7	122	3:48
Middle:	6442	70.4	120	
Forward:	5519	70.9	120	

Directions: I-480 to Exit 37 for SR 91 (Darrow Rd.); south on SR 91; left (east) on Middleton Rd. for ½ mile; on left.

PRIVATE

Description As this Geoffrey Cornish design nears the 30-year mark, it only gets better. The layout has always been a good one, but the course was built on Summit County farmland—and on high ground, as well. With no trees, it had a "Scottish links" look and all the challenges wind can bring. But the thousands and thousands of trees subsequently planted here are now slowing the wind, defining holes, and adding more character every season.

Eight ponds dot the course, and the greens, usually kept to a 9 on the Stimpmeter, can reach 10 and faster. No. 11 is the signature hole here, a classic par 4 of more than 400 yards. It narrows near the green, which has bunkers on both sides and white stakes on the left. Bud Nauffts, a good player in these parts for many, many years, birdied No. 14 last year but said it took him a driver and a 3-wood to get on.

Better-known players who have golfed here include John Daley and Phil Mickelson, who were winners in the annual Junior Invitational played here.

Country Clubs of Fox Meadow (Meadow Course)   ☎ (330) 723-4653

Area: **Southwest**   City: **Medina**   Difficulty: ● ● ◐

Address: 6416 Wadsworth Rd. (SR 57), Medina   **Pro:** Scott Campbell, PGA

Tees	Ydg.	C/r	S/r	Pace
Back:	6877	73.0	123	3:58
Middle:	6345	70.1	118	
Forward:	5801	67.7	114	

Directions: I-71 to Exit 218 for SR 18; west on SR 18; left (south) on River Styx Rd.; right (west) on Sharon-Copley Rd.; left (south) on Wadsworth Rd. (SR 57); on right.

Description This brand-new track, designed by Steve Burns and built on softly rolling farmland, is not as challenging as its sister course, Weymouth. Still, to have two distinct courses for a single membership is intriguing. Fox Meadow has almost two dozen homes as part of the development, and plans call for more than 500 once the last roof tile is hammered down. Members at Fox Meadow are also members at Weymouth (see separate listing). The courses share Denny Wolfe, PGA, as golf pro and superintendent Ken Aukerman, who has tended the greens and fairways at Weymouth for a quarter century.

Country Clubs of Fox Meadow (Weymouth)   ☎ (330) 725-6297

Area: **Southwest**   City: **Medina**   Difficulty: ● ● ●

Address: 3946 Weymouth Rd., Medina   **Pro:** Scott Campbell (?), PGA

Tees	Ydg.	C/r	S/r	Pace
Back:	7007	73.7	123	3:58
Middle:	6639	71.9	128	
Forward:	6352	70.6	125	

Directions: I-71 to Exit 222 for SR 3; south on SR 3 (Weymouth Rd.); on right.

Description From 1969 until 1986 this was a pretty good public track. Once it went private, traps were added until the count reached 80, fairways were contoured, trees were moved around, and famous designer Geoffrey Cornish added his two cents. It is now a very good private track. Length is not yet determined, but it will likely play around 6,400 yards from the member tees and par is 72.

PRIVATE

Members at Weymouth are also members at Fox Meadow (see separate listing). The courses share Denny Wolfe, PGA, as golf pro and superintendent Ken Aukerman, who has tended the greens and fairways at Weymouth for a quarter century.

Elyria Country Club   ☎ (440) 323-8225
Area: **Far West**   City: **Elyria**   Difficulty: ● ● ●

Address: 41625 Oberlin-Elyria Rd., Elyria   **Pro:** Rich Casabella, PGA

Tees	Ydg.	C/r	S/r	Pace
Back:	6731	72.1	130	3:47
Middle:	6326	70.4	125	
Forward:	5625	72.0	123	

Directions: I-480 take Exit 1A for SR 10 (I-480 ends here); west on SR 10 for 14 miles; right (north) on Lagrange Rd.; left (west) on Butternut Ridge Rd.; right (north) on Oberlin-Elyria Rd.; on right.

Description   This is among the most beautiful courses in an area blessed with beautiful courses.

The designer was William F. Flynn, whose work includes Shinecock Hills in New York and Burning Tree in Maryland. In the Greater Cleveland area, Flynn also created courses at The Country Club in Pepper Pike and Pepper Pike Country Club.

Play here calls for every stick in the bag, as the course rolls and pitches over ravine and hillock. Two memorable tees are No. 11, an elevated par 3 of 168 yards that shoots down over water, and No. 15, which calls for a big draw over the east branch of the Black River to a tree-lined fairway.

PRIVATE

Fairlawn Country Club   ☎ (330) 836-5541
Area: **Far South**   City: **Akron**   Difficulty:

Address: 200 N. Wheaton Rd., Akron   **Pro:** Frank Wharton, PGA

Tees	Ydg.	C/r	S/r	Pace
Back:	6277	70.4	126	3:42
Middle:	5917	68.6	123	
Forward:	5242	69.7	115	

Directions: I-77 southbound to Exit 138 for Ghent Rd.; right off circular exit (east) on Ghent Rd.; left (east) on W. Market St.; left (north) on N. Wheaton Rd.; on left.
I-77 northbound to Exit 132 (White Pond Dr.); right (north) on White Pond; right (east) on Frank Blvd.; left (north) on W. Market St.; right (east) on N. Wheaton Rd.; on left.

Description This is a classic old course that reeks of character. Greens are small and well bunkered; the Stimpmeter usually measures around 10. Few courses are better conditioned. At just a little under 6,000 yards from the white tees, this course bobs and weaves enough that good scores are posted only by players who make few mistakes.

Firestone Country Club   ☎ (330) 644-8441

Area: **Far South**   City: **Akron**   Difficulty: ●●●

Address: 425 E. Warner Rd., Akron   **Pro:** Mark Gore, PGA

Tees	South				North				West			
	Ydg.	C/r	S/r	Pace	Ydg.	C/r	S/r	Pace	Ydg.	C/r	S/r	Pace
Back:	7139	75.1	128	3:44	7060	74.7	131	3:55	6663	72.4	130	3:46
Middle:	6379	71.2	122		6422	71.8	126		6156	70.1	124	
Forward:			5609	72.1	124		5049			69.9	121	

Directions: I-77 to Exit 120 for S. Arlington St.; north on S. Arlington; left (west) on E. Warner Rd.; on left.

Description If you play the south course of parallel holes from the tips, you'll play 7,139 yards, par 70. Only one type of game plays well here: big and strong.

Harvey Penick used to say, "The woods are filled with long hitters." Here, long hitters can wind up in an adjacent fairway, which, while not the preferred method, is not always a bad place to be.

The signature hole is No. 16, a wonderful and dramatic 625-yard par 5. Sand is found on both sides of the fairway, which buttonhooks around water to get to the green.

This is a three-shotter if ever there was one. In 1979, Lon Hinkle intentionally skipped his ball across the water. He saved par—and he won the World Series of Golf by one stroke.

The North course, thought by many to be more difficult than South for its dramatic changes in elevation, leaning fairways, and "water, water, everywhere," is lots more fun. Middle and low handicaps will find themselves creating shots that they didn't know were in their bags.

Management at this storied course has generously seen fit to add a nine-hole course and allow the hoi polloi to play there. Generosity, thy name is Firestone!

PRIVATE

Glenmoor Country Club   ☎ (330) 966-3602

Area: **Farther South**   City: **Canton**   Difficulty: ● ● ●

Address: 4191 Glenmoor Rd., Canton   **Pro:** Bill Riley, PGA

Tees	Ydg.	C/r	S/r	Pace
Back:	7018	74.5	140	4:15
Middle:	6505	71.6	131	
Forward:	6008	69.6	123	

Directions: I-77 to Exit 109 for Everhard Rd./Whipple Ave.; west on Everhard; right (north) on Brunnerdale Ave.; left (west) on Glenmoor.

Description In the eighties, Jack Nicklaus created courses that no one could play and enjoy.

That era is history. Nicklaus courses are demanding, but not unplayable. Landing areas are large, and the fronts of many greens are open, allowing for bump-and-run shots. With four sets of tee boxes here, the course can play from 5,443 to 7,018 yards. The front nine is noticeably different from the back. The difference is trees. The arbor committee has its work cut out for it on the front nine, and the process of selecting and placing trees is well under way.

Hawthorne Valley Country Club   ☎ (440) 232-1400

Area: **Southeast**   City: **Solon**   Difficulty: ● ● ●

Address: 27840 Aurora Rd. (SR 43), Solon   **Pro:** Dave Pezacov, PGA

Tees	Ydg.	C/r	S/r	Pace
Back:	6340	71.1	133	3:51
Middle:	6102	69.9	131	
Forward:	5753	73.4	126	

Directions: I-271 to Exit 26 for Rockside Rd.; east on Rockside; right (south) on Aurora Rd. (SR 43); on right.

Description This is a hilly course, and two of the outstanding holes use elevation. No. 14 is a 207-yard par 3 that begins at an elevated tee—be ready for 23 wooden steps up to the tee box—and ends at an elevated green. No. 16 inspires awe. A drive of a couple hundred yards on this par 4 leaves an approach of a couple hundred more, as the fairway suddenly leans left and careens steeply to a green.

Kirtland Country Club

☎ (440) 942-4400; (440) 951-8422

Area: **East**   City: **Willoughby**   Difficulty: ●●●

Address: 39438 Kirtland Rd., Willoughby   **Pro:** Tim Bennett

Tees	Ydg.	C/r	S/r	Pace
Back:	6842	73.6	135	3:58
Middle:	6437	71.7	130	
Forward:	6006	69.5	123	

Directions: I-90 to Exit 193 for SR 306; south on SR 306 for ½ mile; right (west) on Kirtland Rd.; on left.

Description The two most difficult consecutive holes in the area are to be found in the Chagrin River Valley, on the back nine of this magnificent course. No. 10 is a par 3 of 225 yards and no. 11 is a par 4 of 440 yards. Uphill. To a double-tiered green. If a great golf hole has to be difficult as well as beautiful, the back nine here easily has more examples— seven, at my count—than any club around. It is the site of the U.S. Open sectional qualifier. From the back tees, the slope is 135 and the course rating a stern 73.6, so don't look for red numbers.

Lake Forest Country Club

☎ (330) 656-3804

Area: **Far South**   City: **Hudson**   Difficulty: ●●●

Address: 100 Lake Forest Dr., Hudson   **Pro:** John Goodson, PGA

Tees	Ydg.	C/r	S/r	Pace
Back:	6736	72.9	129	4:02
Middle:	6337	71.1	125	
Forward:	5709	72.8	126	

Directions: I-271 to Exit 18 for SR 8; south on SR 8; left (east) on Boston Mills Rd.; left (north) on Lake Forest Dr. to dead end.

Description The magnificent clubhouse here was designed by H. O. Fullerton, who cut his design teeth on the Van Sweringen mansion in Shaker Heights. The course was designed by Herbert Strong, the maestro behind Canterbury Golf Club in Shaker Heights.

The club's first pro, Densmore Shute, teamed up with Walter Hagan to challenge Tommy Armour and Horton Smith three days before the course's opening in 1930. At the time, Lake Forest, at 6,890 yards, was the longest course in Ohio.

The foursome arrived by Goodyear blimp on the spectator-lined first hole (now the driving range). Shute and Hagan made short work of their opponents, winning by five strokes. Shute went on to win two

PGAs and the 1933 British Open.

Guests should speak in reverential tones here; the course is purely wonderful. No. 10 is the most striking tee in the area. And No. 14 is a great par 5: 500 yards over two creeks while descending a narrow fairway, with an approach to a two-tiered green.

Lakewood Country Club   ☎ (440) 871-5338
Area: **West**   City: **Westlake**   Difficulty: ●●●

Address: 2613 Bradley Rd., Westlake   **Pro:** Tom Waitrovich, PGA

Tees	Ydg.	C/r	S/r	Pace
Back:	6800	72.9	136	4:00
Middle:	6357	70.9	131	
Forward:	5966	74.4	133	

Directions: I-90 to Exit 156 for Crocker Rd./Bassett Rd.; left (south) on Crocker; right (west) on SR 254 (Detroit Rd.); left (south) on Bradley Rd.; on left.

Description   After all these years, this course remains a challenge.

The 1921 design was done by A. W. Tillinghast, whose other golf treasures include Winged Foot Country Club and Baltusrol Country Club in New York and Baltusrol Golf Club in New Jersey.

Nothing's unfair about the layout, but its route through woods and over water definitely makes it a course for better players.

PRIVATE

Legend Lake Golf Club   ☎ (440) 285-3110
Area: **Far East**   City: **Chardon**   Difficulty: ●●◐

Address: 11135 Auburn Rd., Chardon   **Pro:** Reece Alexander

Tees	Ydg.	C/r	S/r	Pace
Back:	6568	71.0	123	3:47
Middle:	6322	69.7	120	
Forward:	5570	71.5	119	

Directions: I-271 to Exit 34 for US 322 (Mayfield Rd.); east on US 322, past SR 306; left (north) on Auburn Rd. for 2 miles; on left.

Description   Six days out of seven, this Chardon club fulfills its mission: "We help golfers golf." The club is short on pretense and expense, high on course maintenance and promotion of the game.

Madison Country Club

☎ (440) 953-1964

Area: **Far East**   City: **Madison**   Difficulty: ●●●

Address: 6131 Chapel Rd., Madison   **Pro:** Tom Fussaro

Tees	Ydg.	C/r	S/r	Pace
Back:	6458	71.1	127	3:47
Middle:	6145	69.7	124	
Forward:	5288	70.0	116	

Directions: I-90 to Exit 212 for SR 528; north on SR 528 past US 20; left (west) on Chapel Rd.; on left.

Description This was not always Madison Country Club. It began in 1923 as Madison Golf Lakelands, a summer retreat for Pennsylvania families from Pittsburgh and Sharon. When a home was purchased, club membership went along with the deal. Designer Grange Alves laid this course out on rolling terrain. Nearby Lake Erie provides scenery—and warmth. Thanks to the warm lake, the playing season often goes until Thanksgiving. Woods are minimal; sand is substantial. While golf is the club's mainstay, the family is the force behind the activities here, which include swimming, tennis, and excellent dining.

Mayfield Country Club

☎ (216) 382-3958

Area: **East**   City: **South Euclid**   Difficulty: ●●●

Address: 1545 Sheridan Rd., South Euclid   **Pro:** Charlie Wood, PGA

Tees	Ydg.	C/r	S/r	Pace
Back:	6631	73.0	133	3:57
Middle:	6308	71.4	131	
Forward:	5745	73.8	134	

Directions: I-271 to Exit 32 for Cedar Rd.; west on Cedar; right (north) on Richmond Rd.; left (west) on Mayfield Rd.; left (south) on Sheridan Rd.; on left.

Description Want to create a mood for your game? At Mayfield, the historic club tucked away in South Euclid, you can begin by having a cup of coffee with Charlie Wood, the club's longtime pro.

This shotmaker's course was designed by Bertie Way, an Englishman by way of Scotland. There have been a few changes since the dedication round in 1911, but nothing major. Mr. Way, incidentally, also did the original layout at Firestone South as well as the Detroit Country Club.

PRIVATE

Medina Country Club

☎ (330) 725-6621

Area: **Southwest**   City: **Medina**   Difficulty: ●●●

Address: 5588 Wedgewood Rd., Medina   **Pro:** Scott Schreck, PGA

Tees	Blue-Green Ydg.	C/r	S/r	Pace	Blue-Red Ydg.	C/r	S/r	Pace	Green-Red Ydg.	C/r	S/r	Pace
Back:	6935	74.3	134	4:04	6365	70.2	122	3:45	6215	69.5	121	3:49
Middle:	6506	71.7	131		5985	68.3	117		5980	68.4	119	
Forward:	5155	69.1	111		5120	68.9	115		5025	68.2	118	

Directions: I-71 to Exit 218 for SR 18; west on SR 18 to Medina; left (south) on Wooster Pike (SR 3); right (west) on Wedgewood; on left.

Description Nothing wrong with sticking the ol' howitzer in your bag before setting off for this rangy layout of three nines: Blue, Green, and Red. The Red nine was the original when the club started about 30 years ago. Today, tournaments are played on the Blue and Green nines— including the U.S. Open Qualifier, the Women's State Amateur, and the Ohio Senior Open. One of the rare courses to have a graveyard on the premises.

Oakwood Club

☎ (216) 291-0679

Area: **East**   City: **Cleveland Hts.**   Difficulty: ●●●

PRIVATE

Address: 1516 Warrensville Center Rd., Cleveland Hts.   **Pro:** Wink McLaughlan, PGA

Tees	Ydg.	C/r	S/r	Pace
Back:	6709	73.3	128	3:49
Middle:	6289	71.5	125	
Forward:	5609	71.7	122	

Directions: I-271 to Exit 34 for Cedar Rd.; west on Cedar; right (north) on Warrensville Center Rd.; on left.

Description This classic plays long for women players, and it's no pushover for the guys, either. The Donald Ross design has plenty of hazards, but if golfers are playing well, they won't notice most of them.

The last three holes are Oakwood's version of Amen Corner: the approach on the par 4 No. 16 carries water just in front of the green, the par 3 No. 17 has no bail-out opportunities, and No. 18 plays according to the wind. Pro Wink McLaughlan hits a driver, then a 4-iron if the wind is in his face. It's a driver, then a wedge if the wind is behind him.

The Oakwood Club has a big bonus at the end: it boasts one of the area's best kitchens.

Oberlin Golf Club ☎ (440) 774-1891

Area: **Far West**   City: **Oberlin**   Difficulty: ●●●

Address: 200 Pyle Rd., Oberlin   **Pro:** Cliff Pratello

Tees	Ydg.	C/r	S/r	Pace
Back:	6436	71.0	124	3:45
Middle:	6116	70.0	122	
Forward:	5390	66.5	116	

Directions: SR 2 to exit for SR 58; south on SR 58 for 8 miles; right (west) on Morgan St.; left (west) on Pyle Rd.; on right.
OR, I-480 to Exit 1A for SR 10 west (I-480 ends here); west on SR 10 (merges with US 20) to SR 511; west on SR 511; left (south) on SR 58; right (west) on Morgan St.; left (west) on Pyle Rd.; on right.

Description No debutante balls here. No social memberships, either. Oberlin may be a golf club, but it's a modest one. Modesty notwithstanding, the club has lots of very good players. In the Northern Ohio Golf Association's directory, Oberlin players were winners in the following categories: stroke play, best ball match play, two-man scramble, and interclub match play.

Is it experience? Could be. The club was formed in 1899.

On the front side, two holes stand out. No. 2 is a great par 4 that begins from an elevated tee. The landing area is framed by a pair of sand traps, and the fairway rises to the green. No. 8, a par 3 that sounds puny at 151 yards, is an elevated tee to an elevated green; wind is a major influence on club selection. On the back, No. 11 is an old-fashioned, gorgeous par 4 of 405 yards with a demanding green.

Pepper Pike Country Club ☎ (216) 831-9400

Area: **East**   City: **Pepper Pike**   Difficulty: ●●●

Address: 2800 SOM Center Rd., Pepper Pike   **Pro:** Carlo Alaqua

Tees	Ydg.	C/r	S/r	Pace
Back:	6658	72.0	129	3:47
Middle:	6261	70.0	125	
Forward:	5555	71.9	120	

Directions: I-271 to Exit 29 for SR 87 (Chagrin Blvd.); east on Chagrin; north on SOM Center Rd. (SR 91); on left.

Description Ah, Pepper! Last bastion for WASP culture. This would be an ideal club to place in the Smithsonian, reflecting, as it does, the old private club culture. Ver-r-r-r-y exclusive. A backstage pass to a Stones concert is an easier ticket than a membership here.

PRIVATE

While the membership is studded with Northeast Ohio's corporate leaders, the membership doesn't care much for golf. Every season Pepper holds the dubious distinction of fewest rounds played.

It is not a long course, but very demanding. Players failing to pay attention to alignment find their scores ballooning. That includes approaches as well as tee shots; many second and third shots must be made from less-than-level lies.

No. 17 is a short par 4, only 338 yards, but it is a dogleg right and plays uphill, which likely adds 40 or 50 yards to club selection. The greens slope from rear to front and are kept at medium speed. If they were to be cut and rolled, the Stimpmeter could go to double digits.

Conditioning here is best described as magnificent. The fairways are so lush, some roll is lost. When he left Cleveland for Baltimore, Art Modell left his clubs here.

Portage Country Club   ☎ (330) 836-8565
Area: **Far South**   City: **Akron**   Difficulty: ●●●

Address: 240 N. Portage Path, Akron   **Pro:** Rod Johnston, Master PGA

Tees	Ydg.	C/r	S/r	Pace
Back:	6246	70.5	127	4:00
Middle:	6083	69.7	125	
Forward:	5873	72.4	124	

Directions: I-77 southbound to Exit 138 for Ghent Rd.; right (east) on Ghent Rd.; left (east) on W. Market (SR 18); left (east) on Twin Oaks Rd.; left (north) on N. Portage Path; on left. OR, I-77 northbound to Exit 132 (White Pond Dr.); right (north) on White Pond; right (east) on Frank Blvd.; right (south) on W. Market St. (SR 18); left (east) on Twin Oaks Rd.; left (north) on N. Portage Path; on left.

PRIVATE

Description No secrets on this old and revered course. Get a good night's rest before the match, a good breakfast before teeing it up, and swing easy. Plenty of players, amateurs as well as professionals, have drooled when looking at the yardage figures here, imagining a record round in the near future. Wrong. While getting from tee to green is not difficult, getting into the cup is. The greens are as old as the course: 100 years. They are "the claim to fame here . . . very old and very fast," says head golf pro Rod Johnston. "The greens are small, too. And with 78 bunkers, it's a shotmaker's dream."

Quail Hollow Resort & Country Club   ☎ (440) 350-3500

Area: **Far East**   City: **Painesville**   Difficulty: ●●●

Address: 11080 Concord Hambden Rd., Painesville   **Pro:** Danny Ackerman

Tees	Devlin/Von Hogge				Weiskopf/Morris			
	Ydg.	C/r	S/r	Pace	Ydg.	C/r	S/r	Pace
Back:	6712	72.2	130	4:10	6872	73.9	130	4:20
Middle:	6357	70.6	126		6408	71.4	125	
Forward:	4389	65.7	107		5166	70.0	117	

Directions: I-90 to Exit 200 for SR 44; south on SR 44 to Auburn Rd.; left on Auburn Rd.; right (east) on Concord Hambden Rd.; on right.

Description There are only a few ways to get to play this Bruce Devlin/Robert Von Hogge course: be a member of the club, a guest at the resort, or part of an outing. There is no shortage of qualified players: about 27,000 rounds are played annually between April and October. Regardless of mode of entry, playing here can be memorable.

The terrain pitches and rolls on occasion, and the designers took advantage of that. The course is lined with hardwoods, and during spring and autumn the views and scenery can be breathtaking. Instead of the plain ol' white stake at the 150-yard mark, Quail Hollow uses six yardage markers, from 225 yards down to 100.

The greens are kept in tabletop condition because of the many important tournaments played here: the U.S. Amateur Qualifier, the Ohio Open Championship, the World Championship of Blind Golf, and a slew of Ben Hogan and Nike opens.

The scorecard has two features not seen elsewhere. The first is the Stableford scoring system, best used for outings, and the second is pace measurement. By the time the players leave the first tee, only 15 minutes should have passed. Leaving the No. 6 green, the time spent playing should not exceed 1 hour 24 minutes. By maintaining the pace, players finish a round in 4 hours 9 minutes.

The new course, the result of the design skills of Tom Weiskopf (the rudest player on the Senior Tour) and Jay Morrish, is open and winning rave reviews. It should. After Weiskopf's boorish behavior at the U.S. Senior Open at Canterbury GC, it's difficult to remember that the Tour's worst crybaby is one heck of a designer, too. A former pro at the club, speaking of the decision to hire Weiskopf, said, "We were interested in finding the top designer, one who could take the resort to a higher level in the golf world and one to match up the new course to the course we already have." They found the designer they sought. The new Weiskopf-Morrish layout is powerful, very challenging, beautiful, and playable. Carved from stands of mature hardwoods, the course has a classic air to it and no shortage of surprises, including the well-planned use of marshland in the fairway.

PRIVATE

When Weiskopf was in town to lead reporters, investors, and club members around his latest, he said three elements were necessary for a great course design: water, changes in elevation, and trees. At Quail, he got all three and used them well. Of his latest creation, the winner of the British Open and U.S. Senior Open said, "It's not a long-ball hitters' course at all. In fact, it's just the opposite. It's a finesse course. I would truly regard execution and accuracy from the tee to be more important than length. You'll find a lot of pitching and chipping options around the green."

While there is little to fault hitting it long, accuracy is more important than length here. The fairways are sometimes generous, sometimes more demanding, but putting a ball in the woods here is always costly. The greens are medium fast and as time marches on will become delightfully frustrating. The course doesn't return at the turn, but club girls in carts keep players stocked with refreshments.

It is an old-fashioned course. And it is a powerful course. No sleeping at the wheel here. Weiskopf said some of his major design influences were the great private layouts in Northeast Ohio, such as The Country Club and Canterbury Golf Club. The greatest compliment, he said, is to hear his designs called classic. That's what he seeks to build: great courses with all the virtues and none of the gimmicks.

Rosemont Country Club   ☎ (330) 666-1121
Area: **Far South**   City: **Akron**   Difficulty: ●●◐

PRIVATE

Address: 3730 W. Market St., Akron   **Pro:** Kurt Ewing, PGA

Tees	Ydg.	C/r	S/r	Pace
Back:	6327	71.8	124	
Middle:	5932	68.8	118	
Forward:	5100	70.3	119	

Directions: I-77 to Exit 137 for SR 18; east on SR 18 (becomes W. Market St.); on right.

Description For a match at Rosemont, leave the driver in the trunk. And practice, practice, practice those iron shots. This is a layout for players confident in their short-game skills. The only par 5 longer than 500 yards is the home hole, and that 523-yarder is the number 8 handicap hole. On the front side, both par 3s measure only 132 yards from the member tees, and the number one handicap is No. 2, a wonderful and classic dogleg to the left of 388 yards.

Rustic Hills Golf Club ☎ (330) 725-4281

Area: **Southwest**   City: **Medina**   Difficulty: ●●●

Address: 5399 River Styx Rd., Medina   **Pro:**

Tees	Ydg.	C/r	S/r	Pace
Back:	1943	62.5		
Middle:	1778	58.9	91	
Forward:	1599	62.5	98	

Directions: I-71 to Exit 218 for SR 18; west on SR 18; left (south) on River Styx Rd.; on left.

Description What an unusual private club: only nine holes. This layout, put together in the 1960s, is a step above executive length, with four par 3s and five par 4s. Players go around twice, using different tee markers the second time around. No. 7, which often plays about 265 yards, tempts big hitters; the green is surrounded by three ponds, however, so danger lurks. There is a swimming pool, tennis courts, and a large practice green, but no range. The strength of this course is in the greens, which are small, crowned, and fast. Former Ohio Amateur champ Glen Apple is one of about 250 members here. Instead of a pro, club policy has been to hire an aspiring PGA member. Some of these college kids have gone on to positions at Westfield Country Club and Barrington, among others.

Sand Ridge Golf Club ☎ 440-285-8088

Area: **Far East**   City: **Chardon**   Difficulty:

Address: 12150 Mayfield Rd., Chardon   **Pro:** David Scull

Tees	Ydg.	C/r	S/r	Pace
Back:	7088	75.2	138	
Middle:	6502	72.1	133	
Forward:	5078	64.6	112	

Directions: I-271 to US 322 (Mayfield Rd.); east on US 322 past Bass Lake Rd.; on left.

Description Sand Ridge is the result of the stars being perfectly aligned: a vision and the leadership to carry out the vision; a market anxious for just such a venture and willing to pay for it; a big and rangy piece of property natural for golf; and a designer with the time and energy to take on this project.

The place is pure golf. No debutante balls (no ballroom), no tennis or swimming lessons, no outings. No houses lining fairways. Instead, it offers (and encourages the use of) caddies, and the course itself—

Outings: Why You Shouldn't Have One

Let me give you a half dozen reasons why you shouldn't sponsor a golf outing this year.

First, you tie up a course I might want to play. Not just tie it up, but tie it up with morons, half-wits, episodic alcoholics, and poseurs, all of whom would be better entertained on half-price day at Edgewater Park, where they can bob with the chunks of floating fecal matter.

Second, your guests (?) are half in the bag for the ride home. It's difficult enough navigating through the hordes of SUVs, piloted by intensely sincere suburban mothers who need those things like Euclid Avenue needs trolleys. Adding drunks with clubs in the back seat is a recipe for trouble.

Third, do you think you're doing someone a favor? Good golfers don't want to be there, dodging errant tee shots from those mentioned in the second paragraph, or listening at the bar to some sun-scorched hacker brag about almost winning the Long Drive contest. The bad golfers don't want to be here, either. How much pleasure do you think they take in whiffing the ball in front of their colleagues? Or taking four putts to sink a three-foot putt? If they wanted to look stupid, they could pay full price to go to a Cavs game.

Fourth, if this is a way to raise money, I have two or three other, better ideas that don't call for a committee. (Armed robbery springs to mind almost instantly.) No one ever wants to figure out just what an outing costs, but to the golf and carts and liquor and prizes, add the hours and hours of assembling lists of every sort, negotiating with club personnel, creating and mailing the invitations, and then RSVPing the whole mess. I don't care what your bill is, I bet it really cost you three times as much and did about as much good as the Blizzard of '77.

Fifth, golf wasn't designed for mobs. Lynching, voting, and St. Patrick's Day were designed for mobs. Golf was designed to be played alone or with another golfer. Four players at the most.

Sixth, there's no good reason for it. Don't tell me you're having this outing because everyone else has an outing. If everyone else jumped off the Detroit Superior Bridge, I suppose you would, too?

You want to be good to the help? Keep 'em working.

—JHT

designed by Tom Fazio and spread over 380 acres of Geauga County maple forests so naturally and powerfully beautiful that the emotional dimension of golf is drawn out.

Shaker Heights Country Club
☎ (216) 991-3324

Area: **East**   City: **Shaker Hts.**   Difficulty: ●●●

Address: 3300 Courtland Blvd., Shaker Hts.   **Pro:** Joe Haase, PGA

Tees	Ydg.	C/r	S/r	Pace
Back:	6532	72.6	135	3:50
Middle:	6265	71.4	133	
Forward:	5814	74.3	132	

Directions: I-271 to Exit 29 for Chagrin Blvd.; west on Chagrin; right (north) on Warrensville Center Rd.; left (west) on S. Woodland Rd.; left (south) on Courtland Blvd.

Description   It is not unusual for Joe Haase, PGA, to get calls from across the country. "There are players out there who want to play all the Donald Ross courses," the pro explains. Shaker is the Donald Ross course built before World War I as part of the Van Sweringen brothers' development of Shaker Heights. Mr. Ross, the estimable and influential Scotsman, built courses with designs which place a premium on accurate iron play and putting. As it was in 1914, so it is today. Construction costs, however, have risen somewhat in the intervening years; the total bill to build Shaker was $59,233.45. A restoration by architect Brit Stenson took place in 1997.

From the members' tees, the course measures 6,265 yards, but that doesn't mean it plays short. The par 3s and par 5s are short, and the par 4s are long. Even the low handicappers keep the club cover off the driver. Good bunker play here can be worth a stroke or two, and putting, of course, is vital—particularly on No. 5 and No. 7. No. 10 remains Ross's way of telling us a short par 4 can be tough. Only 252 yards, it calls for a mid-iron and a wedge to a steeply elevated green. Easier to bogey than it looks.

The greens on Nos. 11, 16, and 17 on the back side are the holes the club brags about.

A couple of seasons ago, neurosurgeon Yoshiro Takaoka tested the wind, drew his 5 wood at the elevated 11th tee, and knocked the ball in the hole. The card says the par 3 measures 154 yards, though with pin placement and swirling winds, club selection is a matter of two parts judgment and one part luck.

Sharon Golf Club   ☎ (440) 273-2383

Area: **Far South**   City: **Sharon Center**   Difficulty: ●●●

Address: SR 94, Sharon Center   **Pro:** Dwight Axtell

Tees	Ydg.	C/r	S/r	Pace
Back:	7153	74.0	132	3:57
Middle:	6812	72.5	129	
Forward:	5933	68.8	122	

Directions: I-71 to Exit 218 for SR 18; east on SR 18; right (south) on SR 94 (N. Ridge Rd.); on left.

Description   Sharon Golf Club is private in the truest sense of the word. It seeks no publicity; it doesn't advertise. One member has called it "the best club in the country for casual golf." Built in 1964 and designed by George Cobb of Greenville, South Carolina, it opened in 1966 and was a qualifying site for the U.S. Open. It was here that Arnold Palmer once missed the cut. It is a powerful course with four sets of tees. The longest measures 7,153 yards, par 72 with a course rating of 74 and a slope rating of 132. The next longest route is 6,812 yards, course rating 72.5 and slope of 129. As one member of the management team said, "The strength is that Sharon is strictly a golf club, which affords easy access to members at all times." The number of events here is limited.

Silver Lake Country Club   ☎ (330) 688-6016

Area: **Far South**   City: **Cuyahoga Falls**   Difficulty: ●●●

Address: 1325 Graham Rd., Cuyahoga Falls   **Pro:** Tom Atchison, PGA

Tees	Ydg.	C/r	S/r	Pace
Back:	6646	71.8	128	4:10
Middle:	6344	70.5	125	
Forward:	5483	71.5	118	

Directions: I-271 to Exit 18 for SR 8; south on SR 8; exit at Graham Rd. in Cuyahoga Falls; left (east) on Graham Rd.; on left.

Description   The cover shot on the new scorecard is No. 17, a short par 3 of only 126 yards. What it lacks in length it makes up in glamour, running as it does slightly downhill to a small green nestled among dogwood, azalea, rhododendron, and huge oak trees.

Each hole on this young course (1959) sets up well from the tee. There are no blind shots, and the terrain rolls gently. The greens are big and fast, and the conditioning is excellent. (Grass clippings, for example, are picked up from the fairway). The signature hole on the front side

PRIVATE

is No. 6, a downhill par 3 of 189 yards with water behind green. While waiting for players in front to putt out, golfers can survey most of the course from the tee, the highest point on the course.

Spring Valley Country Club   ☎ (440) 365-1411
Area: **Far West**   City: **Elyria**   Difficulty:

Address: 1100 Gulf Rd., Elyria   **Pro:** Michael Caronchi, PGA

Tees	Ydg.	C/r	S/r	Pace
Back:	6166	69.9	124	4:00
Middle:	6006	69.1	123	
Forward:	5553	71.8	118	

Directions: I-90 to Exit 148 for SR 254 (Detroit Rd.); west on SR 254; left (south) on Gulf Rd. for 3 miles; on right.

Description   Few clubs have clubhouses as imposing as this. If a maharajah were being carried down the front steps, the procession would not look out of place. The head pro here is Mike Caronchi, PGA, and it's rare to find a pro more proud of his course. This is a short and tight layout that can be exhilarating or frustrating; hitting the landing area from the tee is vital. Holes 4, 11, and 17 have recently been redone.

Tanglewood Country Club   ☎ (440) 543-3191
Area: **Southeast**   City: **Chagrin Falls**   Difficulty: ●●●

Address: 8745 Tanglewood Trail, Chagrin Falls   **Pro:** Jubal Jerik

Tees	Ydg.	C/r	S/r	Pace
Back:	7029	75.8	144	3:51
Middle:	6313	72.4	137	
Forward:	5320	72.6	125	

Directions: I-271 to Exit 27 for US 422; east on US 422; north on SR 306 (Chillicothe Rd.); right (east) on Tanglewood Trail; on right.

Description   Of this young (1967) Chagrin Falls layout, Fuzzy Zoeller once said, "Let the rough grow and you could play the Open there." Water is a factor on only a few holes, but No. 1, the 520-yard (blue tee) par 5, is one of them. From the elevated tee, a drive must be long and accurate. Fading too much will find a lake on the right, and hooking even slightly will mean no shot to the green. The hole bends left less than 100 yards out and crosses a stream before running up to an elevated green. Nothing wrong with an opening par, so a driver–short iron (to the water) approach is a good plan.

This hilly course has a wealth of beautiful tees, and No. 8 is one of them. The fairway on this 457-yard par 4 runs down a steep hill to a stream. The shallow green has sand in front, and pin position can make for big trouble. It looks shorter and easier than it is; it's the number one handicap. On a course with a slope of 144 and a course rating of 75.0, you know you'll be facing a challenge. Likely you're getting a stroke here anyhow, so approach with caution.

On the back side, Nos. 16 and 17 are testers. Most players would score better on No. 16, the 238-yard par 3, by laying up. A severely canted fairway and trees down both sides make it hazardous. No. 17, another elevated tee, is a big dogleg right. Few players can cut the corner, filled as it is with tall hardwoods, so the player who wants to be in the money goes down the middle or just a bit left of the tee.

Twin Lakes Country Club   ☎ (330) 673-6665
Area: **Far South**   City: **Kent**   Difficulty: ●●●

Address: 1519 Overlook Rd., Kent   **Pro:** Tony Guerreri

Tees	Ydg.	C/r	S/r	Pace
Middle:		70.9	125	
Forward:		73.2	124	

Directions: I-480 to SR 14 east in Streetsboro (I-480 ends here); right (south) on SR 43 (Cleveland-Canton Rd.); left (east) on Overlook Rd.; on right.

Description An invitation to this club means mystery, mystery, mystery! The assistant manager refuses to talk about the club or the course, and swears she can't find a scorecard. That's club life in a college town.

Walden Golf & Tennis Club   ☎ (330) 562-7145
Area: **Southeast**   City: **Aurora**   Difficulty: ●●●

Address: 700 Bissell Rd., Aurora   **Pro:** Mitch Camp, PGA

Tees	Ydg.	C/r	S/r	Pace
Back:	6979	74.4	134	3:59
Middle:	6358	71.2	130	
Forward:	5609	72.4	125	

Directions: I-480 to Exit 36 for SR 82; east on SR 82; right (south) on Bissell Rd.; on right.

Description When he arrived here after a half dozen years as an assistant pro at Fairlawn Country Club in Akron, Mitch Camp thought that the pace would be slower. After all, the bag storage room holds only 100; at

PRIVATE

Fairlawn, 600 were lined up. Walden is a residential community; Fairlawn was a golf club.

Camp was wrong. The pace of play is different from Fairlawn's, but it is relentless. "Play goes on all the time because it's a residential community," he says. "It's peaceful here and that's by design. Members can walk and carry their clubs if they prefer, and more than 200 members have their own golf carts."

The first nine was built in 1969. Today it is the back nine, and the tighter of the two. Back then, the clubhouse was in a barn. Today, The Barn is a gourmet restaurant behind the 11th green. Some nongolfing residents of Walden maintain memberships in this private dining room. The second nine was added in 1973, along with one of the most comfortable and stylish clubhouses in the area.

The U.S. Open qualifier has been held here, and for two years in a row the Northern Ohio PGA assistant pro championship was held here as well. "Both times, par held up," Camp notes.

Westwood Country Club   ☎ (440) 331-3016
Area: West   City: Rocky River   Difficulty: ●●●

Address: 22625 Detroit Rd., Rocky River			Pro: John Sico, PGA

Tees	Ydg.	C/r	S/r	Pace
Back:	6626	73.1	131	3:53
Middle:	6349	71.5	128	
Forward:	5265	66.7	124	

Directions: I-90 westbound to Exit 160 for Clague Rd.; south on Clague; left (east) on Detroit Rd. (SR 254); on right.
OR, I-90 eastbound to Exit 161 for Detroit Rd.; right (west) on Detroit; on left.

Description Who better to advise guests at this West Side club than Gary Eckert, nine-time (and current) champion? The champ never tires of winning, though he says, "Sometimes I feel funny that people might think, 'Is that all he does? Play golf?'" Not at all. He's an accountant.

"Westwood is a fair golf course with no trouble," Eckert says. "Everyone I know who's played likes it. They think they can tear it up and then can't figure out why they don't score better."

It's not overly long, but it plays a bit longer than rookies think. The adrenaline pump doesn't start until the tee at No. 4. This 183-yard par 3 is moderately long, but it's merciless. "You have to carry the ravine, and if you're going to miss the green, miss on the right," the champ advises. The bottomless pit on the left means almost no shot.

Wooster Country Club

☎ (330) 263-1988

Area: **Farther South**   City: **Wooster**   Difficulty: ●●◉

Address: 1251 Oak Hill Rd., Wooster   **Pro:** Gary Welshhans

Tees	Ydg.	C/r	S/r	Pace
Back:	6466	71.8	125	4:02
Middle:	5704	68.6	119	
Forward:	5311	71.0	123	

Directions: I-71 to Exit 204 for SR 83; south on SR 83 (Burbank Rd.) to Wooster; right (west) on Milltown Rd.; left (south) on Oak Hill Rd.; on left.

Description   The back nine at Wooster is a memorable one, tripping and traipsing up and down and around hills, valleys, and old-growth forests. To play it well one has to play here often. The front nine, across the street from the clubhouse, is nice enough, but first-timers definitely will be surprised—and delighted—after the turn. The course serves not only the members, but also the local high-school team and the players from Wooster College.

Youngstown Country Club

☎ (330) 759-1133

Area: **Farther East**   City: **Youngstown**   Difficulty: ●●●

Address: 1402 Country Club Ln., Youngstown   **Pro:** William Cox

Tees	Ydg.	C/r	S/r	Pace
Back:	6577	71.6	126	3:49
Middle:	6350	70.7	124	
Forward:	5687	72.8	117	

Directions: Ohio Turnpike to Exit 15 for I-80 east; I-80 to Exit 234 for SR 7; south on SR 7; west on SR 304 to Logan Way/Wick Ave. extension; left (south) on Logan Way; on right.

PRIVATE

Description   Three tough holes on the back nine of this layout can make heroes of mortals: Nos. 10, 11, and 18. Ten is a 414-yard par 4 that plays to a very small green. A bunker waits on the left side. No. 11 is a longer par 4 (426 yards), just a straightaway test for big hitters. The home hole, a 444-yard par 4, is a downhill dogleg that plays into a bowl. The mounding around the back of the green looks like a TPC course. The green slopes from back to front, and greens are kept very fast here: 10.5 on the Stimpmeter.

Driving Ranges

Airport Greens Driving Range
Area: **East** City: **Willoughby Hills** ☎ **(440) 944-6164**

Address: 28980 White Rd., Willoughby Hills
Tees: 60 **Grass:** 60 **Lighted:** 60 **Covered:** 0
Prices: $4.00–$8.00
Season: Apr 1–Nov 30 **Hours:** 6 a.m.–10 p.m. **Practice facil:** Range, Putting Green, Chipping Green, Sand, Miniature golf **Clubhouse:** Food, Beer, Liquor, Pavilion
Lessons: Available
Directions: I-90 to Exit 187 for Ford Rd./Bishop Rd. in Willoughby Hills; south on Bishop Rd. left (east) on White Rd.; on right.

Azar's New Falls Pro Shop & Golf Range
Area: **Far South** City: **Cuyahoga Falls** ☎ **(330) 929-2573**

Address: 3873 Wyoga Lake Rd., Cuyahoga Falls
Tees: 70 **Grass:** 50 **Lighted:** 0 **Covered:** 12
Prices: $3.75–$14.00
Season: Mar–Sept **Hours:** 11 a.m.–7:30 p.m. **Practice facil:** Range, Chipping Green
Clubhouse: None **Lessons:** Available
Directions: I-271 to Exit 18 for SR 8; south on SR 8; west on Steels Corners Rd.; left (south) on Wyoga Lake Rd.; on left.   OR, SR 8 north to Steels Corners Rd.; west on Steels Corners; left (south) on Wyoga Lake Rd.; on left.

Benko's Driving Range
Area: **Far West** City: **Elyria** ☎ **(440) 458-4386**

Address: 10364 Middle Ave., Elyria
Tees: 20 **Grass:** 20 **Lighted:** 0 **Covered:** 0
Prices: $3.00–$7.00
Specials: Senior discount available
Season: Year-round **Hours:** 8:00 a.m.–dark **Practice facil:** Range, Putting Green, Chipping Green, Sand, Club repair available; authorized Ping fitting center. **Clubhouse:** None **Lessons:** Available
Directions: I-480 to Exit 1A for SR 10 (I-480 west ends here); west on SR 10 (merges with US 20) to exit for Lagrange Rd.; south on Lagrange; left (east) on Butternut Ridge Rd.; left (north) on Middle Ave.; on left after Elyria Airport.

Brookpark Golf Range

Area: **South**   City: **Parma**   ☎ **(216) 351-2239**

Address: 8701 Brookpark Rd., Parma
Tees: 60 **Grass:** 20 **Lighted:** 60 **Covered:** 6
Prices: $4.00–$5.00
Season: Year-round **Hours:** Sunrise–11 p.m.; call for winter hours **Practice facil:**
Range, Chipping Green, Miniature golf, 30-foot-high golf-ball target on range, Covered
tees are heated **Clubhouse:** Food, Beer, Dairy bar, Game room **Lessons:** Available
Directions: I-480 to Exit 15 for Ridge Rd. (SR 3); south on Ridge; right (west) on
Brookpark Rd.; ½ mile on left.

Buzzard Cove Driving Range

Area: **South**   City: **Hinckley**   ☎ **(330) 278-2384; (216) 831-6650 off season**

Address: 1053 Bellus Rd., Hinckley
Tees: 25 **Grass:** 0 **Lighted:** 25 **Covered:** 12
Prices: $4.00–$6.00
Season: Apr–Oct (weather permitting) **Hours:** 8 a.m.–7 p.m. spring; 8:30 a.m.–11
p.m. summer **Practice facil:** Putting Green, Targets on range, 5 elevated greens on
range: 60 yds, 100 yds, 130 yds, 160 yds, 200 yds, with sand traps, 36 hi-tech miniature
golf holes **Clubhouse:** Food **Lessons:** Available **Pro:** Tim Monroe
Directions: I-71 to Exit 226 for SR 303; east on SR 303; right (south) on Stony Hill Rd.;
left (east) on Bellus Rd.; at intersection of Bellus Rd. and Hinckley Hills Rd. (SR 606).

Decile's Driving Range

Area: **East**   City: **Highland Hills**   ☎ **(216) 464-9256**

Address: 4201 Green Rd., Highland Hills
Tees: 70 **Grass:** 35 **Lighted:** 0 **Covered:** 0
Prices: $4.00–$6.00
Season: Mar 12–Nov 15 **Hours:** 8:30 a.m.–10:00 p.m. **Practice facil:** Range, Putting
Green, Chipping Green, Sand **Clubhouse:** Pavilion, Miniature golf **Lessons:** Available
Pro: Bob Hamric
Directions: I-271 to Exit 29 for Chagrin Blvd./US 422; west on Chagrin; left (south) on
Green Rd.; on left.

Downview Sports Center

Area: **Far South**   City: **Cuyahoga Falls**   ☎ **(330) 971-8418**

Address: 1617 Bailey Rd., Cuyahoga Falls
Tees: 32 **Grass:** 25 **Lighted:** 15 **Covered:** 15
Prices: $3.00–$7.50
Specials: Seniors: $2.50–$3.75–$6.50
Season: Mar–Dec **Hours:** Memorial Day–Labor Day: 11 a.m.–11 p.m. Mon–Fri, 8
a.m.–11 p.m. Sat, Sun; Sep–Oct 10 a.m.–8 p.m.; Nov–Dec & Mar–May 11 a.m.–7 p.m.
Practice facil: Range, no grass tees (astroturf); 10 heated tees **Clubhouse:** Food,
Pavilion, (refreshments available) **Lessons:** Available **Pro:** Steve Black
Directions: I-271 to Exit 18 for SR 8; south on SR 8; left (east) on Howe Ave.; "soft" left
(north) on Bailey at six-point intersection; on right, after Kennedy Blvd.

RANGES

Firestone Driving Range
Area: **Far South**   City: **Akron**   ☎ **(330) 724-4444**

Address: 600 Swartz Rd., Akron
Tees: 30 **Grass:** 15 **Lighted:** 30 **Covered:** 10
Prices: $4.00–$8.00
Season: Year-round **Hours:** Summer: 7 a.m.–10 p.m.; winter: 10 a.m.–8 p.m. **Practice facil:** Putting Green **Clubhouse:** Food, Beer, Liquor, Dining room, Pavilion, 50-seat grill
Lessons: Available **Pro:** Rick Schmidt
Directions: I-277 to Exit 3 for S. Main St.; south on S. Main; east on Swartz Rd. (Swartz is directly opposite eastbound exit for S. Main); on right.

Forest Hills Golf Center
Area: **Far West**   City: **Elyria**   ☎ **(440) 323-2632**

Address: 41971 Oberlin Rd. (US 20), Elyria
Tees: 20 **Grass:** 20 **Lighted:** 0 **Covered:** 0
Prices: $4.00–$6.00
Season: Mar 14–Dec 30, weather permitting **Hours:** 7 a.m.–sunset **Practice facil:** Range, Putting Green, Chipping Green **Clubhouse:** Food, Beer, Liquor, Pavilion
Lessons: Available **Pro:** Thomas S. Porter, PGA
Directions: I-480 west to end; becomes SR 10; west on SR 10 (merges with US 20 and SR 301) to exit for Lagrange Rd.; right (north) on Lagrange; left (west) on Butternut Ridge Rd.; right (north) on Oberlin-Elyria Rd.; on right.

Golden Tee Golf Range
Area: **West**   City: **Olmsted Falls**   ☎ **(440) 235-9115**

Address: 27153 Bagley Rd., Olmsted Falls
Tees: 38 **Grass:** 29 **Lighted:** 38 **Covered:** 4
Prices: $3.00–$8.50
Specials: Seniors Mon–Fri open–4 p.m. $1.00 off
Season: Mar 1–Oct 31; Nov–Feb weather permitting **Hours:** Summer, 11 a.m.–10 p.m.; spring & fall, noon–dusk **Practice facil:** Range, Putting Green, Chipping Green, Sand, Target greens **Clubhouse:** None **Lessons:** Available **Pro:** Bob Reid
Directions: I-480 to Exit 3 for Stearns Rd.; south on Stearns to Bagley Rd.; on southwest corner at Stearns & Bagley.

RANGES

TIDYMAN'S TIDBITS #18
Most likely courses for losing balls:
• Thunder Hill
• Berkshire Hills
• The back nine at Brunswick Hills
• The Pine Valley nine at Emerald Woods

Golf Dome

Area: **Southeast**   City: **Chagrin Falls**   ☎ **(440) 543-1211**

Address: P.O. Box 23236, Chagrin Falls
Tees: 34 **Grass:** 0 **Lighted:** 34 **Covered:** 34
Prices: Mon–Fri $7.00 per ½ hour; Sat–Sun & "prime time" $8.00 per ½ hour
Specials: Juniors (18 and under) Mon–Fri $5.75 per ½ hour; Seniors 8:30 a.m.–5 p.m.
Mon–Fri $5.75 per ½ hour
Season: Year-round **Hours:** 8:30 a.m.–9:30 p.m.; Sat–Sun "prime time" 8:30 a.m.–9:30
p.m. **Practice facil:** Range, Putting Green, Chipping Green, Sand, Target Greens,
Distance Meters **Clubhouse:** Food, Vending machines **Lessons:** Available **Pro:** Jim
Chapman
Directions: I-271 to Exit 27 for US 422; east on US 422 to SR 306; left (north) on SR
306; left (west) on E. Washington St. for ½ mile; on right, behind Chagrin Cinemas.

Description There is no snack bar here, but just about everything else
golfers need to keep the ol' swing lubed is: clubs, balls, putters, gloves,
sweatshirts, wind shirts, towels ... and an indoor range of the first order.
For $15, your swing can be videotaped and analyzed by one of three
teaching professionals. In the middle of a long Northeast Ohio winter,
what better treat than to have a golf pro focus on your cut? The video
also uses a microwave measuring device that locks in on the spin, direc-
tion, and velocity, so you know what the ball would have done had it
plowed through the ceiling. Rates are charged by time, not buckets:
$6.50 per half hour, an extra buck on weekends. Seniors and juniors can
play for $5.25 per half hour, but only until 5 p.m. on weekdays. About 35
percent of the patrons are women. No membership fee, no reservations.

Golfer's Inn

Area: **South**   City: **Hinckley**   ☎ **(330) 225-9933**

Address: 1429 W. 130 St., Hinckley
Tees: 24 **Grass:** 12 **Lighted:** 0 **Covered:** 0
Prices: $3.00–$5.50
Season: Year-round **Hours:** Sunrise–sunset **Practice facil:** Range **Clubhouse:** Food,
Beer, Liquor, Volleyball, Horseshoes **Lessons:** Available **Pro:** Tim Monroe
Directions: I-71 to Exit 226 for SR 303; east on SR 303; right (south) on W. 130 St.; on
left.

Highlander Golf & Tennis

Area: **Far South**   City: **Akron**   ☎ **(330) 867-5664**

Address: 2782 Ridgewood Rd., Akron
Tees: 38 **Grass:** 20 **Lighted:** 38 **Covered:** 28
Prices: $4.00–$8.00
Season: Year-round **Hours:** Summer: 9 a.m.–10 p.m.; winter: 9 a.m.–6 p.m. **Practice
facil:** Range, 12 heated tees **Clubhouse:** None **Lessons:** Available **Pro:** Mike Bittner
Directions: I-77 to Exit 133 for Ridgewood/Miller Rds.; west on Ridgewood; on left.

RANGES

Hillcrest Golf Range
Area: **Far West**   City: **Avon**   ☎ **(440) 937-6622**

Address: 32575 Detroit Rd. (SR 254), Avon
Tees: 35 **Grass:** 20 **Lighted:** 0 **Covered:** 0
Prices: $2.50–$4.00
Specials: Mon–Fri 11 a.m.–1 p.m. $1.75–$2.50; Tue "Ladies Day" ½ price
Season: Mar–Oct **Hours:** 9:30 a.m.–sunset **Practice facil:** Putting Green, Chipping Green, Miniature golf **Clubhouse:** Food, Vending machines **Lessons:** Available **Pro:** Omar Jonas
Directions: I-90 to Exit 156 for Crocker-Bassett Rds.; south on Crocker; right (west) on Detroit Rd. (SR 254); on left.

Description Why they call this Hillcrest is not clear. No hills. But for practicing the swing, this old-fashioned range is one of the best. The small shack has a few clubs, a cash register, and a television set. Pro Omar Jones, old as dirt, is available for lessons as well as chewing the fat. No natural gas heaters, no covered tees. Mostly grass tees, and greenery all around. It's quiet. No distractions except songbirds. The best value on the West Side.

Hol-Hi Driving Range
Area: **Far South**   City: **Akron**   ☎ **(330) 644-9815**

Address: 81 Vaughn Rd., Akron
Tees: 27 **Grass:** 10 **Lighted:** 27 **Covered:** 0
Prices: $4.00–$5.00
Season: Mar–Dec **Hours:** 8 a.m.–9 p.m. **Practice facil:** Range, Putting Green, Chipping Green, Sand **Clubhouse:** Food, Beer, Dining room **Lessons:** Free group lesson with large bucket of balls **Pro:** Mike Kosar
Directions: I-77 to exit for I-277; I-277 to Exit 3 for S. Main St.; south on S. Main; right (west) on Vaughn Rd.; on right.

Indoor Links
Area: **East**   City: **Bedford Hts.**   ☎ **(440) 232-6600**

Address: 24748 Aurora Rd., Bedford Hts.
Tees: 6 **Grass:** 0 **Lighted:** 0 **Covered:** 0
Prices: $25.00 per hour
Specials: Senior discount Mon–Fri 8 a.m.–4 p.m.
Season: Year-round **Hours:** Daily 8 a.m.–midnight **Practice facil:** Range **Clubhouse:** Food, Beer, Liquor **Lessons:** Available **Pro:** Jim Jackson
Directions: I-271 to Rockside Rd. exit. Indoor Links is directly behind Red Roof Inn, located just off the exit.

Description In some ways, indoor golf is like bowling. The weather, for example, is not a factor. In neither game do players lose balls. Drinking beer between shots is nice. No sunburn.

Some purists look down on computer-generated fairways, but con-

RANGES

verts are made every season. If there is no real golf to be played, indoor golf provides a fascinating alternative.

Indoor Links Golf Club started life as Indoor Fairways in Warrensville Heights. It was sold it and moved in November 1997.

Lost Nation Sports Park
Area: **East**   City: **Willoughby**   ☎ **(440) 602-4000**

> **Address:** 38630 Jet Center Dr., Willoughby
> **Tees:** 7 **Grass:** 0 **Lighted:** 0 **Covered:** 0
> **Prices:** $28.00 per hour, $15.00 for 30 minutes
> **Specials:** Senior discount Mon–Fri 8 a.m.–4 p.m.: $18.00 / hour, $10.00 / 30 minutes
> **Season:** Year-round **Hours:** Daily 8 a.m.–midnight **Practice facil:** Range **Clubhouse:** Food, Beer, Liquor **Lessons:** Available **Pro:** Tom Kochensparger
> **Directions:** SR 2 to exit for Lost Nation Rd; north on Lost Nation; right (east) on Jet Ctr.

Mr. Divot's Driving Range
Area: **South**   City: **North Royalton**   ☎ **(440) 237-2226**

> **Address:** 13393 York Rd., North Royalton
> **Tees:** 50 **Grass:** 20 **Lighted:** 30 **Covered:** 8
> **Prices:** $4.00–$6.75
> **Specials:** Seniors $.50 off each bucket
> **Season:** Year-round **Hours:** 9 a.m.–11 p.m. in summer; varies with weather **Practice facil:** Range, 8 covered tees are heated; 18-hole miniature golf, 6 batting cages, bumper boats **Clubhouse:** Food, Beer, Liquor, Dining room, Patio **Lessons:** Available Corey Brayer
> **Directions:** I-71 to Exit 231 for SR 82 (Royalton Rd.); east on SR 82; left (north) on York Rd.; on right.

The Oaks
Area: **Southwest**   City: **Columbia Station**   ☎ **(440) 236-5060**

> **Address:** 24240 Royalton Rd. (SR 82), Columbia Station
> **Tees:** 80 **Grass:** 50 **Lighted:** 40 **Covered:** 24
> **Prices:** $4.50–$9.00
> **Specials:** Bucket and range passes available
> **Season:** Year-round **Hours:** Daily 10 a.m.–9 p.m. **Practice facil:** Range, Putting Green, Chipping Green, Sand, Custom club repair available; Lighted & heated tees **Clubhouse:** Food **Lessons:** Available **Pro:** Dave Moskal, PGA
> **Directions:** I-71 to Exit 231 for SR 82 (Royalton Rd.); west on SR 82; on right.

Description If the temperature is above 30 but still too cold to play, the heated stalls at this range are an acceptable compromise. In each stall is a map detailing the number of yards to the target flags. You can try every stick in the bag here. The quality of the range balls is notably high. Good pro shop, even if it's pricey.

RANGES

Pancake Creek Miniature Golf & Driving Range
Area: **Far South**   City: **Norton**   ☎ **(330) 825-3422**

> **Address:** 5337 S. Cleveland-Massillon Rd., Norton
> **Tees:** 40 **Grass:** 30 **Lighted:** 0 **Covered:** 10
> **Prices:** $3.00–$7.50
> **Season:** Mar–Oct **Hours:** 9:00 a.m.–sunset **Practice facil:** Range, 10 covered mats,
> 18-hole miniature golf **Clubhouse:** Club regripping **Lessons:** Available
> **Directions:** I-77 to Exit 135 for SR 21; south on SR 21 to Norton; left (east) on Eastern
> Rd.; left (north) on S. Cleveland-Massillon Rd.; on left.
> OR, I-76 to SR 21 south; follow directions above from SR 21.

Pine Valley Sports
Area: **Far South**   City: **Akron**   ☎ **(330) 928-2669**

> **Address:** 1870 Akron-Peninsula Rd., Akron
> **Tees:** 65 **Grass:** 40 **Lighted:** 65 **Covered:** 10
> **Prices:** $2.00–$6.00
> **Specials:** Seniors $1.75–$5.50
> **Season:** Mar–Dec **Hours:** 10 a.m.–5 p.m. winter; sunrise–10 p.m. summer **Practice
> facil:** Range, Putting Green, Chipping Green, Sand, Miniature golf course **Clubhouse:**
> Food, Beer **Lessons:** Available **Pro:** Brian Unk
> **Directions:** I-77 to Exit 138 for Ghent Rd.; west on Ghent; right (east) on Yellow Creek
> Rd. under I-77; right (east) on W. Bath Rd.; right (south) on Akron-Peninsula Rd.; on
> right.

The Practice Greens at Bobick's
Area: **East**   City: **Willoughby**   ☎ **(440) 942-4051**

> **Address:** 38882 Mentor Ave., Willoughby
> **Tees:** 80 **Grass:** 50 **Lighted:** 80 **Covered:** 30
> **Prices:** $4.00–$7.00
> **Season:** Year-round **Hours:** Summer: 9 a.m.–10 p.m.; winter: 9 a.m.–6 p.m. **Practice
> facil:** Range, Putting Green, Chipping Green, Sand, 30 heated tees **Clubhouse:** None
> **Lessons:** Available **Pro:** Joe Whelan
> **Directions:** I-90 to Exit 190 for SR 306; north on SR 306 to Mentor Ave. (US 20); left
> (west) on US 20 for ³/₄ mile; on left.

RANGES

Description The practice range at Bobick's Pro Shop in Willoughby goes where driving ranges have never before gone. On a series of grass tees, players look out to multiple greens, broad fairways, and swaying trees. It looks much more like a golf course than a range.

"I don't even like to call it a driving range, because that brings up the image of somebody just getting up there beating balls," owner George Brown says. Between the multiple tees are practice sand traps. Behind the tee boxes is a grove of tall trees. The trees serve as a buffer against highway noise. For people serious about their games, an annual membership fee of $500 allows unlimited practice on a restricted tee.

The facility was designed by Arthur Hills Associates and built by McCurach Construction—both Florida firms—but it was Brown's idea. He is delighted when equipment reps visit the store, inspect the range, and tell him "I've never seen anything like it."

In addition to the grass tees, Bobick's also has covered mats with natural-gas heaters for year-round practice. Brown has 180,000 golf balls in use there.

Pro Tour Indoor Golf

Area: **Southwest**   City: **Middleburg Hts.**   ☎ **(440) 243-5055**

> **Address:** 18330 Bagley Rd., Middleburg Hts.
> **Tees:** 20 **Grass:** 0 **Lighted:** 0 **Covered:** 0
> **Prices:** $14.00 per ½ hour, $28.00 per hour
> **Specials:** Seniors Day (Mon–Fri) 2-for-1 8 a.m.–2 p.m.; Gift certificates available
> **Season:** Year-round **Hours:** 8 a.m.–midnight **Practice facil:** Range, Putting Green
> **Clubhouse:** Food **Lessons:** Available
> **Directions:** I-71 to exit for Bagley Rd.; west on Bagley; ½ mile on right.

Description   Thanks to interactive golf, winter's icy grip no longer seems so cruel. Players, bags of clubs clutched to their chests, bow to the wind as they walk from the parking lot to this indoor club. Once inside, the weather becomes a non-issue.

There are six golf simulators at this new club, and 20 courses are available, among them Troon North, Banff, Harbour Town, Torrey Pines, and a fantasy course called Devil's Island.

It's a smoking facility. Who wants to go indoors and inhale cigarette smoke? The staff can be rude and the price is getting high—$28 per person per hour. The tee is not adjustable, so everyone has to hit from the same height and the same place. If you're a lefty, you have to pull up the carpet and insert the plastic tee for every tee shot. And remove it as soon as you're done before other players trip on it. The booths are too small to hit longer drivers in.

The Range at Avon

Area: **Far West**   City: **Avon**   ☎ **(440) 937-9464**

> **Address:** 1325 Center Rd. (SR 83), Avon
> **Tees:** 140 **Grass:** 100 **Lighted:** 140 **Covered:** 40
> **Prices:** $2.75–$6.75; prices increase by $1 during winter season
> **Specials:** Frequent player program available: up to 35% discount available for buying balls in advance; Lunch special: Mon–Fri (11 a.m.–3 p.m.) 80 balls for $2.75
> **Season:** Year-round **Hours:** Summer hours: daily 8 a.m.–10 p.m.; winter hours: daily 9 a.m.–9 p.m. **Practice facil:** Range, Putting Green, Chipping Green, Sand, Short game area, fully lit, with 3 bunkers and 4 greens **Clubhouse:** Food, Beer, Liquor, Dining room
> **Lessons:** Available **Pro:** Mark Weitendorf
> **Directions:** I-90 to Exit 153 for SR 83; north on SR 83 (Center Rd.); on right.

Description   There's nothing like family. The Range at Avon is the sister of the Range at Boston Hills, where heated stalls, grass tees, and target greens make practice almost as much fun as playing. At both ranges, top-of-the-line irons and woods are available for demo purposes, so if you always wondered if it's possible to buy a game, here's your chance to find out. The West Side facility offers more heated stalls: 40 compared to the East Side's 29. There are 100 grass tees. There is also a chipping green, putting green, and sand. Arriving for night practice is fun—from a distance, the lighted greens look like an alien landing.

The Range at Boston Hills Country Club
Area: **South**   City: **Hudson**   ☎ **(330) 463-7888**

> **Address:** 124 E. Hines Hill Rd., Hudson
> **Tees:** 100 **Grass:** 70 **Lighted:** 100 **Covered:** 30
> **Prices:** $4.00–$8.00
> **Specials:** Frequent-player program: up to 35% discount for buying balls in advance
> **Season:** Year-round; tees are individually heated in winter **Hours:** 7 a.m.–11 p.m. summer; 8 a.m.–9 p.m. winter **Practice facil:** Range, Putting Green, Chipping Green, Sand, Landscaped, laser-measured target greens; Tee markers to each target area; 30 heated tees **Clubhouse:** Food, Beer, Liquor, Dining room, Club repair **Lessons:** Available **Pro:** Ron Burke, PGA
> **Directions:** I-271 to Exit 18 for SR 8; south on SR 8; right (west) on E. Hines Hill Rd.; on right. OR, I-80 to exit 12, ¼ mile north, turn left at E. Hines Hill Rd.

Description Building a range has traditionally involved shooing the cows away, planting a few colored pennants, and tossing down some mats. As the golf market grows more sophisticated, however, that approach is being left behind. Way behind.

The new practice facility located next to Boston Hills Golf Course is special enough to qualify for proper noun status: The Range. The Range features more than 80 natural grass tees and 30 covered and heated tees. Five target greens lie before players. More than 400 laser measurements went into yardage compilations (yardage is measured to each target and is listed at the tees).

One of many inspirations is the replica of the infamous No. 17 at Sawgrass, the island hole that frustrates Tour players.

The practice greens—there are two totaling 13,000 square feet—can be more difficult than the greens on the nearby course.

Shawnee Hills Driving Range
Area: **South**   City: **Bedford**   ☎ **(440) 232-7184**

> **Address:** 18753 Egbert Rd., Bedford
> **Tees:** 29 **Grass:** 0 **Lighted:** 29 **Covered:** 0
> **Prices:** $2.00 for 34 balls; $5.00 for 68 balls
> **Specials:** Special deals for groups; contact manager
> **Season:** Apr 1–Mid-Nov **Hours:** Sunrise–10 p.m.; Autumn, sunrise–sunset **Practice facil:** Range, Putting Green, Chipping Green **Clubhouse:** Food, Beer, Club repair
> **Lessons:** Available **Pro:** Jeff Staker
> **Directions:** I-77 to Exit 153 for Pleasant Valley Pkwy.; east on Pleasant Valley (becomes Alexander Rd.); left (north) on Dunham Rd; right (east) on Egbert Rd.; on left.

RANGES

Silver Tee Driving Range
Area: **West**   City: **Westlake**   ☎ **(440) 871-9225**

Address: 29300 Center Ridge Rd., Westlake
Tees: 70 **Grass:** 30 **Lighted:** 70 **Covered:** 20
Prices: $2.50–$9.00
Season: Apr 1–Nov 1 **Hours:** 8 a.m.–10 p.m.; Autumn hours: 11:30 a.m.–7:00 p.m.
Practice facil: None **Clubhouse:** Food, Miniature golf **Lessons:** Available
Directions: I-90 to Exit 156 for Crocker-Bassett Rds.; south on Crocker; left (east) on Center Ridge Rd.; on left, opposite Porter Rd.

Southwest Golf Center
Area: **Southwest**   City: **Berea**   ☎ **(440) 234-3034**

Address: 1005 W. Bagley Rd., Berea
Tees: 60 **Grass:** 32 **Lighted:** 60 **Covered:** 12
Prices: $3.00–$12.00
Specials: Senior rates: $2.25/$4.25/$5.25
Season: Mar–Oct **Hours:** 9 a.m.–11 p.m. (summer) **Practice facil:** Range, 19-hole championship putting course; 3 lighted targets **Clubhouse:** Dairy Queen-Brazier
Lessons: Available **Pro:** John Kennedy
Directions: I-71 to Exit 235 for Bagley Rd.; west on Bagley (becomes W. Bagley); on left.

Description You can get a lot of golf in at this pro shop/driving range/custard stand/miniature golf/teaching facility. Lessons are offered by PGA members and go for $25 per half hour. Speaking of lessons, owner Dick Straub says, "Women students are on the increase, and juniors, too, both boys and girls." The driving range here has a unique feature: lighted target greens.

Sports Haven
Area: **Far East**   City: **Novelty**   ☎ **(440) 338-5301**

Address: 9887 Kinsman Rd. (SR 87), Novelty
Tees: 45 **Grass:** 30 **Lighted:** 45 **Covered:** 0
Prices: Not available
Season: Apr–Nov **Hours:** 8:00 a.m.–dark **Practice facil:** None **Clubhouse:** None
Lessons: Not available
Directions: I-271 to Exit 29 for SR 87 (Chagrin Blvd.); east on SR 87 (becomes Kinsman Rd.); 3 miles of SR 306, on left.

RANGES

Strongsville Golf Center

Area: **Southwest**   City: **Strongsville**   ☎ **(440) 238-6443**

Address: 15919 Pearl Rd. (US 42), Strongsville
Tees: 60 **Grass:** 40 **Lighted:** 60 **Covered:** 10
Prices: $3.00–$6.50
Specials: Senior discount with Buckeye card
Season: Year-round **Hours:** Summer: 9 a.m.–11 p.m.; Winter: noon–8 p.m. Mon–Fri, 10 a.m.–8 p.m. Sat, Sun **Practice facil:** Range, Sand, Target greens **Clubhouse:** 18-hole miniature golf **Lessons:** Available **Pro:** Frank DiSanto
Directions: I-71 to Exit 231 for SR 82 (Royalton Rd.); west on SR 82; south on Pearl Rd. (US 42); on left.

Tiny Pines Golf Center

Area: **Far West**   City: **Elyria**   ☎ **(440) 324-4052**

Address: 6604 Lake Ave., Elyria
Tees: 17 **Grass:** 10 **Lighted:** 0 **Covered:** 0
Prices: $3.00–$6.00
Specials: Seniors $2.50–$4.50
Season: Mar–Dec **Hours:** 10 a.m.-dusk **Practice facil:** Range, Putting Green, Chipping Green, Miniature golf **Clubhouse:** None **Lessons:** Available **Pro:** Kevin Lukz
Directions: I-90 to Exit 145 for SR 57 (Lorain Blvd.); south on SR 57; right (west) on Griswold Rd.; right (north) on Lake Ave.; on left.

Description A Mom-and-Pop place: a place for lessons, practice, and custom clubs. Nothing fancy. The Elyria range has 17 stalls, some adjacent grass tees, and a pitching and chipping green.

Valley View Family Golf Center

Area: **South**   City: **Valley View**   ☎ **(216) 573-4990**

Address: 6060 West Canal Rd., Valley View
Tees: 176 **Grass:** **Lighted:** 176 **Covered:** 176
Prices: $4.00–8.00
Specials: Practice membership $79.00; Senior membership $29.00; Junior programs available
Season: Year-round **Hours:** Daily 9 a.m.–10 p.m. **Practice facil:** Range, Putting Green, Chipping Green, Sand, Both outside and inside the dome. **Clubhouse:** Lockers, Custom club fitting: certified Titleist, Ping, and Tour Edge fitting center. **Lessons:** Available **Pro:** Jeff Hogge
Directions: I-77 to Exit 155 for Rockside Rd.; east on Rockside; left (north) on Canal Rd.; on left.

RANGES

Description From the nearby I-480 bridge, it looks like a moon-sized golf ball from outer space plugged in the rough near the Ohio Canal. This unique training facility has a fiber roof supported by air, 80 feet high in the center of the round structure, 320 feet in diameter.

Inside are almost five dozen hitting stations on two levels, a sand hazard, and a putting green. It is open to the public, and memberships are available (they range from under a hundred dollars to more than a thousand). A wide selection of lessons is available.

Hitting a ball under the dome feels strange at first, but once a few balls have been driven into the fabric wall—a hundred yards away—the dome's value as a practice facility becomes evident. There is just enough space between tee and wall to see where the ball is going.

The facility is for players of all abilities.

At various times 80 lighted outdoor tees can be used for practice. A two-tiered deck has 40 hitting stations below featuring mats and synthetic grass and 40 upper-level stations with individual mats. Inside the dome, 57 lighted tee stations, with mats, are available.

West Pines Golf Range

Area: **Far West**   City: **Avon**   ☎ **(440) 871-1414**

Address: 34455 Chester Rd., Avon
Tees: 116   **Grass:** 70   **Lighted:** 20   **Covered:** 20
Prices: $3.00–$6.50
Specials: Lunchtime special Mon–Fri until 2:00 p.m.: medium bucket for $3.00
Season: Mar 1–Nov 1   **Hours:** 8 a.m.–10 p.m.   **Practice facil:** Range, Putting Green
Clubhouse: Custom club fitting and repair   **Lessons:** Available   **Pro:** Bob Barto and Jerry Boykin
Directions: I-90 to Exit 153 for SR 83; north on SR 83 (Center Rd.); SR 83 will turn right, then left; instead of turning left, go straight on Chester Rd.; on right.

Westlawn Golf Range

Area: **Far South**   City: **Akron**   ☎ **(330) 836-0011**

Address: 1423 Collier Rd., Akron
Tees: 50   **Grass:** 40   **Lighted:** 0   **Covered:** 8
Prices: $3.00–$5.00
Specials: Summer special: $1.00 extra get 2 buckets of same size; winter special: 30 balls for $1.00
Season: Year-round   **Hours:** 9:00 a.m.–sunset   **Practice facil:** Range, Putting Green, Chipping Green, Sand, 2 heated tees   **Clubhouse:** None   **Lessons:** Available
Directions: I-77 to Exit 131 for Copley Rd.; west on Copley; left (south) on Collier Rd.; on right.

RANGES

TIDYMAN'S TIDBITS #19
Best driving ranges that are part of a course:
• StoneWater
• Hawks Nest
• Sand Ridge

Edwin Preisler

The first time Edwin Preisler saw Arnold Palmer, the young man from Latrobe, Pennsylvania, who would become golf's most beloved son, was in a sailor suit at Highland Park Golf Course. Coast Guard uniform, more accurately. The last time Preisler saw Palmer, the two were playing golf at Canterbury Golf Club. When they finished their round, Palmer looked at the irons in Preisler's bag. He suggested new irons were needed and within a couple weeks, Palmer's club fitter called Preisler.

Ed Preisler won the Ohio Amateur in 1946. He has played in more than 50 since then. He is a member of the Cleveland Sports Hall of Fame and winner of the Cleveland District Golf Association's Platinum Putter Award. He made ten trips to the U.S. Amateur, three to the U.S. Open, and a half dozen to the U.S. Senior Amateur.

This guy has a game.

He also has a lot of stories, delivered amiably at his kitchen table or in front of his Beechmont locker. Most come from the golf community of the 1940s, '50s and '60s.

It was after he won the Ohio Amateur that he gave the pro tour a try. For two weeks. "I could understand how these guys got to be great. I saw Hogan spend all day in a sand trap. All he stopped for was lunch. I got there at 7:30 in the morning, played two rounds, and when we left, he was still there."

Sometimes Preisler shakes his head and chuckles softly, still amazed at the characters of golf. He played with Moe Norman, the Canadian thought by many to be the greatest ball striker in the history of the game. "I thought he was a little goofy when I first met him. He would talk very fast and repeat everything he said two or three times." Norman's behavior, which included sleeping in his car and walking off the course in a number of tournaments he was leading, lead some to believe he suffered some sort of a mental breakdown.

Norman and Preisler were getting ready to tee off at Beechmont's first hole, a long and difficult par 4. The Canadian asked his host what was necessary to play the hole. "A driver and a wedge," Preisler answered, giving credit to his guest's length off the tee.

Norman teed off with his pitching wedge then used his driver to reach the green.

Another uncommon golfer is Ivan Gant, who, while playing with Preisler, once dove head first into a sand trap. He was that angry at having put the ball in the bunker. His punishment for missing putts was more severe; he would strike himself in the head with his brass putter until the blood ran.

Terrible Tommy Bolt, whose temper inspired him to counsel other players to throw clubs down the fairway so as to retrieve them easily, once hammered a three wood into the ground while playing with Preisler. But it was Bolt's cursing that made an impression on Preisler. "Quite loquacious and he managed to slip in the names of a few players he didn't like."

Tommy Armour had a way with words, too. He had been told about Preisler's yips problem, which lasted for six years, during which Preisler tried putting right-handed, left-handed, cross-handed, one eye closed, eye on the cup instead of the ball, and both eyes closed while he putted and prayed at the same time. During one of the matches they played, Armour said, "Ed, you're playing great. You haven't missed one of those short ones yet."

He did then.

It was Armour, as Preisler's guest, who told a group of Beechmont members he could shoot par every time. He took bets and three thousand dollars was on the line. On the 18th green, Armour studied an 8-foot putt. If he made it, he shot par. He looked at the group standing on the fringe and offered to cancel the bet. No deal, they said. "He knocked it right in the back of the cup."

Preisler took a lesson from Sam Snead at White Sulphur Springs. It cost $15 and was worth it. "He taught me one thing. I was gripping the club a little strong, not letting my legs get into the swing."

It was the irascible Snead who said, apropos of the grip, "If a lot of people gripped a knife and fork like they do a golf club, they'd starve to death."

Preisler has studied thousands of golf swings and finds Snead's to be the best. "It was so smooth and looked so easy. It didn't look like he was putting any force into it. By the way, I was surprised he wasn't a good dancer, because dancing is nothing but timing and tempo."

The homeliest swing belongs, he says, to Miller Barber. "A bad swing. But going through the ball, none of them is bad."

When Preisler's son Michael was a child, the two went to Toledo, home of Inverness Country Club. On the elevator were Ben Hogan and Jimmy Demaret. Pointing to Hogan, Preisler told Michael, "That's Ben Hogan and Jimmy Demaret! How would you like their autographs?"

Hogan said, "I don't give autographs," and continued staring at the elevator door. Demaret, however, said, "Hey, son, take mine. I'm not quite as famous, but maybe I will be someday."

It is quite a fraternity to which Preisler belongs, including names like Palmer, Hogan, Hagen, Armour, Snead, Nelson. Beechmont pro Charlie Stone, PGA says Preisler fits right in with them. "I don't think we realize all that Ed's done for golf." In 1998, the Northern Ohio PGA awarded him with a special President's Award.

—JHT

Golf Organizations

Blue Tee Golfer
8304 Dogwood Ln., Cleveland • Phone: (440) 779-5311

Blue Tee Golfer helps companies, charities, and other groups plan golf outings and fundraisers. They also sponsor the Blue Tee Classic, one of the larger public golf tournaments in Northern Ohio. (It is held from June through the end of September, rotating among various courses.) A newsletter that goes out to members contains updates on tournaments, golf resort and travel package information, and golf discount advertising. The services of Blue Tee Golfer are also available to individuals.

Executive Women's Golf Association
P.O. Box 31704, Independence • Phone: (216) 999-9664

The Executive Women's Golf League (EWG) was formed to help women take up the game of golf, network with other female executives, and learn how to make the game an effective tool for business and personal success.

The Cleveland chapter, formed in 1992 with 80 members playing at Sweetbriar Golf Club, was the first chapter formed outside of Florida, where the league was established in 1991. Now, the EWG has more than 500 Northeast Ohio members, with chapters in Cleveland, Akron, Canton, and Youngstown. Cleveland members tee it up at Pine Hills, Pine Ridge, The Links, and Highland; Akron members play at Boston Hills and Mayfair; Canton members play at Clearview and Tam O'Shanter.

Regular league season membership ($100) includes local and national membership in the EWG, weekly handicap calculations, monthly events, and prizes during the season. Off-season activities include golf-related networking events and educational programs. The membership fee does not include weekly greens or cart fees.

League members are expected to attend regularly scheduled play for the entire season. National members receive EWG's national newsletter, *From Tee to Green*; all members receive Northeast Ohio EWG's newsletter, *The Clubhouse*.

OTHER

For a membership application, call Cindy Darwal, Eastern Great Lakes Sectional Director, at (216) 736-5406.

Inter-Club Public Golf Association
3959 Walter Rd., North Olmsted · Phone: (440) 779-1923

The Inter-Club Public Golf Association (ICPGA) serves public golfers and golf groups by sponsoring a regular series of tournaments at public and private courses throughout the season.

All golfers 18 years of age or older are welcome to participate. Events use both gross and net scores by class. A nominal entry fee covers prizes and an optional skin game. Greens fees are collected on the day of play; cart fees vary from course to course. For dates, advance tee time reservations, and general information, call the "Reservation Hotline" at (440) 954-4069.

ICPGA annual membership is $5.00. Handicap service and a monthly newsletter are also available for $5.00 and $7.00, respectively. To request information and a membership application, or to obtain a free sample copy of the newsletter, send a self-addressed, stamped envelope to the above address.

Northern Ohio Golf Association
10210 Brecksville Rd., Brecksville · Phone: (440) 838-8733

The Northern Ohio Golf Association (NOGA), founded in 1917, provides administrative support to its members, 44 private golf clubs around the area. It is also the area liaison for several national golf-related associations, including the United States Golf Association. As the USGA designee for Northeast Ohio, NOGA maintains unified handicapping, course, slope, and pace ratings, and oversees the rules and officiating for USGA tournaments. It also sponsors a variety of special tournaments and events, in addition to hosting seminars for golf-course managers and pros. It publishes *NOGA Fairways*, a bi-monthly magazine. Information about NOGA is available on the Internet at http://www.noga.org, or via e-mail at noga@usga.org.

Northern Ohio PGA
38121 Euclid Ave., Willoughby · Phone: (440) 951-4546

The Northern Ohio PGA (NOPGA) organizes and sponsors tournaments for PGA professionals from area country clubs and public courses. The series of tournaments runs from mid-April through October. Play is scheduled for every Monday and rotates among area courses. The NOPGA provides no services to other golfers except an invitation to watch the area pros.

Ohio Golf Association
4701 Olentangy River Rd. #200-A, Columbus · Phone: (614) 457-8169

The Ohio Golf Association sponsors and promotes five tournaments each year for the 157 private golf clubs in its membership. The premier event is their Amateur Championship, scheduled every July. In June, there is a junior tournament; the seniors' championship is held in September. Inaugurated in 1997 is the Senior Amateur Championship for golfers over 55 with handicaps under 7.

Ohio Golf Course Owners Association
6478 Fiesta Dr., Columbus · Phone: (800) 761-4394

The Ohio Golf Course Owners Association serves more than 275 member courses throughout the state by helping course owners and managers improve their golf operations. It recently affiliated with the National Golf Course Owners Association and offers dual membership.

Director Allan Whaling and his staff travel extensively to courses across the country in search of new ideas and innovative solutions to common problems. They share them with members at regular round-table meetings.

OGCOA sponsors two statewide junior golf events annually for young men and women. The events are open to players who have not reached their 20th birthday on or before the end of August during the tournament year.

The OGCOA maintains a website: www.ohio-golf.com. It also offers a Workers Compensation Savings Group for club owners and discounts for member courses from over 90 major golf course suppliers. It sponsors a three-day general membership meeting and trade show in March for both members and nonmembers interested in joining up.

Ohio Women's Golf Association
4813 Rean Meadow Dr., Kettering · Phone: (937) 435-9311

The Ohio Women's Golf Association (OWGA) sponsors one tournament a year, a 36-stroke amateur championship for women residents of the state of Ohio. Players are handicapped according to flight. The championship is held on the first Monday and Tuesday after Labor Day every September and rotates among Ohio state park courses. More than 100 women take part each year. There is also a senior division for women 50 years and older. In 1997 the "Jane Climer Super Seniors" division will be inaugurated. Entry applications are available in June from the OWGA. They are also available at local public courses. Entry deadline is mid-August.

OTHER

Women's Ohio State Golf Association

4221 High Point Dr., Medina · Phone: (330) 723-0598

The Women's Ohio State Golf Association (WOSGA) sponsors the Women's Ohio State Golf Invitational Championship. This event is open to members of private clubs that belong to WOSGA, but low-handicap (0–8) public links golfers are also invited to participate. The field is limited to 96 golfers. The Championship is held every July; the location rotates among courses throughout the state.

WOSGA recently inaugurated a state seniors' championship. Golfers over the age of 50 by June of the tournament year are eligible. There's also the Ohio State Juniors Championship held at the Marion Country Club each July. Any young woman under the age of 18 may participate.

TIDYMAN'S TIDBITS #20

Stuff every public course should offer:

- Complimentary tees
- Scorecards and pencils on the second tee
- Complimentary handicapping service
- Refreshment cart
- Starters who have some idea of what it is to serve as starter

OTHER

Indexes

ALPHABETICAL INDEX

INDEXES

GEOGRAPHICAL INDEX

Notes